FROM TIRPITZ TO GORBACHEV

Also by Peter Mangold

NATIONAL SECURITY AND INTERNATIONAL RELATIONS

SUPERPOWER INTERVENTION IN THE MIDDLE EAST

From Tirpitz to Gorbachev

Power Politics in the Twentieth Century

Peter Mangold

First published in Great Britain 1998 by
MACMILLAN PRESS LTD
Houndmills, Basingstoke, Hampshire RG21 6XS and London
Companies and representatives throughout the world

A catalogue record for this book is available from the British Library.

ISBN 0–333–67352–2

First published in the United States of America 1998 by
ST. MARTIN'S PRESS, INC.,
Scholarly and Reference Division,
175 Fifth Avenue, New York, N.Y. 10010

ISBN 0–312–21219–4

Library of Congress Cataloging-in-Publication Data
Mangold, Peter.
From Tirpitz to Gorbachev : power politics in the twentieth
century / Peter Mangold.
    p.   cm.
Includes bibliographical references and index.
ISBN 0–312–21219–4 (cloth)
1. World politics—20th century.   I. Title.
D443.M289 1997
909.82'9—dc21   97–38347
                                                          CIP

This book is printed on paper suitable for recycling and made from fully managed and
sustained forest sources.

10   9   8   7   6   5   4   3   2   1
07   06   05   04   03   02   01   00   99   98

Printed in Great Britain by
The Ipswich Book Company Ltd
Ipswich, Suffolk

To Val – who knows the background

Contents

Acknowledgements   viii

1   A Deadly Anachronism   1

2   'Militarism Run Stark Mad'   15

3   'This Isn't War'   35

4   A Flawed Experiment   53

5   The Remastery of Power   68

6   A Nuclear Education   85

7   'Great in What?'   104

8   Peace in Their Time   123

9   No Other Choice?   142

10 A Conditional Achievement   159

References   174

Index   200

Acknowledgements

My thanks are due to Syed Mahmud Ali and Professor Jim Richardson for reading individual chapters in draft; to John Eidinow for his continuous flow of ideas, comments and encouragement; and to Professor James Mayall and the Centre for International Studies at the London School of Economics for their hospitality.

PETER MANGOLD

1 A Deadly Anachronism

In 1898 Admiral Alfred von Tirpitz introduced his first naval bill in the *Reichstag*. Its aim was to secure the necessary finance to build up a German navy as an instrument of *Weltpolitik*. Europe's newest and most dynamic power was challenging the long-standing predominance of the Royal Navy and thus, by implication, the larger international *status quo*. It was the opening act of a great and terrible drama which would continue, with only one real interval, from the German defeat of 1918 to Hitler's accession to power fifteen years later, for nearly nine decades. International politics was entering an unprecedented predatory phase in which a succession of three hegemonial challenges would result in two world wars and one cold war.

The costs of these remarkable exercises in power politics are literally almost incalculable. Power politics was to prove one of the great killers of the modern era. The death toll in the two world wars amounted to somewhere between 60 and 70 million.[1] Zbigniew Brzezinski puts the number of civilian and military deaths from war in the twentieth century at 87 million.[2] Power politics shaped and misshaped the 'most terrible' century in Western history, far more profoundly than any revolution or ideology.[3] It destroyed or fundamentally weakened all the Great Powers active in 1914, resulting in the division of Europe and its relegation from the century-long placement at the centre of the international system. It generated an intense feeling of insecurity, a sense of living perilously close to the edge of an abyss. It was a prime cause of domestic upheaval and authoritarian reaction. The First World War was a direct cause of the Russian Revolution and an indirect cause of Nazism and the Holocaust. Only in the mid-1980s, when Mikhail Gorbachev introduced *perestroika* in the Soviet Union and accepted the principles of international law as the basis for Soviet foreign policy, did coercive diplomacy cease to be central to the conduct of international affairs.

Power politics is an evocative rather than a precise concept. Although frequently used as 'a colloquial phrase for international politics', it is with its more sinister usage, as a translation of the German *Machtpolitik* – the politics of force – with which we are here primarily concerned.[4] It is the politics of international anarchy, of an essentially untramelled competition between the most powerful of all political units, in which the only operative rules are those which states themselves choose, as a matter of

1

self-interest, to observe. Its guiding principle is that of *raison d'état*, which entitles the state to use whatever means are necessary to further its interests and ambitions, regardless of moral scruple or restraint.

Although neither *raison d'état* nor *Realpolitik*, which came into currency in the middle of the nineteenth century, are synonyms for war, that is certainly what they imply.[5] Might is right and coercion is the norm. This is a Hobbesian world characterised by war and preparation for war, a world in which power is at a premium, and in which one state's gain is *ipso facto* another's loss. 'Who gains nothing,' remarked Catherine the Great, 'loses'.[6] J. P. F. Ancillon, tutor to Frederick William IV of Prussia and State Secretary for Foreign Affairs, wrote: 'In the society of large states in which law does not enjoy an external guarantee, we take as our point of departure the possible or even probable misuse of force. What will be the result? Mutual distrust, fear and restlessness, always recurring and always effective.'[7] A century earlier Montesquieu had complained of a 'new malady in Europe affecting our princes and causing them to maintain 'an inordinate number of troops. As soon as one state increases the number of troops it calls up, the others immediately increases theirs, so that nothing is gained, but all are ruined.'[8]

Power politics therefore is politics in one of its crudest, rawest and most primitive forms, which has long been superseded at the national level where laws are firmly established, and the exercise of force prevented by state monopoly. Its survival into the modern era raises profoundly disturbing questions – not just about the sheer scale and destructive intensity of modern international predation, but the irresponsibility and recklessness with which power has often been handled, and, particularly in an era of nuclear overkill, about the closeness to which the international system was operating to the margins of controllability. The shadow of Sarajevo, of sudden and seemingly unintended systemic breakdown, has overshadowed much of the century. Yet however frightening, however morally reprehensible, our attitudes towards power politics remain ambivalent. Taming the dragon of power politics is not an objective which has been pursued with either political persistence or intellectual rigour.

This failure cannot simply be explained in terms of the very real difficulty of devising alternatives. There is also the more uncomfortable fact that power politics give rise to conduct – courage, sacrifice, comradeship – which is admired and valued. Whether we like to admit it or not, power attracts at least as much as it repels. Theodore Roosevelt is said to have viewed power politics as the most exciting game in the world, and found big game hunting in Africa, which he later took up, to be a poor substitute.[9] Churchill and Henry Kissinger were equally fascinated by power.

So too are the very many readers of war histories, and the crowds that come out to cheer a departing fleet. Power politics has immense romantic appeal. It is associated with 'greatness', with empire, with military show. It excites and quickens the blood, it taps deeper, more atavistic instincts which, as citizens of humane, civilised states we prefer not to admit to. For power is not simply instrumental, a means in the Clauswitzian sense. It can all too easily become an end in itself. The pursuit of power at the international level, as the twentieth century has so amply demonstrated, frequently takes us outside the realm of careful diplomatic calculations into some of the most irrational and destructive areas of human behaviour.

The prevalence of this pathological extreme provides us with our first major clue to the explanation of the peculiar virulence with which power politics was pursued in the years between Tirpitz's naval bill and the advent of the 'new thinking' in the Soviet Union. The twentieth century was crippled from the outset by the failure to reconcile a contradiction which had emerged right at the end of the nineteenth century between a new intensity of predatory purpose and developments in warfare, notably the massive increase in the size of armies and a revolution in firepower, which were rendering power politics a deadly anachronism. In a book published in 1899, originally entitled *The Future of War*, Ivan Bloch foresaw both the kind of war which would be waged some 15 years later on the Western Front, and some of the social and political catastrophes which would flow from it. War, he argued, had become 'impossible, except at the price of suicide'.[10] The implications, though he did not draw them, were profound. If war had become suicidal, and power politics a deadly anachronism, the armoury of the state was drastically depleted. Fundamental change was necessary, not just in the conduct, but in the culture of international affairs. States must scale down their ambitions, and adopt a more restricting, more tolerant code of international behaviour. They would have to accommodate one another's interests.

This, however, was precisely what they did not want to do. States were finding it difficult enough to modernise their domestic political systems in response to the Industrial Revolution. But however great the reluctance to introduce or extend the franchise, the institutional mechanisms for effecting such change did at least exist, along with some sense of shared values and obligation to which it was possible to appeal. If all else failed, then the centres of power which revolutionaries needed to seize were clearly defined. Imposing change within the international system was by contrast a herculean task. In 1899 the ideas, the institutions and the structures were simply not there. More important, there was not even the beginning of an effective consensus for the kind of radical reform which Bloch's prognosis pointed towards. For if a deadly anachronism militarily, and indeed, according to Norman Angell's widely-read *The Great Illusion*, which he subtitled *A Study of the Relation of Military Power to National Advantage*, also economically, power politics was still very much in keeping with the political temper of the time. The progressive moral counterargument, that men were becoming too civilised for war, was more a reflection of wishful thinking than of empirical observation. At the time of the Franco-Prussian war Gladstone had chosen to speak of a new law of nations

> taking hold of the mind, and coming to sway the practice of the world; a law which recognises independence, which frowns upon aggression, which favours the pacific not the bloody settlement of disputes, which aims at permanent not temporary adjustments; above all which recognises as a tribunal of paramount authority, the general judgement of civilised mankind.[11]

Similar sentiments were being expressed by liberals, radicals and socialists up until the eve of the First World War. 'In this,' notes Nicholas Stargardt, 'Lenin was at one with Lytton Strachey, German Marxists with the clergy of Basle.'[12]

Yet far from encouraging reform, the early stages of the Industrial Revolution, coinciding as they did with the rise of nationalism, served to intensify international rivalries. The result was a resurgence of power politics after the long period of quiescence which had followed the Congress of Vienna in 1815. The progress that had been made towards the establishment of a coalition of powers, founded on a European public law for the defence of that law, was in the process of being reversed. Although formally still in existence – the last conference of ambassadors met in 1912 – the Concert of Europe was in terminal decline. In its day it had been remarkably effective. In what involved, if not a refutation, then certainly a modification of *raison d'état*, the leading states of Europe had abjured unilateral action, accepting that problems could only be settled by common consent.[13] Bismarck's jibe that Europe was simply a geographic expression of which statesmen spoke when they wanted 'something from a foreign power which they would never venture to ask for in their own name', was at most a half-truth.[14] The powers allowed their actions to be subjected to the scrutiny of their peers (though not of course of small states), and permitted the Concert to establish a 'standard for responsible statesmanship'.[15]

It could not, and did not last. This was a voluntarist system dependent on the principle of enlightened self-interest, whose only sanction was moral suasion. It was effectively only so long as there remained a consensus in favour of the highly conservative domestic *status quo*, and that the conflict of interests between its members remained limited. Peace may have maintained the Concert, as much as the Concert maintained peace.[16] Certainly the Concert did not prevent the Crimean War of 1854 or, much more important, the Franco-Prussian War of 1870. Defenders of the system, such as the historian F. H. Hinsley, argue that while the underlying principles were suspended during these two conflicts, the governments concerned deliberately restricted their aims and controlled the forces of nationalism 'from a continuing respect for the international system and a concern to preserve order'. Italy and Germany, Europe's newcomers, regarded themselves, in Bismarck's phrase, as 'historical states entitled to a place in the historical state system'.[17] Having unified Germany 'by blood and iron', Bismarck subsequently went out of his way to uphold the international *status quo*.

The damage however had already been done. As one unsympathetic biographer remarks, Bismarck undermined the recent improvement in international morality, 'throwing the nineteenth century back (dragging the young twentieth century with it) to the level of Louis XIV or Frederick the Great'.[18] This was the morality according to which his successors would operate. Dissatisfied, unstable, Wilhemine Germany was no more willing to adapt its international ambitions to the constraints imposed by military change, than it was ready to share power with the emergent working class. The new state in other words regarded the old game of power politics as a part of its inheritance, without stopping to consider how much more dangerous it had become since the German victories of 1866 and 1870.

The mood of this newly-unified, newly-industrialised state, with its immature leadership and institutions was, however, in no sense unique. The temper of the Continent as a whole can be gleaned from the way Herbert Spencer's phrase 'the survival of the fittest', gained a rapid and sinister prominence. In the last decades of the century a dangerous assertiveness was making itself felt. It expressed itself through a particularly aggressive form of nationalism which was to reach its climax in the great outburst of popular rejoicing which greeted the outbreak of the First World War. The spread of the Industrial Revolution to Continental Europe in the two decades after 1850 had changed much more than the balance of power. It changed the mood and context. It generated energy, exuberance, a drive to expand. It also dislocated societies on a massive scale, creating social tensions and frustrations which were all too frequently diverted or sublimated through Social Imperialism, instead of being defused through social and political reform.

The result was the fateful combination of a world increasingly preoccupied with power at a time when power was becoming increasingly
destructive, a group of modern industrial nation-states, whose citizens at
least when it came to their ideas about war and their national histories,
espoused romantic, pre-industrial values. These contradictions however,
only became evident in 1914, with the outbreak of what George Kennan
has described as the 'seminal catastrophe' of the twentieth century.[19] The
Great War, to use its original name, marked the first of a series of systemic breakdowns. Things fell apart. The international, and later in some
countries also the domestic order, the norms of civilised behaviour, the
safe fabric of daily life, all collapsed. Having lost their footing in July
and August 1914, the great powers failed to regain it for almost another
thirty years. One failure led to another. The early war of movement initiated by the German attack on France, quickly degenerated into trench-
warfare which the generals did not know how to fight, except at the cost
of horrendous casualties. These casualties in turn fuelled the mood which
contributed first to the punitive Versailles settlement, later to
Appeasement. The Second World War merged into Cold War and the
nuclear arms race.

Eventually the crisis brought about by the wilful pursuit of power politics
into an age where power outstripped statecraft, was brought under control
as the stabilising impact of modernisation began to assert itself. But it was
a slow and difficult process, which only seriously began in the mid-1940s.
While the First World War did indeed generate a strong reaction against
power politics, there were as yet neither the political ideas, nor the economic means, to fashion an effective alternative. Like Germany, power
politics had suffered a serious, but by no means fatal defeat. For the
victors at least war had been deprived of its old glamour. The volunteers
who had gone to fight for their countries, found themselves killing, and
being killed in bewildering and senseless numbers. They died not
gloriously as Rupert Brooke had naively envisaged, but rather, in
Wilfred Owen's disparaging phrase, 'like cattle'.[20]

The reaction was nowhere near as good news as it originally seemed.
For it undermined the capacity to re-establish a balance of power, without
however substituting anything fresh in its place. The new preoccupation
with peace was as obsessive and unthinking as the prewar bellicism had
been. New concepts, such as collective security, were never subject to adequate public scrutiny or debate. There was a moral progress, in that
Woodrow Wilson internationalised the rejection of power politics embodied in the idea of American exceptionalism, and provided political impetus

to a set of international norms which firmly delegitimised *raison d'état* and war as an instrument of policy, other than for defensive means. But Wilson was much stronger in articulating a new international morality, than in tackling the old problems of anarchy and self-help. This might have mattered less had the Versailles peace conference succeeded in removing the underlying political and economic causes of conflict in Europe. But the failure then, as indeed of more serious efforts in the 1920s, to provide the bases for a new stability, placed an unrealistic burden on a fundamentally flawed system. Arbitration, by which the League set much store, could only cope with relatively minor disputes. The crucial fall-back of collective security never commanded more than rhetorical support.

What made these failings so critical was not simply Hitler and his far-reaching ambitions, but the fact that the First World War had facilitated a remastery of power. While public opinion in Britain and France remained transfixed on the horror of the trenches, the German General Staff focused their attention on the period of mobile warfare which had followed Ludendorff's breakthrough on the Western Front of March 1918. While the outcome of the First World War had been politically inconclusive, the hard fact was that war could once again achieve decisive results without suicidal consequences. The full potency of the technology of *Blitzkrieg*, which was refined over the next 20 years, was shown by the extraordinary successes of the German army, which between September 1939 and November 1942 had established control of Europe from the Atlantic to the outskirts of Moscow. But it was with the Second War War that the decline of power politics really begins. For in overreaching himself, Hitler created conditions in which any similar exercise of power would become impossible to repeat. The reaction this time was not confined to the victors, as it had been after 1918. Although demilitarisation was imposed on Germany, as on Japan, the Allies were in large measure preaching to the converted. The vanquished had learned their own lessons. The decisiveness of their defeats, and in the case of Germany the nature and excesses of Nazism, served to discredit the whole of that aggressive late nineteenth-century *Weltanschauung* which had come to a head with Fascism, and made the pursuit of power over the preceding four decades so demonic.

Here, for the first time, was a real opportunity for change; and, thanks in large measure to the United States, it was seized with alacrity. The years between 1944 and 1957 saw an unprecedented series of initiatives, starting with the Bretton Woods monetary conference and ending with the signature of the Treaty of Rome. As Francois Duchene remarks in his biography of Jean Monnet, the points of European statecraft, traditional since the late Middle Ages, were finally switched.[21] It was a period of moral as much as of material recovery, of a belated reassertion of the political will to mould and control events rather than be controlled by them. The sense of fatalism and drift, the willingness to let wishful thinking substitute for policy which had marked so much of the interwar years, was gone. Important lessons had been learned from the political and economic disasters of the last 30 years. There were new ideas on the table, ideas characterised by a combination of vision and pragmatism which had been conspicuously missing after 1918.

But while power was more ably and imaginatively managed, it had also become much more manageable. Modernisation and economic development were reaching the point where they were finally beginning to exert an ameliorating influence on the conduct of international affairs. As economies became more productive, sophisticated and interdependent, and as societies became more concerned with the well-being of their members than the symbols of nationhood, the whole state-centric system in which war was regarded as normal and legitimate, began to look increasingly crude and anachronistic. The community of states which now emerged in the West could neither afford the use of force in their mutual relations (its military attentions were entirely taken up the Soviet Union), nor had any need for it. It had no unresolved political or territorial disputes. It had no economic incentives for war. On the contrary, technological advance, an open international trading system, and a period of unprecedented economic growth served to render the economic rationale for conquest – whether it was a question of *Lebensraum*, markets, or with the partial exception of oil, raw materials – obsolete.

This however was not just an affluent peace, but a democratic one. If democracy is not incompatible with power politics, it has certainly proved generally far more antipathetic towards it than have more authoritarian systems. Power politics originated in pre-industrial, pre-democratic societies. It was pursued by sovereigns unfettered by considerations of public opinion. The sovereigns declared war. Their subjects fought – and died. With the spread of the franchise the soldier and his family began to have, if not a direct say in foreign policy, then a certain veto power. This was not important before 1914 when franchises were still narrow and, more important, public opinion was strongly, and unusually, nationalist. In the aftermath of the First World War however, public opinion imposed peace as the priority of democratic governments. Chamberlain was lionised when he declared 'peace in our time'. It was what the public wanted to believe. While the Second World War created a new popular realism about power, this went alongside the demands for social reform and a better life.

Germany and Japan emerged in the vanguard of the group of the world's most economically and technologically advanced states which had come to reject the old heroic, nationalist values in favour of the more mundane, and personal concerns of peacetime. In this *accommodatory* culture, a concept which we will elaborate in Chapter 8, power was losing its glorificatory overtones and greatness was being redefined away from its traditional associations with empire and military domination. Democratic and material progress on the one hand, and the decline of power politics on the other, were two sides of the same coin.

Here at last was a workable alternative to power politics – a community of states which accommodated one another's interests on the basis of an agreed set of rules, norms and rights. Indeed in the sophisticated form which rapidly developed in Western Europe from 1950 onwards, it was not so much an alternative, as an antithesis. The new accommodatory politics expressed more than a change of national purpose. It was the reflection of the triumph of the civilised view of human nature championed by nineteenth-century progressive thinkers over the predatory warrior ethic.

But it did not of course exist within a strategic vacuum. There was also another very much more restrictive form of accommodatory politics based on the necessities of military constraint rather than changed values and new economic opportunities, which at first sight did not appear to differ notably from more traditional forms of power politics. The idea that scientific advance would one day render war so terrible that it ceased to be a political option has a long history. In 1829 the poet Robert Southey had suggested that, in matters of warfare,

> the chemist and the mechanist will succeed where moralists and divines have failed ... the novel powers which, beyond all doubt, will be directed to the purposes of destruction, are so tremendous, and likely to be so efficient, that in their consequences they may reasonably be expected to do more towards the prevention of war than any or all other causes.[22]

If there was any doubt that this point had finally arrived with the advent of the atomic bomb, and both the Americans and the Russians showed some initial reluctance to acknowledge the fact, it was dispelled by the explosion of the first hydrogen weapons. A scientist who visited the site of the first Soviet H-bomb test in 1953, described its impact as transcending 'some kind of psychological barrier. The effects of the first atomic bomb had not inspired such flesh-creeping terror, although they had been incomparably more terrible than anything seen in the still recent war.'[23]

The implications of this are perhaps best summarised in the story which the American Secretary of State, Dean Rusk, tells at the end of the chapter on the Cuban missile crisis in his memoirs published nearly 30 years later.

After the crisis ended, John Kennedy gave each of the Excomm members a small desk calendar with the thirteen days of October high-lighted. I have that calendar still, and whenever I glance at it, I remember a question that haunted me throughout the missile crisis and since. The question actually comes from the Westminster Shorter Catechism of the Presbyterian Church, which I had to memorize as a small boy growing up in Atlanta. It reads, 'What is the chief end of man?' The catechism gives a theological answer: 'To glorify God and enjoy Him for ever.'

During the early days of the crisis, before Kennedy's speech to the nation, as I drove through the streets of Washington and saw people walking on the sidewalks and riding in their cars, not knowing what was going on, and as I thought about my own family, equally ignorant, I could not help remembering that question. It really asks, 'What is life all about?' And I realized that this first of all questions had become an operational question before the governments of the world.[24]

Still however the superpowers were not ready to give up. If war was precluded as a rational instrument of Great Power politics, the threat of war was not. Each side could hope to play on the other's fear of their irrationality – in other words, to gain by bluff and intimidation. Thus while the rules of power politics were immediately changed, with both the United States and the Soviet Union forced to respect one another's vital interests, the larger question, of whether the game itself would have to be abandoned, was still very much open. Stalin and his successors sought to prove that it need not. They failed. In retrospect the Cold War emerges as a rearguard action by men determined to try and devise means whereby strategic power could still be harnessed to traditional political purpose. The slow and uneasy progression from crisis and confrontation to *detente* and arms control and finally some four decades after Hiroshima, to the radical 'new thinking' of Mikhail Gorbachev, mark the main stages in their defeat.

This progress was not inevitable. Things might have gone differently had Western nerve not held in the face of Soviet nuclear intimidation. But the lessons of brinkmanship taught by Western willingness to stand up to Soviet pressure during the 1950s and early 1960s, were clear to both sides – nuclear diplomacy was just too dangerous. States could not go on taking this level of risk. By the late 1970s there was also a growing body of evidence to suggest that, despite the initial successes of *detente*, the Soviet Union had also failed in its alternative strategy of seeking to convert nuclear arms into political influence. Power in other words was no longer 'fungible'. A decade later Gorbachev came to the conclusion that the military costs of superpower status were no longer worth the disproportionate price which the Soviet Union had been paying.

Once the Soviet Union had taken the decision to become a more open society, with close links with the international economy, it was bound to abandon the attempt to try and find new rules to play the old game of power politics in the nuclear age. The 'new thinking' proved thus to be a badge of international modernism, the signal that the Soviet Union had accepted the conclusions reached by Japan and Germany 40 years earlier. Power no longer paid, whereas economic investment and international cooperation did. *Raison d'état* was an anachronism in an interdependent world which the Soviet Union could not hope to dominate.

The end of the Cold War therefore represented a second and highly visible watershed in the decline of power politics. This was more than confirmation and reinforcement of an immensely welcome and necessary trend, a reprieve from what had at one point seemed an inexorable and potentially catastrophic cycle of conflict and destruction. Unwilling as we seem to recognise the fact, it is one of the great achievements of the age, a moral as well as a political step forward. Although the progress has been slower than that in other fields – the prevalence of liberal democracy over its rivals or the taming of the extremes and the cruelties of Capitalism, the fact remains that the last great bastion of Hobbesian politics was finally giving way to something much closer to an international society in the sense defined by Hedley Bull and Adam Watson.[25]

That said, however, the process is by no means complete or assured. The immediate prospects are for consolidation rather than substantial further advance. In contrast to the end of the Second World War, the end of the Cold War has provided relatively little impetus for further progress. In 1990 George Bush raised considerable excitement with his reference to 'a new world order ... a new era, freer from the threat of terror, stronger in the pursuit of justice, and more secure in the quest of peace. An era in which the nations of the world, East and West, North and South, can prosper and live in harmony.'[26] Beyond the immediate issue of the Gulf War, however, neither the United States nor indeed any other members of international community were prepared to accept this vision as a programme for long-term action. The rich states of the accommodatory order balked at the complexities and costs of resolving the new disorder which had broken out in countries such as Rwanda, Somalia and the former Yugoslavia. While encouraging the spread of democracy and free markets, providing limited support to some peace-keeping operations, and keeping a close eye on the more dangerous threats posed by the proliferation of weapons of mass destruction, they had no stomach for any kind of new Marshall Plan or any other grand design. A residual role for power politics was something which they, as indeed many Third World countries who had other immediate priorities or objected to seeing the rules of the Post-Cold War world laid down by the West, seemed to be willing to live with.

Yet if power politics posed much less of a threat than it did for the first 90 years of the century, the residual dangers are still too serious to ignore. While the threat of a breakdown of the accommodatory order built up after the Second World War may not be immediate, the ravens of Realism do have a point.[27] With the partial exception of the European Union, the major changes which we have been describing have occurred not in the structure of the international system – this is still a world of states, subject to at least some of the tensions and insecurities created by the underlying condition of anarchy – but within states or in the economic and strategic circumstances which condition their behaviour. Were these to revert or deteriorate, power politics could be expected to stage a dangerous comeback. There is no guarantee that the institutional barriers, such as the IMF, World Bank or G7, can prevent or contain future major international economic or financial upheavals, or that an erstwhile Great Power such as Russia will avoid the hardship and humiliation which are the traditional breeding grounds of assertive nationalism. While nuclear weapons might be expected to provide a safety-net, ensuring the maintenance of minimal standards of accommodatory behaviour, the likely presence of right-wing nationalist forces would create additional pressures and tensions to which decision-makers were not subject during the Cold War. Power politics could also make a comeback by default – by an incremental erosion of the habits of cooperation and accommodation which have characterised relations within institutions such as the European Union, NATO or the WTO.

The more immediate danger, however, lies outside the accommodatory order. Power politics has already gained a new lease of life in the Third World, where the majority of states take a much more traditional and Hobbesian approach to international affairs. All the 'new' states which have gained independence in the wake of the break-up of empires which stretched from the end of the First World War to the break-up of the Soviet Union in the 1990s, are members of the United Nations and therefore, formally at least, subscribe to the charter with its proscription of power politics. What many do not enjoy – and are not likely to have for some time – is the combination of economic prosperity and domestic stability which helped their erstwhile imperial masters to put power politics behind them. On the contrary, many live in an environment where power is highly relevant to political purpose. The influx of modern weaponry into the Third World has not been accompanied by a transfer of modern ideas about the control or elimination of power politics. The 'lessons' of other people's wars do not travel easily. The superpowers' experience with nuclear weapons will not automatically apply to other nuclear adversaries who, with less rational and sophisticated governmental machines, but more vulnerable nuclear forces, find themselves operating in closer geographical proximity and under much greater political pressures.

We are thus faced with the prospect of a long and uneasy coexistence of two very different political cultures. The first, the hard-earned privilege of the world's most developed states, is accommodatory, a culture disposed to compromise and negotiation which explicitly rejects the use of force – and indeed has no particular use for it. It is a culture characterised by a degree of convergence between the norms of domestic and international politics. This is not quite a 'post-power politics' culture, if only because power continues to provide security and clout, and because at least some members of the 'pacific' community, continue to set store by it for reasons of prestige. But it is a culture in which power is under stringent control. The second culture is the one with which we are so historically familiar.

How these two cultures coexist in a highly interdependent system in which communication is constant and instantaneous, but in which even unsophisticated states can gain access to highly sophisticated weapons, is likely to be one of the key issues of international politics in the early decades of the twenty-first century. This is a drama which will play for a long time over a large and complex stage. If the favourable postwar economic trends continue, and if potentially dominant states such as China can avoid the internal dislocations which may tip the balance away from the choice of an accommodatory role, then the auguries may be favourable. Power politics would be contained, if not actually squeezed out of the system. It would survive at the regional level, and in the bilateral relations of some secondary states, without providing any larger threat to the system as a whole. It is also possible to foresee conditions in which power politics seep back into the mainstream of international politics with potentially catastrophic results.

These risks are worth emphasising because of what seems a tendency, at least as far as public opinion is concerned, to assume that the worst is now over. While this may indeed be true. it is essential to recognise how hard won this victory over power politics was, and to draw the necessary lessons from the dangerous and tumultuous years that separated the advent of the adventurous German admiral from that of the last Soviet leader. As the following chapters will try to show, it is a story which is much too fascinating, and too important, to consign to a bad and bygone past. It is a story too, though we may not often pause to reflect on the fact, which is all too close to our own lives; for we are once both its victims and its beneficiaries.

2 'Militarism Run Stark Mad'

In the last week of July 1914 the crowds began to come onto the streets. Nearly four weeks after the assassination of Archduke Franz Ferdinand at Sarajevo, the Austrians had suddenly presented Serbia, which they believed to have been behind the killing, with a very tough ultimatum. When the inevitable rejection came the popular response in the German capital was immediate. 'All,' reported the Berlin daily, the *Taegliche Rundschau*, 'are seized by one earnest emotion: War, war, and a sense of togetherness. And then a solemn and festive sound greets the evening: (the patriotic song) "*Es braust ein Ruf wie Donnerhall*"' ('A roar like thunder sounds.')[1] Five days later, on 30 July, with the crisis rapidly worsening, the crowds reappeared, remaining a virtually permanent feature of the German capital over the next week.

Similar demonstrations took place elsewhere in Germany and in other major European capitals. The jubilant face of the 25-year-old Adolf Hitler can be seen in a surviving photograph of a demonstration on the Feldherrnplatz in Munich. From St Petersburg the French ambassador sent a late glimpse of the old order. 'Everywhere ... the same popular demonstrations, the same grave and religious enthusiasms, the same impulse to rally round the Tsar, the same faith in victory, the same exultation of the national conscience.'[2] The British ambassador reported from Vienna that news of the breach with Serbia had been greeted with 'a frenzy of delight, vast crowds parading the streets and singing songs till the small hours of the morning'.[3] Although the response in Britain was somewhat more muted, Bertrand Russell spent the evening of 3 August walking through the streets around Trafalgar Square 'noticing cheering crowds, and making myself sensitive to the emotions of passers-by. During this and the following days I discovered to my amazement that average men and women were delighted at the prospect of war.'[4]

There is no parallel in modern history to these popular expressions of the will of the nation-state. In the days before the franchise had become general in Europe, they were the equivalent of a landslide vote for war. It was a remarkable spectacle, moving to contemporaries, intelligible today perhaps only to those of a much later generation who witnessed the sailing of the British taskforce for the Falklands in 1982. It is best described by the German word *Wahn* – folly, madness, or more cruelly, in the image of lemmings heading towards the cliffs.

This, however, was no sudden or inexplicable aberration. It was the out-pouring of sentiments which had been developing since the end of the nineteenth century and which would ensure that the ensuing war would continue well beyond the point where, on any rational calculation of *Realpolitik*, a compromise peace should have been negotiated. What is remarkable is that it took the politicians, who had feared a much more unfavourable popular reaction, by surprise. But so did the whole crisis. European opinion and European politicians were mentally oddly unpre-pared for a war which had been long in the making. Political assassina-tions were not unusual during this period, and there was no hint of the 'blank cheque' which Germany had extended on 5 July to Austria against the possibility of Russian intervention in an Austro-Serbian war. The Kaiser had duly departed on a cruise; other key leaders were out of Berlin which the American ambassador described on 8 July, as being as quiet as the grave. The French President and Prime Minister saw no reason to put off a visit to Russia a week later. The British were no more perceptive. The day before the Serbian ultimatum, the Chancellor of the Exchequer, David Lloyd George, told the House of Commons, that relations with Germany were better than they had been for years.[5]

The fundamental problem, however, lay not in the success of the German and Austrian diplomatic smoke screens, but in the way in which Europeans had allowed themselves to be lulled into a false sense of secur-ity in what some at least consciously or subconsciously realised, was an increasingly insecure era. They had convinced themselves (to paraphrase a character in John Buchan's novel, *The Power House*, published the previ-ous year) that a wall 'as solid as the earth' separated civilisation from bar-barism, whereas in fact the division was 'a thread, a sheet of glass'.[6] Something of the ambivalence of a world in which war was perceived as both inevitable and impossible is captured by Churchill:

> Those whose duty it was to watch over the safety of the country lived simultaneously in two different worlds of thought. There was the actual visible world, with its peaceful activities and cosmopolitan aims; and there was a hypothetical world, a 'world beneath the threshold', as it were, a world at one moment utterly fantastic, at the next seeming about to leap into reality – a world of monstrous shadows moving in convul-sive combinations through vistas of fathomless catastrophe.[7]

Progressive nineteenth-century wishful-thinking explains part of the optimism. It was assumed, or hoped, that the better off men became, the more science allowed them to understand the world and to improve their living conditions, the less aggressive they would be. War would become a thing of the past, an atavism unworthy of civilised European men. It was the fact of war, rather than any premonition of the scale of the impending conflict which led Henry James to reflect on 4 August that the

> plunge of civilization into this abyss of blood and darkness ... is a thing which so gives away the whole long age during which we have supposed the world to be, with whatever abatement, gradually bettering, that to have to take it all now for what the treacherous years were really making for and meaning is too tragic for any words.[8]

At the same time there was also a complacency, compounded of a certain fatalism. Europeans had become used to tension and crisis they felt unable to do anything about. They had been living with high levels of armaments for nearly four decades – a period almost exactly as long as the Cold War. During this time the general staffs had been preparing war plans of increasing complexity while, according to A. J. P. Taylor, gravely talking 'of the conflict which would break out when the snow melted on the Balkan mountains. Navies were built and rebuilt; millions of men were trained for war. Nothing happened.'[9] The crisis of July 1914 was the fifth major international crisis in nine years. The previous four had all been successfully weathered. 'It was natural to hope, even expect', Sir Edward Grey wrote in his memoirs, 'that the same methods which had preserved peace hitherto, when it was threatened, would preserve it still.'[10]

It was a candid, but damaging admission. A more perceptive diplomatic observer would have recognised the progressive deterioration in the international situation. The intensification of the arms race from 1910 onwards was one symptom.[11] But it was reflection as much as cause of the tensions which had become increasingly marked since 1905, when Germany's decision to challenge the extension of French control in Morocco produced the most serious strains in Franco-German relations for 20 years – along with much talk of war. The next crisis, this time over Bosnia in 1908 was more serious. In a Europe increasingly polarised around the rival Triple Alliance and Triple Entente, it raised the spectre of a larger conflict which would set Austria–Hungary against Russia, supported by Germany on the one hand, and France and Britain on the other.[12] During the second Agadir crisis of 1911 the British put discreet military preparations into effect. Only a year later there was more trouble in the Balkans in which the Great Powers repeatedly came close to blows. This left a particularly dangerous legacy. It had, in David Stevenson's words:

> cankered European politics. More men had been called up in time of peace than ever before, and many taboos had been broken. In 1911

France and Germany had both stood down their senior conscript class, but in 1912 Russia kept its class on, and the Austrians partially recalled theirs. 'Trial mobilisations' at times of crisis were a new feature of the scene. There were now two players in the game of armed diplomacy in Eastern Europe, and everywhere there were greater spillover effects than previously as the two halves of the Continent were drawn more tightly together.[13]

Only the fact that nobody then saw advantage in direct involvement, and more specifically that the German military believed this would be the wrong war at the wrong time, prevented the outbreak of a larger conflict.[14]

If Grey and the British Foreign Office did not recognise this downward trend toward to war, others were more perceptive. The images of impending disaster can be found in the works of artists such as the Wassily Kandinsky, Ludwig Meidner and Franz Marc. Meidner's *Apocalyptic Landscape* of 1913, painted against the background of the Balkan crisis, reflected a general sense among painters of different schools that the world might soon be threatened by awesome destruction.[15] Visiting the French town of Tours in spring 1914, the Austrian dramatist Stefan Zweig was startled by the depth of antagonism evoked by a newsreel film. The moment the Kaiser had appeared in the screen

> a spontaneous wild whistling and stamping of feet began in the dark hall. Everybody yelled and whistled, men, women and children, as if they had been personally insulted ... I was frightened. I was frightened to the depths of my heart. For I sensed how deeply the poison of the propaganda of hate must have advanced through the years, when even here in a small provincial city the simple citizens and soldiers had been so greatly incited against the Kaiser and against Germany that a passing picture on the screen could produce such a demonstration.[16]

An American diplomatic envoy Colonel Edward House, who had come to Europe to investigate the possibility of a US mediation mission, was equally disconcerted by what he found. Writing from Berlin less than two months before the Archduke's assassination, House reported to President Wilson that the situation was 'extraordinary. It is militarism run stark mad. Unless someone acting for you can bring about a different understanding, there is some day going to be an awful cataclysm.'[17]

Colonel House was visiting Europe at the high noon of power politics. It was a Europe of Powers preoccupied with power to the point of obsession. In no other period was power so popularised. In no other period was it thought about so uncritically, or were its dangers treated with such insouciance. As rivalries had intensified and international politics become increasingly militarised, the 'perpetual quadrille' of the balance of power had given way to something on a much larger, more menacing scale. The caution and constraint which characterised international relations for much of the nineteenth century had long been a thing of the past. The aggressive and antagonistic forms of hypernationalism exposed during the Franco-Prussian War of 1870, in which love of country turned into hatred of other nations, had been more or less held at bay under Bismarck's iron chancellorship. Bismarck had possessed an unusually acute awareness of the limits of power, a sure sense of where it was in Prussia's, and later on in Imperial Germany's, self-interest to stop.

After his removal however German power was managed with a much less sure hand. His successors became willing prey to a force with a quasireligious quality inimical to the rational, if cold-blooded calculation which had been the hallmark of Bismarck's *Realpolitik*; the popular sentiments it tapped were too intense, the ideology it inspired too preoccupied with the exclusive rights of their particular state. 'If the flag of the State is insulted,' wrote the German nationalist historian, Heinrich von Treitschke, 'it is the duty of the State to demand satisfaction, and if satisfaction is not forthcoming, to declare war, however trivial the occasion may appear, for the State must strain every nerve to preserve for itself the respect which it enjoys in the state system.'[18]

Hypernationalism, and the intense emotions which surrounded it, were by no means a German monopoly. The rather more familiar term, 'jingoism', had been coined in Britain as early as 1878 to describe the extreme and distorted patriotic enthusiasm for Disraeli's use of the British fleet in Turkish waters to resist Russian advances. The liberal theorist, J. A. Hobson, linked this phenomenon to the dislocations and disorientations caused by industrialisation and urbanisation. The urban population of Britain increased from 11.2 million in 1890 to 15.8 million in 1913; that of Germany from 5.6 million to 14.1 million over the same period.[19] In his *Psychology of Jingoism*, published during the Boer War, Hobson argued that:

> the neurotic temperament generated by town life seeks natural relief in stormy sensational appeals, and the crowded life of the streets, or other public gatherings, gives the best medium for communicating them. This is the very atmosphere of Jingoism. A coarse patriotism, fed by the wildest rumours, and the most violent appeals to hate and the animal lust of blood, passes by quick contagion through the crowded life of cities, and recommends itself everywhere by the satisfaction it affords to sensational cravings.[20]

Europe was a restless, uncertain and, in the final analysis, dangerously unstable place, whose mood alternated, in L. L. Farrar's term, between arrogance and anxiety.[21] Violence, whether in the form of anarchist's bomb, syndicalists' strike as well as international crisis, was never far from the surface. But the Industrial Revolution had not simply disorientated; it had generated an extraordinary outburst of energy and expansionism. Between 1870 and 1910 the population of Europe grew from 290 to 435 million. National incomes doubled or tripled.[22] Iron and steel production of the major European Powers increased from 15.93 million tons in 1890 to 38.23 million in 1913; energy consumption increased from 287.1 millions of metric tons of coal equivalent to 558.9 over the same period.[23] The result was a will to power, which led states to behave, in H. G. Wells' words, like 'ill-bred people in a crowded public car,' who begin 'to squeeze against one another, elbow, thrust dispute and quarrel.'[24] Looking back on the causes of the war many years later, Stefan Zweig believed that:

> It had nothing to do with ideas, and hardly even with petty frontiers. I cannot explain it otherwise than by this surplus of force, a tragic consequence of the internal dynamism that had accumulated in those forty years of peace and now sought release. Every State suddenly had the feeling of being strong, and forgot that every other State had the same feeling, each wanted more and wanted something from the other.[25]

The most tangible expression of this assertive dynamism was Imperialism. World conquest preceded world war. In the Far East, Japan had begun to establish its Asian empire in Korea. The United States had taken the Philippines. France, Russia, Britain and Germany were all engaged in competition for empire and domination. From 1876 to 1914 the colonial powers annexed over 11 million square miles of territory.[26] Even a liberal like Herbert Asquith believed that expansion was 'as normal, as necessary, as inescapable and unmistakeable a sign of vitality in a nation as the corresponding processes in the growing human body'.[27] Cecil Rhodes, an avowed imperialist, put a more specifically political gloss on this. The lesson, as read by Rhodes, was that 'expansion was everything, and that the world's surface being limited, the great object of present humanity should be to take as much of the world as it possibly could'.[28]

This intensely competitive environment found its ideology in the crude social and political extrapolations from Darwin's *Origin of Species*, encapsulated in Spencer's neat phrase, 'the survival of the fittest', or '*der Kampf des Daseins*'. The notion of Social Darwinism (though the term itself was not in fact used during the nineteenth century), gained vogue after the Franco-Prussian War.[29] It appealed to a Europe living off its nerves, in which competition at all levels often seemed almost literally a life and death affair. The rhetoric tells its own story. 'The strong and the hungry,' argued one British writer, warming to the theme of the Empire's need to look to its defence, 'will eat the weak, fat and defenceless whenever they can get a chance'.[30] The German writer, Clauss Wagner, taking the higher theoretical ground, declared that:

> The natural law, to which all law of Nature can be reduced, is the law of struggle. All intra-social property, all thoughts, inventions, and institutions, as, indeed, the social system itself are a result of intra-social struggle, in which one survives and another is cast out. The extra-social, the super-social, struggle, which guides the external development of societies, nations, and races, is war.[31]

Hunold von Ahlefeld, Director of the Imperial German dockyards at Kiel, took a more immediately practical view when he saw the struggle for survival raging 'between individuals, provinces, parties, states ... there is nothing we can do about this, except to join in. He who doesn't will perish.'[32] Karl Marx too had taken the point, although Darwin declined the offer of having the English edition of *Das Kapital* dedicated to him.

Implicit in the thinking of Social Darwinists was a world in which resources were finite, so that the gains of one state would be automatically denied to others. Colonies and markets came very much into this category. Social Darwinists saw trade not in terms of a peaceful exchange of nations but rather as a relationship between acquisitive tribes, where if one robs the other is robbed, thus making them enthusiastic subscribers to protectionism and mercantilism. States in other words could not afford to live and let live. Nor did they particularly wish to do so. Social Darwinism was more than a symptom of troubled times and the acute sense of insecurity which went with it. It also served to legitimise ruthlessness in the name of the laws of science and nature. Those who survived had a right to dominate, since in the struggle between nations and empires, the victors had *ipso facto* proved themselves morally superior. War, and this of course was a remarkably convenient doctrine for those seeking to disguise old-fashioned ambitions and land-hunger, ceased to have a merely political function as an instrument of policy. It was now seen as a means of 'selection', an integral part of the larger process of evolution, an instrument of progress.

This view of war was part of a set of anti-liberal nineteenth-century values which placed a premium on the heroic, on sacrifice, on the ennobling deed as a counter to the greed and the growing materialism of the age. Already in the middle of the century, at the time of the Crimean conflict, there existed a 'redemptive' view of war whose supporters included no less respectable a figure than Tennyson:

> We are noble still
> It is better to fight for the good than to rail at the ill;
> I have felt with my native land, I am one with my kind,
> I embrace the purpose of God, and the doom assign'd.[33]

The theme proved perniciously tenacious. War represented 'motion and life'. Perpetual peace, growled the elder von Moltke after receiving a copy of a model law of war produced by the Institute of International Law in 1880, is 'a dream, and not even a beautiful dream. War is an element of the divine order of the world. In it are developed the noblest virtues of man ...'[34]

There were of course dissenters. There was an active peace movement. Norman Angell's *The Great Illusion* sold more than two million copies between 1910 and 1913.[35] Some 250 000 people attended an anti-war demonstration in Berlin in September 1911 at the time of the second Agadir crisis.[36] Nevertheless the prevailing mood was one of what Michael Howard has described as 'bellicism' – a cultural disposition to war.[37] This mood had never been as prevalent in the past; it would never again, not even in Nazi Germany, be so intense in the future. The evidence is to be be found in a wide range of sources – not just in the press and public speeches, but in the emphasis which school history syllabuses placed on war and the preoccupation of popular history with battles. There was an outpouring of novels and stories with such titles as *La Guerre de Demain*, *The Invasion of of 1910* or *Der Weltkrieg*. The genre provided, what I. F. Clarke describes as the 'perfect para-utopias for an era of exaggerated nationalism. Politics and self-persuasion combined to create a vision of the glorious nation imposing its will on the unspeakable enemy'. The novelists also turned their attention to the military implications of aviation far more quickly than did the general staffs.[38]

In general, however, fact and fiction proved disconcertingly close. The links between nationalism and the army were carefully cultivated. The armed forces had come to be regarded as the embodiment of the nation. Military parades, bands and ceremonial provided an image with which all classes could identify, and through which social order and cohesion could be maintained.[39] The influence of the armed forces was reinforced by the militarised chauvinism promulgated by such bodies as the German *Flottenverein*, the English Navy League, the public schools and indeed the Boy Scouts founded in 1908 by a hero of Mafeking, Lt Colonel Robert Baden-Powell. Within two years there were 100 000 scouts in Britain.[40] Their motto, 'Be prepared', had overtly military connotations.

But prepared for what? The contemporary image of war was a highly romantic, and romanticised one. The long immunity from the realities of warfare, as G. P. Gooch noted in 1901, had blunted the public imagination. It thought of wars in terms of excitement and victory.[41] When war eventually came in 1914, therefore, it was welcomed not just as the fulfilment of nationalist purpose, but as a great romantic adventure. Hitler later wrote how on leaving Munich he first saw the Rhine:

> as we rode westward along its quiet waters to defend it, the German stream of streams, from the greed of the old enemy. When through the tender veil of the early morning mist the Niederwald monument gleamed down upon us in the gentle first rays of the sun, the old *Watch on the Rhine* roared out of the endless transport train into the morning sky, and I felt as though my heart would burst.[42]

Many of the young men who rushed to the colours in 1914 sought a means of escape from the dull, meaningless regimentation of life in a modern industrialised society. It was an odd choice – the swapping of one form of regimentation for another, but then the recruits of 1914, like the generals and politicians, were remarkably ignorant about the reality of modern warfare. During those feverish, hysterical days when Europe slid so willingly into disaster, it was possible to write poetry beginning

> *Frohlockt, ihr Freunde, dass wir leben,*
> *Und dass wir jung sind und gelenk*

(Rejoice, friends that we're alive, And that we are young and nimble!)[43] Rupert Brooke's sonnet, *Peace*, has proved as lasting a memorial to the spirit of August 1914, as have the villages stones and crosses to the blood-letting which followed:

> Now, God be thanked Who has matched us with His hour,
> And caught our youth, and wakened us from sleeping,
> With hand made sure, clear eye, and sharpened power,
> To turn, as swimmers into cleanness leaping,
>
> Glad from a world grown old and cold and weary,
> Leave the sick hearts that honour could not move,
> And half-men, and their dirty songs and dreary,
> And all the little emptiness of love!
>
> Oh! we who have known shame, we have found release there,
> Where there's no ill, no grief but sleep has mending,
> Naught broken save this body, lost but breath;
> Nothing to shake the laughing heart's long peace there

But only agony, and that has ending;
And the worst friend and enemy is but Death.[44]

If death was to become the great leveller, then the idea of war was grasped at in 1914 as the great unifier, a force which would transcend class barriers and create that sense of community which the societies of this dynamic, insecure and regimented Continent felt to be so conspicuously lacking.[45]

The crisis of 1914, therefore, broke in a Europe already in crisis, or rather in a series of crises. European society had lost its traditional anchor points, its shared values and common constraints. The mood, the climate of ideas, the clash of national ambitions all pointed to the need for governments to maintain an unusually clear head in their management of power; they also made it very unlikely that this would happen. It is difficult to avoid the conclusion that politically and psychologically the First World War was a war waiting to happen – the eventual explosion of pressures which had been building up for decades. By 1914, men, in Churchill's phrase, 'were everywhere eager to dare'.[46] But it was the public rather than governments which were spoiling for war. Power, as we have seen, had been popularised. The diplomats, as we are about to see, tended to be much more cautious. The key exception, and the countries where the pressures were most marked, were Austria and Germany. This is not to argue that Germany 'caused' the First World War. The story is rather more complicated than that. But it was the challenge posed by Europe's newest and most restless Power around which the diplomacy of the prewar years centred, and the future place of Germany over which the eventual war was fought.

What made Germany so dangerous was not so much the power it had at its disposal, as the way this politically unstable, ill-led state handled that power. Wilhemine Germany prized and accumulated power, without ever understanding its nature and limitations. Some of the general reasons for this have already been touched on, but there is also something more exclusively German. Henry Kissinger ascribes the obsession of German statesmen with naked power to the fact that,

> in contrast to other nation-states, Germany did not possess any integrating philosophical framework. None of the ideals which had shaped the modern nation-state in the rest of Europe was present in Bismarck's construction – not Great Britain's emphasis on traditional liberties, the French Revolution's appeal to universal freedom, or even the benign universalist imperialism of Austria. Strictly speaking, Bismarck's

Germany did not embody the aspirations of a nation-state at all, because he had deliberately excluded the Austrian Germans. Bismarck's Reich was an artifice, being foremost a greater Prussia whose principal purpose was to increase its own power.[47]

German leaders never came to grips with the dangers of their position as Europe's middle Power, at once easily strong enough to upset the balance of power, but unable to impose its will on the Continent. They never for a moment recognised that the very Industrial Revolution which had made them powerful, was transforming the power politics to which they instinctively turned into a deadly anachronism. They never, prior to September 1914, defined a clear set of objectives, let along a strategy for achieving them.

Much had changed since 1870 and the days when Bismarck had conducted foreign policy on the premise that the new Germany was a satisfied Power with a strong stake in the continuing stability of Europe. At the time of unification, Germany had been a largely rural state, only slightly less rural and slightly more industrialised in character than Prussia had been in 1816. By the 1890s, it was well on the way to being one of the world's foremost industrial powers, its population having grown by 25 million in less than that number of years. Small wonder therefore that the country should start to set its sights rather higher than it had done in Bismarck's day; small wonder too that this should first be reflected in colonial policy where Germany was heavily disadvantaged. 'The question,' Prince Bernhard von Buelow, chancellor from 1890–1901 declared, 'is not, whether we want to colonise or not, but that we *must* colonise, whether we want it or not'. (Emphasis in original.)[48] Kurt Riesler, foreign policy assistant to Bethmann Hollweg, and a man very much influenced by both Nietzsche and Social Darwinism. spoke of a young nation 'of enormous energy and capacity' and a rapidly growing population which had 'awakened to activity ... External capacity and internal vitality force it to engage in *Weltpolitik*'.[49]

By the end of the 1890s the urge to *Weltpolitik* had crystallised into something more dangerous – the establishment of a German battlefleet. Naval power was internationally fashionable. Its best known exponent, the American, Alfred Mahan, argued that seapower, commerce and colonies were inseparably connected, the indispensable foundation of national wealth and prosperity. The Kaiser, who was among Mahan's wide circle of readers, had translations of his works placed aboard every vessel in the German fleet. Seapower increasingly meant battleships, the contemporary symbol of national pride, which embodied the technological achievement of the whole nation, world reach and, of course, with their huge guns, immense destructive power.[50] 'A really Great Power with a seaboard', Bethmann Hollweg insisted, 'could not be a *Landratte* (landrat): she *must* have a fleet and a strong one, not merely for the purpose of defending her commerce but for the general purpose of her greatness.'[51]

But the fleet also had a much more specifically defined purpose, which its architect, Admiral Alfred von Tirpitz, was careful to hide when piloting his first naval bill through the *Reichstag*. The British empire had expanded by one third in the last 15 years of the nineteenth century, to the point where it was no less than 40 times the size of its German counterpart.[52] Tirpitz believed that Britain was determined to prevent Germany becoming a world power. And it was the Royal Navy which was the real target of the new fleet. This did not mean that Tirpitz was planning war. But a German fleet would provide an important instrument of pressure, especially if it could be constructed 'to unfold its greatest military potential between Heligoland and the Thames'. In wartime, Britain would then be forced to recall squadrons from the Mediterranean and Far East, leaving these vulnerable to attack by other powers. And this, or so Tirpitz believed, would encourage Britain to seek accommodation to Germany's advantage.[53]

Tirpitz is a remarkable figure. The photo of this man with his bold domed head, forked beard and penetrating eyes bears witness to his reputation for ruthlessness, aggressiveness and above all an obsessive belief in German seapower. Determination and strategic insight, in the broadest sense of the word, did not, however, go together. Tirpitz had embarked on a very dangerous strategy, one which puts him at the front of a line of German leaders, culminating with Hitler, who consistently miscalculated British policy. Tirpitz was posing a direct challenge at the point of Britain's greatest power – and vulnerability. His object was to intimidate Britain. Unlike Hitler, at least until 1939, he only succeeded in provoking her.

The British were worried about the rise of German power. They sensed that the period of their pre-eminence was passing, indeed the idea if not the phrase of *Weltmacht oder Niedergang* (world power or decline) was as prevalent in Britain as it was in Germany. The preoccupation of the British official class with Social Darwinism reflected this defensive pessimism.[54] But while they would negotiate over secondary issues, such as the future partition of Portuguese colonies, they were in no mood to engage in appeasement. They had no inkling of the price of defeating Germany in a protracted land war which they never expected to fight. But in so far that the appeasement option was considered, it was dismissed as tactically unsound. In his famous memorandum of 1907, the senior clerk at the Foreign Office issued a warning which a future generation of British policy-makers in the 1930s was to ignore at its cost. 'To give way to the blackmailer's menaces enriches him,' wrote Eyre Crowe,

> but it has long been proved by uniform experience that, although this may secure for the victim temporary peace, it is certain to lead to renewed molestation and higher demands after ever-shortening periods of amicable forebearance. The blackmailer's trade is generally ruined by the first resolute stand made against his exactions and the determination rather to face all risks of a possibly disagreeable situation than to continue in the path of endless concessions.[55]

The implications of this were ominous. Germany's relations with the other European states were reaching an *impasse*. The boorish, blustering diplomacy of Europe's *parvenu* power, particularly noticeable in the Agadir incidents, had only succeeded in provoking antagonism and making others feel threatened. Germany had effectively isolated itself; Britain had abandoned its 'splendid isolation' in favour of its old rivals, France and Russia to form the Triple Entente. It had also entered into tentative, though important, staff talks with the French. But if the existing powers would not accommodate the new arrival, if Germany lacked the diplomatic finesse to establish its position by less threatening means, if the whole ethos of the period served to emphasise the military dimension of power, there could only be trouble.

Given more far-sighted leadership, it is possible that things might still have worked out differently. But the hard fact is that there were no sustained efforts to defuse the situation, or to establish a basis for a new European *modus vivendi*. There were Anglo-German naval talks which yielded nothing. There were the two Hague disarmament conferences of 1899 and 1907 – a third scheduled for 1915 never met. Disarmament conferences were a new feature on the diplomatic scene. As rapidly became clear however, they were significant as a symptom of the growing importance attached to the military dimensions of the balance of power, rather than as a cure for the problems they were ostensibly intended to address. Few of the powers, other than Russia, whose interest had originally been motivated by the increasing economic burden of armaments, showed any enthusiasm. Indeed much of the European political class objected to the vary principle of discussing arms limitation, insisting on untramelled sovereignty in defence matters.[56] The Hague conferences did nothing to slow the arms race, and one of the few agreements reached, on the limitation of the use of poison gas in warfare, was promptly broken in 1915. The old

Concert of Europe had a final success in 1912 in defusing the Balkan crisis, but this was a one-off achievement which proved impossible to repeat when Grey tried to resurrect the idea two years later. If there was a diplomatic option for the resolution of the German problem in the years before 1914, nobody succeeded in finding it.

The situation was further aggravated by domestic politics. During the first Hague conference, the German military delegate had refuted Russian and Dutch claims that the arms race was imposing an impossible burden on the countries of Europe. The German people, he declared, were 'not crushed beneath the weight of armament expenditure ... They are not hastening toward exhaustion and ruin.'[57] As the new century drew on, however, the burdens of the Anglo-German arms race began to tell politically. The question of how revenue to pay for the new ships was to be raised became increasingly contentious in a country where the form and phenomenal speed of industrialisation was straining political stability. *Weltpolitik*, as indeed the whole naval programme, had been at least in part a deliberate strategy by the traditional ruling classes to defuse these tensions. As Chancellor von Buelow had put it, 'only a successful foreign policy can hope to reconcile, pacify, rally, unify'.[58]

But the policy had not been successful. The European Powers, as we have had already noted, were no more willing to accommodate Germany than the Kaiser and the Junkers were disposed to share power with the Social Democrats. Both the Powers and the German establishment felt threatened; both dug in their heels. Meanwhile the arms race had to be paid for. The result was an increasingly acrimonious argument about how the burden of taxation was to be shared.[59]

As the failures of domestic and foreign policy increasingly fed on each other, they created a mood of intense pessimism in Berlin. The confidence of the 1890s was giving way to a sense of paranoia. Bismarck's '*cauchemar des coalitions*', an affliction, he had once written, which German ministers were liable to have for the indefinite future, began to weigh more and more heavily on those now in office.[60] They became obsessed with the idea of encirclement, and obsessed with the expansion of the French, and above all the Russian, armies. No matter that the Russians had no offensive designs, that their military expansion was a reaction to that of Germany and that they themselves remained much more conscious of the internal weaknesses which had contributed to their defeat at the hands of the Japanese in 1905, and would lead to revolution and defeat in 1917. All these considerations were ignored as the Germans concentrated on the Russian railway building programme, and the manpower reserves of a country whose population of 171 million people, was close to three times their own. Bethmann-Hollweg, looking over the park at his estate of Hohenfinow north east of Berlin, gloomily wondered whether there was any point in planting new trees, since in a few years' time 'the Russians would be here anyway'.[61]

This was the background against which the idea of a preventive war began to take shape. But the point was not just that it would be better for Germany to attack before she was attacked; war was also seen as a way of breaking out of what seemed an increasingly impossible domestic and international situation. The arguments were of course couched primarily in military terms. In conversation with a senior official at the German Foreign Office in May 1914, the Chief of Staff, the younger von Moltke, expressed deep concern about what would happen when Russia completed her armament programme in two to three years. The military superiority of Germany's enemies would then be so great that he did not know how to cope, whereas now the Germans would still be more or less a match for them. Only a week before the assassination of the Archduke, the Kaiser was speculating whether it might not be better to attack than to wait. A few days earlier Colonel House had warned Grey that Germany 'would strike quickly when she moved; that there would be no parley or discussion; that when she felt that a difficulty could not be overcome by peaceful negotiation she would take no chances but would strike'.[62]

In the event the Germans acted with less decisiveness than House had anticipated. Isolation had forced Berlin into an increasingly close alliance with Vienna, capital of what one German officer called 'the hotch-potch Danubian monarchy'.[63] While nationalism had united Germany, it threatened the Austro-Hungarian Empire with dissolution. In December 1913, the French ambassador, in a comment which might also have been applied to Germany, had reported that Austria 'finds herself in an impasse without knowing how she is to escape ... People here are becoming accustomed to the idea of a general war as the only possible remedy.'[64] But when a potential *casus belli* presented itself six months later, the Austrians reacted with an understandable caution. They welcomed the chance for a 'final and fundamental reckoning' with the government in Belgrade, which they saw as posing a direct threat to the integrity of the empire. But they were also well aware of Serbia's alliance with Russia, and would only take action if assured of German support.[65]

The Austrians had a clear grievance and reasonably clearly defined objectives. The underlying issues for Germany, as indeed for all of the other major Powers by contrast, were at once more nebulous and much more far-reaching. This was a crisis about power and the balance of power in which one side gambled and the others felt compelled to react.

None of them deliberately set out to start a general European war, but nor were they disposed to take extraordinary measures to prevent one. The crucial phase at the very end of July, from the point of the initial Russian partial mobilisation on 25 July, occurred without any serious exchange between Berlin and St Petersburg regarding the political substance of the crisis.[66]

The German records of what happened next are incomplete. But there was no formal discussion of the issues and options, as there had been, albeit imperfectly, in Vienna. The key decisions in a remarkably erratic and ill-coordinated administration lay with the impulsive figure of the Kaiser whom Grey, six years earlier, had likened to 'a great battleship with steam up and the screws going but no rudder and you cannot tell what he will run into or what catastrophe he will cause'.[67] Wilhelm's decision was in part motivated by monarchical solidarity and outrage at the assassination of a comrade. But he had already promised to back military action against Serbia the previous autumn and was well aware both of Russia's growing military strength and the implications of an Austrian–Hungarian collapse. The Chancellor saw diplomatic opportunities extending well beyond the Balkans, in the event of a localised or even a wider Continental war.[68]

By 5 July, when Count Szogyeny, the Austrian ambassador, presented Franz-Joseph's hand-written request for German support, the die appears to have been cast. The Kaiser's opening response was cautious. It was only after lunch that the mood changed, when, in one of the most gratuitously irresponsible acts of twentieth century history, the Kaiser extended his infamous 'blank cheque'. It was here at the New Palace in Potsdam, rather than in Sarajevo, that Europe's fate was decided. The ambassador's account of what happened next, addressed to the Austrian Foreign Minister, conveys little or no awareness of the momentous nature of the occasion:

> The Kaiser authorised me to inform our gracious Majesty that we might in this case, as in all others, rely upon Germany's full support. He must, as he said before, hear first what the Imperial Chancellor has to say, but he did not doubt in the least that Herr von Bethmann Hollweg would agree with him. Especially as far as our action against Serbia was concerned. But it was his (Kaiser Wilhelm's) opinion that this action must not be delayed. Russia's attitude will no doubt be hostile, but to this he had been for years prepared, and should a war between Austria–Hungary and Russia be unavoidable, we might be convinced that Germany, our old faithful ally, would stand at our side. Russia at the

present time was in no way prepared for war, and would think twice before it appealed for arms.[69]

The Kaiser reverted to this last point in subsequent discussions with his advisers. The Tsar, he believed, would not place himself on the side of 'the regicides'. As to Russia's long-standing ally, France, it would 'scarcely let it come to a war as it lacked the artillery for the field armies'.[70] But there was a risk of a larger conflict. The Kaiser had acknowledged this, at least implicitly, when he instructed the military to be ready for all eventualities. Bethmann Hollweg spoke privately of the possibility of world war, as did the only other civilian to attend the meeting with the Kaiser on the afternoon of the 5 July, the Under-secretary of State in the Foreign Office, Arthur Zimmermann. This was indeed a 'leap in the dark'; it was hardly however, as some of those involved chose to believe, a calculated risk.[71]

In making these unduly sanguine assessments, the German leadership may have subconsciously chosen to downplay the danger. In contrast to previous crises they were now disposed to take decisive action, and may not have wanted to dwell too much on what this entailed. What is quite clear is that the risks they were running were forseeable and had not been carefully thought through. The Germans made a series of miscalculations, the first of which concerned the Russian reaction to the Serbian ultimatum. In encouraging Austria to take on Serbia, the Germans were throwing down a challenge which their rivals simply could not afford to ignore. Russian policy had been generally passive in recent years. But by early 1914, under the influence of the growing military strength which the Germans so feared, there was a feeling in Moscow that it was time for Russia to reassert its interests.[72] They were no longer willing, the words are those of the Tsar, to let themselves 'be trampled upon'.[73] Russian policy, the Russian Foreign Minister Sergei Sazonov warned the Austro-Hungarian Ambassador just before the delivery of the ultimatum to Serbia, *'est pacifique mais pas passive'*.[74] This did not mean that they actively sought war. The order for partial mobilisation given on 25 July was intended only as a warning to Austria; full mobilisation was authorised by the Tsar five days later with the greatest reluctance. But the Russians had reached the point where they felt they no longer had any alternative. As Sazonov argued to his colleagues in the Council of Ministers on 24 July, to make concessions now would only mean that Russia would face similar forceful German challenges in the future. The time had come to show such methods could no longer be effective.[75] (This was precisely the same argument which Eyre Crowe had put forward seven years earlier.)

Once Russia was involved, the crisis was bound to escalate. This was not because of anything the Triple Entente had previously agreed. Military cooperation was limited and the alliance was not intended to act as a deterrent. Its real existence, as Sazonov had remarked a few months earlier, was no more proved than that 'of the sea serpent'.[76] The crucial link between Russian mobilisation and British intervention which ensured that this would be a Continental War, lay rather in the Germans' own military planning. What is truly extraordinary about the events of July 1914 is not that the Germans gambled; it is that they did so on the assumption that a war could be localised when they had no plans to fight a limited engagement.

In advancing the 'blank cheque', the Kaiser appears to have taken inexcusably little account of the rigidity of his army's military planning. Once again the record is incomplete, but it appears that in 1913 Moltke had discarded *Grosse Ostaufmarsch*, which provided for the deployment of the main German force to the east, and had until then had been kept up to date in the General Staff files.[77] The only plan available in 1914 therefore was the one drawn up by the former Chief of Staff, Count Alfred von Schlieffen. War against Russia would begin with a knock-blow against French forces in the west, after which the German forces would turn their attention to the lumbering military giant in the east. The political risks of an operation involving the violation of Belgian neutrality had not been ignored. But while Schlieffen assumed British hostility, he also assumed that the British land force would be too small, and arrive too late to be effective. None of this, however, was ever subjected to proper scrutiny, although leading political figures, including Bethman Hollweg, appear to have long been aware of, and approved of, the plan's outlines, if not of all the details. According to David Stevenson, Bethmann Hollweg 'knew enough to realize that German mobilization would set all Europe ablaze'.[78] But this did not induce caution during the July crisis.

One reason for this may have been that, unlike Schlieffen, Bethmann Hollweg believed that Britain could be persuaded to stay out of a Continental quarrel. It was a fundamental misreading of British policy and history but it was one to which, in the short-term at least, the British contributed. For it was only very late in the crisis that they began to warn Germany of the dangers of a European war. Grey was missing a vital piece of intelligence – he did not know of the 'blank cheque' and despite a veiled warning from the German ambassador, Prince Lichnowsky did not recognise the the German hand behind the Austrian ultimatum.[79] His initial assumption on the contrary was that British mediation might defuse the crisis. There were in consequence no military signals such as the mobilisation of the Fleet to warn the Germans off.[80]

By 3 August British policy had changed dramatically, but it had taken considerable political effort to bring this about. In the run-up to the final crisis, the bellicose sentiment of earlier years was notably evident. As the cabinet shifted its attentions from Ulster to the European situation, opinion was overwhelming pacific.[81] It took the German declaration of war on France and, a matter of particular sensitivity in London, violation of Belgian neutrality of which Britain was a guarantor, for the government to accept that Britain's standing as a Great Power was at stake. To ignore its obligations and stand aside would leave the country's reputation in tatters. No less important, it would violate that cardinal principle of British foreign policy, the maintenance of the European balance of power. Had the Germans really worked out the risks, they would have realised that it was inconceivable that Britain would allow them to get into a situation where they would dominate Europe and control the Channel ports. Nor, although this was only spelled out in the privacy of the Foreign Office minutes, could she afford to stand aside only to find herself faced with a French and Russian victory. Such an outcome would raise very awkward questions about the future of the British position in India and the Mediterranean.[82]

During the last stages of the crisis, as the full implications of what was happening became clear, there were attempts to draw back. 'We must decline', Bethmann Hollweg declared early in the morning of 30 July, 'to let ourselves be dragged by Vienna, wantonly, and without regard to our advice, into a world conflagration'.[83] On 1 August, after the order for general mobilisation had been given, a telegram arrived in Berlin which appeared to suggest that if Germany undertook not to attack France, Britain would guarantee that France would not enter war against Germany. Bethmann Hollweg and the Kaiser were delighted. 'Now,' said the latter, 'we need only wage war against Russia! So we simply advance with the whole army in the east!' His Chief of Staff was horrified. Such a reversal, von Moltke replied, was

> impossible. The deployment of an army a million strong was not a thing to be improvised; it was the product of a whole year's hard work and once planned could not be changed. If His Majesty were to insist on directing the whole army to the east, he would not have an army pre-pared for the attack, but a barren heap of armed men disorganised and without supplies.[84]

The telegram turned out to have been based on a misunderstanding, and von Moltke's categorical assertion was subsequently disputed by a senior logistics expert on the German General Staff.[85] (He was in any case temporarily and partially overruled.) Europe was now to pay an appalling price for the way all classes, from the generals and politicians who 'managed' the crisis, to the intellectuals and workers who first celebrated and then volunteered to fight, had become intoxicated with the idea of power, while failing to grasp its military realities.

3 'This Isn't War'

The military, like the politicians and public, found themselves at once prepared and quite unprepared for war. A great deal of military planning had taken place in the years before 1914, and the mobilisation plans in particular had been developed in considerable detail. But the armies in Europe were completely unprepared for the prolonged military stalemate in which they were about to engage on the Western, though not, it should be added, the Eastern, Front. Although they did not immediately realise it, the Powers had gone to war at a time when their instruments of national coercion had been temporarily blunted. They now found themselves with the wrong weapons, the wrong plans, the wrong tactics. Their generals were to take an inordinately long and bloody time before they learned how effectively to fight, let alone win, a modern war on this quite unprecedented scale.

Although much has been made of the importance of the 'railway timetables' during the final phase of the July crisis, the military pre-history of the First World War has received far less attention than it deserves. This is unfortunate because while, as Marc Trachtenberg has argued, the influence of the generals in the final days of the peace may have been exaggerated,[1] the pre-war failures of the military were to exert a desperately debilitating influence over the course of the conflict, the repercussions of which were to make themselves felt long after the fighting was over. As in other cases where states have been surprised such as Pearl Harbor or the German attack on the Soviet Union in 1941, the danger signs had been there for those who were prepared to see them. Although there had been no major conflict in Europe since the Franco-Prussian War of 1870, a good deal of evidence had accumulated to suggest that a war between the Powers would now be something very different from the short, sharp shock of conventional wisdom. From the 1880s onwards a number of commentators began warning of the military crisis to come. They included Friedrich Engels, historians such as Sir Charles Dilke in Britain and Jean Colin in France, as well as a few military writers. Among the latter were Colonel Frederick Maurice, author of a celebrated essay entitled *War* published in 1891 and General Colmar von der Goltz, who eight years later predicted that a future war would be waged with 'a destructive force such as has hitherto never been displayed. War is now an exodus of nations and no longer a mere conflict between armies.'[2]

Concern extended to the most senior military levels. General Joffre is recorded in 1913 as noting privately that the next war would last several years. Kitchener too expected a longer war. Two of Germany's most prestigious officers took an even gloomier view. As early as 1879 the elder von Moltke had ceased to believe in the possibility of a repeat of the knock-out blow which he had delivered against France at Sedan. As time went on he became increasingly pessimistic, to the point where he believed that a future war might last between seven and fourteen years.[3] Before his appointment as Chief of Staff in 1906, von Moltke's nephew told the Kaiser that the next war would be one between peoples which would not be concluded with a single battle. It would be a 'long, weary, struggle with a country that will not acknowledge defeat until the whole strength of its people is broken; a war that even if we should be the victors will push our people, too, to the limits of exhaustion'. As late as 29 July 1914 the Younger von Moltke warned that without an eleventh hour miracle almost the whole of European civilisation would be annihilated for 'decades to come'.[4]

These, however, were no more than generalised warnings. There was only one man who studied the issue in real detail. Born of humble Jewish parents in Poland, Ivan Bloch had made his name and fortune as a banker, financier and large-scale railway contractor. But his key claim to lasting fame lies in his role as a crusader against war, 'a Polish Richard Cobden – desiring peace, free trade, and the triumph of commerce and industry over war'. He brought to the study of armed conflict an entirely new mind which combined the analytical skills of the engineer, economist and sociologist.[5] Although he had had practical experience of military logistics – he had been responsible for organising the Russian railway supplies in the war against Turkey of 1877 – he was not a military man. This, however, was in many respects an advantage. As he told his English translator, Wickham Stead, it was precisely the bystander who is the better able to see 'the drift and trend of things than those who are busily engaged in the actual detail of the operation'.[6] The result was a six volume study, which took eight years to research and ran to no less than 3085 pages, whose full English title, (it was originally published in French) was *The Future of War in its Technical, Economic and Political Relations*. It provided a bleakly pessimistic assessment. Bloch saw the war of the future as a long drawn out conflict. It would be a war of entrenchments in which the advantage would lie with the defensive, a war which would drain Europe to the point of famine and revolution.

Among the most important factors of which Bloch had taken account, was the greatly increased size of European armies which had followed the growth in population over the nineteenth century. Bloch estimated that in a war between the two rival alliances some ten million men would be under arms. Such forces posed challenges of logistics, command and control, and it was still to be proved 'whether the human brain, or at least human organisation was capable of directing the movement and sustenance of such numbers'.[7] The general of the future would require managerial, as well as the more traditional military, qualities. And when he made mistakes, as undoubtedly he would do, they would prove unprecedentedly expensive in human lives.

Bloch also paid considerable attention to the revolution in firepower. Smokeless powder, patented by Alfred Nobel in the late 1880s, opened up and extended the battlefield. It cleared the field of vision and made possible the concealment of guns, speeded their reloading and increased the range and accuracy of artillery five or six fold. An army could now be brought under fire before it had even come into sight.[8] Although Bloch made relatively little of the machine gun, he was quite clear how devastating other changes in rifle design which allowed for much more rapid rates of fire, immensely longer range and far greater precision, would prove. So great had the power of rifle fire become, that Bloch believed that it was now impossible for combatants to close in on each other. One hundred men in a trench could, he estimated, put out of action 336 out of 400 attackers trying to cross a fire zone only three hundred yards wide.[9]

Bloch was by no means ignored. His book was widely read and translated and is credited with helping influence the Tsar's call for the the first disarmament conference in the Hague in 1899. His critics however were unimpressed. In Germany Bloch was dismissed as a dilettante whose lack of *first hand* military experience seriously impaired the value of his work. From the 'scientific' standpoint Hans Delbruck declared, 'the work does not have much to recommend it ... the conclusions are extremely faulty and hastily drawn'. Such favourable reaction as there was among military professionals appears to have been confined to the small and unprestigious technical services. Infantry and cavalry officers resisted statistical analysis of casualties which suggested that bayonet, sword and lance had become obsolete.[10] Bloch's thesis went against the whole ethos of the period. His conclusions were altogether too radical and too unpalatable to meet ready acceptance. Whether Bloch would have had more influence had he lived to pursue the debate must be a matter of guesswork; he died two years after the book was published.

The problem, however, lay not simply with the unwelcome nature of his prognosis. Bloch's military audience also had a much narrower view of military power. Most of them took little account of economic, technical or political factors. Nor were they under pressure to do so. Remarkably for an era of high military spending and growing international tension, coordination with the politicians and diplomats was poor. The military were left very much to their own devices. Their judgement was insufficiently questioned; their planning and thinking were subjected to inadequate scrutiny or supervision.

This failure was particularly acute in Germany where the military had long developed a formidable power base. Even Bismarck had had difficulties in ensuring military subordination to civil authority. Military leaders succeeded in protecting their establishment from any effective measure of civilian control, maintaining the army as what the chief of the military cabinet described as an 'insulated body into which no one dare peer with critical eyes'.[11] This was not too difficult in the segmented and ill-coordinated structure of the German governmental machine. The military were readily allowed to concentrate on their professional responsibilities. The Chancellery, Foreign Office and the Reichstag all showed a dangerous indifference to the details of warmaking.[12] As Arden Bucholz notes, the Foreign Ministry did not concern itself with the technical plans of another department. Specialisation, document classification and need-to-know rules, compartmentalised knowledge. Each specialist respected the technical judgement of his peers. Political leaders deferred to specialists. In Germany, as indeed elsewhere in Europe, national leaders betrayed a 'bland ignorance' of defence questions.[13]

In Britain, they didn't want to know. Senior ministers allowed the army planners to go ahead with staff talks with the French without challenging their assumptions that the war in which the British Expeditionary Force (BEF) would participate would be short, or that a small force some four or five divisions strong could make any significant impact. On only one occasion, in August 1911 did the Committee for Imperial Defence discuss matters of grand strategy or strategic coordination. Asquith often did not understand defence issues, and had an evident distaste for the idea of intervention in a Continental war.[14] Grey too appears to have had an aversion to military affairs. He 'neither understood nor wished to understand' the way in which from the beginning of the Anglo-French staff talks in 1906 officers were taking decisions which would limit his diplomatic options. *The Times* military correspondent attributed the government's failure to recognise the implications of these talks to 'a complete disbelief of both great political parties that such war would ever came, and their determination that we should never take serious part in it ... if it came. The chance that such aggression might be forced upon us by the aggression of a foreign power,' he tellingly adds, 'was too inconvenient to be considered.'[15] When the cabinet did finally begin to wrestle with the crisis at the very end of July 1914, it did not solicit military opinion, nor was any meeting of the Committee of Imperial Defence held.[16]

This was foolhardy. Military plans and assumptions had important political implications, a point which at least one senior officer had noted 22 years before the outbreak of the First World War. In the course of the Franco-Russian negotiations which led to the formation of the Dual Alliance, the Russian Adjutant General, Nikolai Obruchev, warned that the armaments of European countries had been developed to

> extreme limits, while their preparedness for mobilization is now measured not in weeks but in days and hours. Success on the battlefield now depends (other things being equal) on the most rapid deployments of the greatest possible mass of troops and on beating the enemy to the punch. Whoever first concentrates his forces and strikes against a still unprepared enemy has assured himself of the highest probability of having the first victory, which facilitates the successful conduct of the whole campaign. The undertaking of mobilization can no longer be considered as a peaceful act; on the contrary, it represents the most decisive act of war.

'All diplomatic decisions,' he went on to warn, 'must be taken in advance on the basis of an entirely clear recognition of the military–political side of the struggle.'[17]

This however is precisely what did not happen. The pre-eminent example of this failure is of course the Schlieffen Plan. Although never a great military commander, Count Alfred von Schlieffen who had been Chief of the German Staff from 1891 to 1906, can lay claim to have had as much if not more impact on European history than any of the more famous fighting figures. Schlieffen had taken over and revised the plans of his predecessor, which had fitted in closely with Bismarck's view of Germany as a satisfied Power. If Germany *had* to fight a two-front war, then Moltke's strategy was for a limited offensive in the east, while standing on the defensive along the Rhine. Schlieffen's strategy, as we have already seen, was altogether more ambitious and aggressive – a two-front campaign with the initial attack now concentrated on France in order to take advantage of the relatively slow pace of Russian mobilisation. It was also to be a very quick war. This was partly because Schlieffen believed, rightly, that in a long drawn-out campaign the superiority of combined French and Russian numbers would eventually tell against Germany. But he also shared the more widely-held misapprehension that European economies could not survive a lengthy conflict. What he and others failed to foresee was that it was precisely the underlying economic strength of the Powers which would make a long war possible.[18]

Schlieffen drew up the final version of his plan almost in isolation. He made no attempt to coordinate with the Austro-Hungarian General Staff, and it is uncertain whether the plan was taken up with other Prussian army planners. According to Gerhard Ritter, even the War Ministry in Berlin was kept in ignorance about it until 1912.[19] And yet Schlieffen was preparing what was in effect an immense gamble, the risks of which were inconsistent either with the stakes, or with the consequences of failure.[20] Its audacity masked Germany's underlying weakness. Geography, along, as already indicated, with the relative inferiority of its manpower resources meant that the only prospect for victory in a two-front war, lay in a high risk strategy. Political considerations were to drive the Kaiser and his chief military and political advisers to a very similar conclusion in 1914. What is perhaps more remarkable is that this was an enterprise which, by Schlieffen's own admission, was beyond Germany's strength, and for which the planning was at best incomplete.[21] Schlieffen had failed to make adequate provisions in at least two crucial areas – he had provided insufficient reserves, and he had not taken adequate account of the immense logistic problems of the operation. It would have taken 14 000 more trucks than Germany possessed in 1914 to transport the right wing alone of the invading force. Although the supply arrangements worked reasonably well to the Marne, subsequent evidence suggests that the state of the railways would have prevented the Germans from following up a victory had this been achieved.[22]

Not surprisingly, historians have been harsh in their verdict. Martin van Creveld, who has subjected the logistic side of the plan to extensive scrutiny, notes that Schlieffen well understood the difficulties he was likely to encounter, but made no systematic attempt to solve them. 'Had he done so, he might well have reached the conclusion that the operation was impracticable.' To Avner Offer, the Schlieffen Plan represents 'a wilful rejection of material constraints'.[23] Schlieffen reflects the ambiguities and contradictions of pre-war thinking. He knew that the conditions in which the next war would be fought would be different from anything which had gone before, indeed the kind of war he describes in an essay published in 1909 is quite similar to that foreseen by Bloch.[24] Schlieffen was aware of the challenge posed by the revolution in firepower; by 1900 there was indeed widespread agreement that frontal assault would be very difficult.[25] He had given much thought to the problems of handling mass armies. But in the final analysis his response evaded rather than met the problems. Like the rest of his contemporaries, he had no radically new solutions.

Military thinking prior to 1914 had failed to resolve, or indeed properly to recognise, the crisis in land warfare which by the turn of the century was already at hand. As the long peace which followed the Franco-Prussian War progressed, the outpouring of professional military literature which had followed that conflict was drying up. Tactical manuals and field exercises were beginning to show a lack of realism.[26] The best known strategist of the period was a sailor, Alfred Mahan, but he too, was looking backwards rather than forwards. Mahan was writing at the end of the period in which sea power played a decisive role in history. His arguments, which drew heavily on examples from the seventeenth and eighteenth centuries, were based on the questionable thesis that the past provided a good guide to a technologically dynamic future.[27]

Without the impetus of unambiguous new evidence to the contrary, which the Boer War and the Russo-Japanese War of 1905 failed to provide, the prevailing orthodoxies remained, albeit uneasily, in place. The predictions and fears of the von Moltkes' and Glotzs had no more influence on military plans and thinking than those of Bloch. There were no attempts even to sketch out on a contingency basis, the logistical or tactical requirements for a long war. The case for the defensive was dismissed out of hand.[28] 'The defensive is never an acceptable role to the British,' declared one British major-general, 'and he makes little or no study of it.'[29] In France Colonel de Grandmaison, prewar chief of the Operations Section of the General Staff, announced that the French army no longer 'knows any other law than the offensive ... All attacks are to be pushed to the extreme'.[30] This was not simply a matter of bravado; organisational bias, doctrinal oversimplification, along with political considerations, were at least as influential. The French military was strongly opposed to a strategy which would involve the professional army being turned into a training cadre for a mass army composed of strategic reserves. But there was also the fact that the offensive spirit provided an antidote to the many ills afflicting the army, including deficiencies in armaments, political division and lack of doctrine; it was something all Frenchmen, whether on the left or the right, whether pro or anti-Dreyfusards, could agree on.[31]

Last but by no means least there was a widespread reluctance to face up to the implications of the revolution in firepower. We return again and again to the fact that while the weapons were modern, the armies of the prewar years, and above all, their tactics, were not. They remained conservative institutions, 'pre-industrial' in their composition and thinking. A high proportion of the officer corps continued to be drawn from the landed aristocracy. Its values, which were very much in line with those inspiring the broader spirit of European bellicism, led it to champion will and courage, rather than the technical skills which modern weaponry was increasingly coming to require. In the words of a British cavalry general, speaking in 1910 – and the cavalry continued to enjoy the highest prestige – 'What we should seek in war is to produce moral rather than material effect; indeed, the only object of material effect is to produce moral effect on the enemy, and to get his nerves ... into such a state that he will acknowledge defeat.'[32]

Behind such sentiments in Britain lurked another, rather different set of concerns about the impact of industrialisation. How would city-based recruits face up to modern warfare? Steadily improving standards of living were expected to enhance their instinct for self-preservation and diminish the spirit of self-sacrifice. It was a not unreasonable, but in the event totally misplaced fear, which weighed heavily in the minds of officers who expected heavy casualties.[33] And yet while they worried about about firepower and casualties, the British, along with other European armies consistently neglected the weapon which was to dominate the Western Front. Richard Gatling, who produced one of the earliest machine guns, claimed that the new weapon bore 'the same relation to other firearms that McCormack's Reaper does to the sickle, or the sewing machine to the common needle'.[34] It certainly offered a staggering increase in firepower. The point was repeatedly demonstrated first in Africa and then during the Russo-Japanese War. No European army however came anywhere near recognising its potential importance. Once again there are no simple or single explanations for this failure. Earlier technical flaws and the weapon's heavy use of ammunition provide part of the answer; financial parsimony and uncertainty about its tactical role were also factors. According to Tim Travers, while most senior British officers accepted the new technology, the army then made the mistake of directing the weapon into 'acceptable and traditional patterns. The problem was not getting the gun accepted as a piece of technology, but what was done with it.'[35]

That however may not have been the full story. The machine gun was seen, if subconsciously, as a threat not to the ability of armies to conduct war, but to a traditional concept of warfare which had stressed the decisiveness of personal courage and individual endeavour; a threat not just in Bloch's sense that it made war 'impossible, except at the price of suicide', but that it implied the total subordination of men to the machine. The response of the old-style gentlemen officers who were to fight the new-style industrial war, was simple. The machine gun was ignored. At the Staff College an officer who presented a paper which argued that future tactics should be based on the power of the machine gun and rapid firing rifle rather than the experience of military history, was severely criticised. In manouvres just before the war young officers who asked what to do with the weapon were told 'to take the damned thing to the flank and hide it'.[36]

With the benefit of hindsight it is easy to highlight mistakes and under-estimate the difficulties facing traditionally-minded institutions in the process of the transition to modern warfare to which they were neither technically nor psychologically atuned. One cannot discount what I. F. Clarke describes as 'the now familiar time-lag between the rapid development of technology, and the belated abandonment of ideas, mental habits and social attitudes that the new machines and the new industries had rendered out of date'.[37] The long peace which followed the Franco-Prussian War had proved treacherous. It allowed armies to convince them-selves that the nature of war had not radically altered, just as it had allowed liberals to convince themselves that mankind had become too civilised for war. The key changes had been cumulative. They did not depend on any single weapon, certainly not one 'visible' or revolutionary enough to force itself onto their attention. Unlike the navy, where innova-tions in the areas of propulsion, fire-control and design, were public and pressing, there was no pressure for radical change. Money was short; there was no public debate about the future of warfare; political supervision, was inadequate. The generals were never asked to explain their plans, let alone the thinking on which they were based.

The fact remains however that they were the professionals. It was their job to keep up to date with the changing nature of armed conflict, to study the trends, to see that the right lessons were drawn from the Boer and the Russo-Japanese Wars. In the final analysis the generals of the pre-1914 years share with diplomats and politicians of the 1930s, a deep-seated reluctance to face up to unpalatable facts of war in the industrial age. They misread and ignored the evidence, with the result that they not only planned for the wrong kind of war, but failed to alert the politicians to the dangers they were increasingly running. The great tragedy of the prewar period is that Europe had in fact a formidable deterrent which it totally failed to recognise. If the power of the machine gun had been more widely recog-nised, if Bloch's predictions had become part of the conventional wisdom, then the events of July 1914 might have turned out very differently.

Some sense of the disaster at hand did exist. Grey would later write that each time the danger of conflict had loomed in earlier crises, he had been 'more and more impressed with the feeling of the unprecedented catastrophe that a war between the Great Powers of Europe must be under modern conditions'. It 'seemed impossible' that other leaders would not be equally impressed by this danger. Late in the July crisis he warned the German ambassador that war would result in 'total exhaustion and impoverishment; industry and trade would be ruined, and the power of capital destroyed. Revolutionary movements such as those of ... 1848 due to the collapse of industrial activity would be the result.'[38] The private comments attributed to Bethmann Hollweg suggests that he, like the younger von Moltke, shared at least part of this assessment.[39] But these were not the thoughts which predominated in the Chancelleries, or indeed on the streets, where there appears to have been little or no awareness of the revolution in firepower and the casualties it was likely to cause. In the final analysis this was a war which resulted from ignorance, in part wilful. In that sense it must be seen as an unnecessary war.

With the outbreak of fighting in August 1914, reality asserted itself with a vengeance. The crisis in land warfare now became glaringly evident, resulting in a four-year-long war which permanently fractured the pre-1914 consensus in support of power politics. What emerged was a highly damaging mismatch between the extraordinary, and unanticipated capacity of states to mobilise men and resources, and their inability to translate the great destructive power at their disposal into an effective coercive force. Overwhelmed by this new experience of industrialised warfare, national leaderships pitted men against materiel in a conflict from which neither side would disengage, and which for the first three and half years, nobody knew how to win. European societies were both literally, and metaphorically bled. The war took over. In his account of Verdun, *The Price of Glory*, Alistair Horne notes how after three months of fighting the battle 'seemed to have somehow rid itself of all human direction and now continued through its own impetus'. In the diaries and journals of both sides, it is the war itself which increasingly comes to be seen as the real enemy, as a monster, a Moloch, a Minataur, a creature with an insatiable appetite 'for its daily ration of lives, regardless of nationality'.[40]

The underlying explanation for this state of affairs, as Horne's title implies, was political. It was now that the hypernationalisms of the late nineteenth century did their real damage. The logical response to the stalemate of the Western Front was a compromise peace. But what might have been possible for eighteenth-century statesmen, responsible only to their princes, was impossible in nation states roused to high states of popular enthusiasm and indignation. The old monarchies had made decisions on war and peace on a more rational calculation of gain and loss. They had known where to stop, whether to secure their gains or, no less important, to ensure that they lived to fight another day. Here however was a clash of popular wills in which national hatreds and anger rapidly became a substitute for policy.[41] Once involved in war, notes George Kennan, regardless of the specific circumstances that gave rise to the involvement in the first place, the nation state fights for vague, emotional, essentially punitive purposes. *They*, the opponents, must be punished, made to regret their recalcitrance, made to be sorry. *We*, on the other hand, must be vindicated by victory ... *our* admirableness must be documented by *their* ultimate recognition of our superiority.

Under such circumstances compromise equated with defeat.[42]

If the Powers were proud and self-righteous, they were also greedy. War aims on both sides reflected a drive to annex territory and establish spheres of influence. An Allied peace imposed on Germany in February 1917 before the United States entered the war, would have been much harsher than the one which actually emerged at Versailles.[43] But Germany was the revisionist, and the most ambitious Power. Just how ambitious only became clear once war had broken out. For German military planners meeting in January 1914, victory meant less the destruction of the entente as its neutralisation. It was a matter of breaking not the capacity to resist, but the will to use that capacity. Germany sought pre-eminence in Europe, not hegemony over it.[44] With the onset of hostilities however, the diffused and vague sentiments associated with *Weltpolitik* were quickly translated into a much more ambitious set of demands.[45] According to an internal working document formulated in September 1914, when it was still believed that peace negotiations would open shortly, Germany would seek a permanent solution to the security problem which had come to obsess it in preceding years. France 'must be so weakened as to make her revival as a great power impossible for all time. Russia must be thrust back as far as possible from Germany's eastern frontier and her domination over the non-Russian vassal peoples broken'. Germany would seek the establishment of an integrated continental economic system including Germany, Austro-Hungary, the Low Countries and Poland as well as possibly France, Italy and Scandinavia. Germany would definitely want the French iron ore field of Briey, and consider taking the western slopes of the Vosges, and a coastal strip from Dunkirk to Boulogne. France should pay a war indemnity high enough to prevent her spending 'any considerable sums on armaments for the next 15–20 years'.[46]

There was no reference at this stage to extensive annexations – Bethmann Hollweg was still seeking to organise the Continent from the centre around what an associate described as Germany's 'undemonstrative leadership'. Others, however, had less subtle ideas which became increasingly prominent as power shifted from the Chancellor to the military. By the terms of the 1918 treaty of Brest-Litovsk, Russia lost almost a third of its territory and was reduced to the size of Muscovy before the days of Peter the Great. By the end of the war, and the country's war aims continued to expand right up until August 1918, the German leadership under the military dictatorship of Lundendorff and Hindenburg was planning for a Germany stretching from the Caucasus to the Channel.[47]

With a a compromise peace ruled out, the politicians were dependent on the generals' ability to adapt to the kind of war which they had insisted would never take place. And as Kitchener despairingly admitted, they did not know what to do. This simply wasn't war.[48] The stalemate had begun almost immediately after the battle of the Marne at the beginning of September, when soldiers of both sides began digging in. The original entrenchments were rudimentary, intended simply to provide troops under fire with shelter and allow for a breathing space. Nobody in the autumn of 1914 realised that they would become a permanent feature, a continuous static front running the whole way from the Channel to the Swiss border. No General Staff had the technology or the tactical know-how to suppress, overrun and penetrate 'a well-sited defence system some four miles deep, the front edge of which was only a short distance from one's own, protected by massive wire entanglements and fired by the flanking fire of machine guns and a wall of artillery and mortars of all calibres sited in depth'.[49]

The response was crude. The armies tried to bludgeon their way through, relying heavily on the use of artillery. The British commander, Sir John French, believed that breaking through the lines was largely a matter of 'the expenditure of high explosive ammunition. If sufficient ammunition is forthcoming, a way can be blasted through.' The infantry, it was assumed, would then simply walk in and 'take possession'.[50] But it was never as simple as that. Initially there was a shortage of shells – nobody after all had planned for a long war. Subsequently it was discovered that the guns were not accurate enough, that they could not penetrate the heavily-defended German lines, but ploughed up the ground across which the infantry had to advance.

The British and French did sometimes succeed in breaking into the German trench system, but the bridgeheads they established could never be held long enough or reinforced quickly enough, to resist German counterattack. The generals nevertheless stubbornly persisted in pursuing the same ineffective strategy in the face of repeated failure and appalling losses, unwilling to admit even to themselves that decisive success was beyond their powers. They kept on believing that the next big push, supported by yet more artillery, would provide the elusive breakthrough.[51] When in September 1916 Lloyd George queried how the cavalry, kept ready to charge through the gap about to be made through the lines by the Guards, could operate succesfully on a front bristling with machine guns, the generals, or so he later claimed, 'fell on me'.[52]

It took three and half years to resolve which Michael Geyer calls 'the riddle of the trenches.'[53] While it was common to all the armies on the Western Front, the British were particularly badly placed to do so. 'From the highest to the lowest', as the official war historian later privately wrote, 'we were all amateurs.' Generals and staffs had no experience of Continental warfare or of handling such large numbers of troops. They were short of trained officers and NCOs capable of expanding the original expeditionary force of some 160 000 to an army which by 1917 would number some one and a half million men. The extraordinary sight of waves of men advancing slowly, as though on an Aldershot parade ground, towards the German lines at the Somme, is to be explained by Britain's prewar unpreparedness. Senior officers feared that their new recruits would be unable to emulate the more flexible tactics employed by their allies. French forces advanced by rushing in small groups from one piece of dead-ground to the next; British troops, their officers feared, would either take cover and stay there or disintegrate into uncoordinated groups.[54]

The real problem however was at the top. Haig and other senior officers brought to the Western Front obsolete ideas of warfare which they had learned at Staff College 20 years earlier, and which they took much too long to discard.[55] In his novel, *The General*, C. S. Forester unflatteringly compares a meeting of British generals in the aftermath of the battle of Loos to

> a debate of a group of savages as to how to extract a screw from a piece of wood. Accustomed only to nails, they had made one effort to pull out the screw by main force, and now that it had failed they were devising methods of applying more force still, of obtaining more efficient pincers, of using levers and fulcrums so that more men could bring their strength to bear. They could hardly be blamed for not guessing that by rotating the screw it would come out after the exertion of far less effort; it would be a notion so different from anything they had ever encoun-tered that they would laugh at the man who suggested it.[56]

To compound their difficulties, commanders lacked an effective staff system to handle tactical and operational problems, analyse data, experi-ment with new methods, and perhaps above all, to encourage open discus-sion which would make it possible to challenge received wisdom. The Royal Navy suffered from a similar handicap when trying to cope with the threat posed by German submarines in 1917.[57]

The ideas for breakthrough when it was finally achieved, did not come from the general staff. Generals were not on the whole interested in the primitive but essential tactics of small units. But it was here, rather than the field of grand strategy or in new weaponry such as the tank, that salvation initially lay. In a pamphlet entitled *The Attack in Trench Warfare*, written in 1915, a French officer, Captain Laffargue, advocated a strategy of infiltrating rather than frontally assaulting enemy lines. Laffargue's ideas may have had some influence on the French commander, General Robert Nivelle;[58] they certainly appear to have influenced the Germans who captured a copy and first employed similar tactics on the Eastern Front in the assault on Riga in September 1917.[59] By then all armies were becoming more innovative, but the Germans were still more adaptable than their enemies. When in late 1917 Ludendorff began to plan the first German offensive on the Western Front since Verdun, he did something which the British, with their much more hierarchical system, would not have thought of doing. He brought together the best tactical thinkers of the army regardless of rank, charging them with the task of learning from the lessons of previous campaigns in order to devise a way of finally breaking the stalemate.[60]

With the launching of the March 1918 offensive, the Germans abandoned the unsuccesful practice of the frontal assault in favour of infiltration by storm groups, who advanced under the cover of a creeping artillery barrage designed to punch channels through the enemy lines to the immediate rear. They did not worry about maintaining a continuous line of assault or overcoming points of resistance. The rigid adherence to plans laid down beforehand was gone. Larger units then dealt with remaining defensive positions and consolidated gains against enemy counterattack.[61] Although the Germans failed to follow through their dramatic initial success – on 5 June the British Cabinet was discussing the speed with which troops could be pulled out of France in the face of a German victory – [62] mobile warfare had at last been restored. It continued, with tanks now playing an increasingly prominent part, until the German surrender in November.

The long-term damage had, however, already been done. There had been heavy casualties during the initial phase of fighting which ended with the battle of the Marne. There were again very heavy casualties during the fighting of the summer and autumn of 1918. The heaviest losses, however, were a result of the siege warfare on the Western Front. Horne estimates that nearly one and a quarter million men were killed and injured on both sides during the prolonged battle of Verdun. German and British forces suffered one million casualties in an area of just seven square miles during the battle of the Somme.[63]

Such losses were accepted at the time. In the early years of the war, high casualty lists were regarded as indicators of national resolve and fitness to rank as a Great Power, rather than of national incompetence.[64] The only serious incident, the French army mutiny of 1917, was less a revolt against the war than a protest caused by lack of confidence in the French high command's ability to deliver victory. That was not how it seemed later. Postwar appeasement has its roots on the Western Front. One million, four hundred thousand Frenchmen had been killed. Half of the six and a half million Frenchmen who survived the war had sustained injuries. Such losses left the country both materially weakened and psychologically exhausted. Patriotism, as Eugen Weber puts it 'died in the trenches, on the Marne, at Verdun'. After the war it gave way to pacifism in the 'ever more weary, ever more desperate search for impossible solutions to insoluble problems'.[65]

In the British case numbers tell only part of the story. There was the also the element of shock to a society which had known little worse than the limited losses of colonial campaigns and was totally unprepared for the unequal struggle between man and technology waged on the Western Front. Even then the impact might have been less debilitating had it not been for the sense of futility and waste which the war left. The casualty lists were read against the few miles of ground gained in the great battles, rather than the real but invisible achievement of wearing down the German armies. This ultimately is the most telling case against the only strategy available to the generals. Long-term attrition did bring victory. The Somme proved the muddy grave of the old German field army, which by end of the battle was, by Ludendorff's own later admission, 'utterly worn out'.[66] But because it took so long and because there was no obvious link between the earlier losses and the final victory, an immense political cost had later to be paid. What was remembered in the 1920s and above all the 1930s, was the sheer horror of the war. 'No pen or drawing', wrote the painter Paul Nash in November 1917, 'can convey this country – the normal setting of the battles taking place day and night, month after month. Evil and the incarnate fiend alone can be master of this war ... It is unspeakable, godless, hopeless.'[67] 'I cannot attempt', wrote a British gunner subtaltern during Passchendaele, 'to describe the conditions under which we are fighting. Anything I could write about them would seem an exaggeration but would, in reality, be miles beneath the truth. The whole battle field for miles is a congested mess of sodden, rain-filled shell holes which are being added to every moment. The mud is not so much mud as a fathomless sticky morass.'[68]

Then there was that peculiarly horrible, if militarily ineffective innovation – gas. Gas did not change the war, but it did help change attitudes to war. One of Wilfred Owen's bitterest poems, *Dulce et Decorum Est*, describes the aftermath of a gas attack:

> If in some smothering dreams, you too could pace
> Behind the wagon that we flung him in,
> And watch the white eyes writhing in his face,
> His hanging face, like a devil's sick of sin;
> If you could hear, at every jolt, the blood
> Come gargling from the froth-corrupted lungs,
> Obscene as cancer, bitter as the cud
> Of vile, incurable sores on innocent tongues, –
> My friend, you would not tell with such high zest
> To children ardent to some desperate glory,
> The old Lie; Dulce et decorum est
> Pro patria mori.[69]

The great tragedy was that this change of sentiment from the bellicism of the pre-1914 years, was in its turn also to do great harm, making it much more difficult to deal with the ambiguous and unsatisfactory outcome of the war. For while Germany had been defeated, its power had not been broken. The dangerous contradiction between its immediate underlying strength, and its long-term weakness, remained. The country's military machine had proved formidable, a well equipped, well trained army with a strong sense of discipline and an excellent General Staff. Its officers adjusted much more quickly to the conditions of modern warfare than did their enemies. Against the handicap of the two-front war, the Germans enjoyed the advantages of good inner lines of communication, readily defensible positions in the west, and the open space for mobile warfare in the east. In 1917 the army succeeded in pushing the French army to the point of mutiny, while the navy came close to starving Britain into surrender.[70]

In the final analysis, as Schlieffen had foreseen, the balance of resources told against her. The Allies were able to mobilise far more men, and had had much greater economic muscle. Allied war expenditure, at some 57.7 billion dollars, was more than double the 24.7 billion of the Central Powers.[71] It was this imbalance, this sense of not being strong enough which accounts for the succession of German gambles – the Schlieffen Plan, the 'blank cheque' and in early 1917, the decision to launch all-out submarine warfare against the United States despite warnings that it would bring the US into the war. Kurt Riesler, using the same phrase which he had used to describe the 'blank cheque' of 5 July 1914, referred to the decision as 'a leap in the dark. We all have the feeling that this question hangs over us like a doom. If history follows the laws of tragedy, then Germany should be destroyed by this fatal mistake, which embodies all its earlier tragic mistakes.'[72] Ludendorff's March offensive, undertaken with the knowledge of the 'enormous quantities of material of all kinds' becoming available to the Allies in the aftermath of the American declaration of war, was the result.[73]

In the immediate circumstances prevailing in the autumn of 1918 therefore, the Allies could and arguably should have done better. If the arguments against the punitive peace imposed at Versailles are compelling, there is a stronger case for saying that they should have pressed their military advantage on the battlefield when the Germans, facing an increasingly desperate situation sought an armistice. Advocates of a policy of unconditional surrender at the time included the American commander, General Pershing, and Lloyd George. At a meeting on 13 October 1918, the British Prime Minister raised the question whether

the actual defeat of Germany, and giving the German people a real taste of war, was not more important, from the point of view of the peace of the world, than a surrender at the present time, when the German armies were still on foreign territory ... In twenty years' time the Germans would say that they made this mistake and that mistake, and that by better preparation and organization they would be able to bring about victory next time.[74]

In the event German soldiers were able to march home in formed units with bands playing and carrying personal arms, often receiving a welcome more appropriate to a victorious than a defeated army.[75] Poor intelligence provides part of the explanation. Neither the British nor the French realised just how bad the state of the German army was, and feared that the fighting would continue through into 1919. This worried the British less for humanitarian reasons, than because they feared that they would have to bear a disproportionate burden of future fighting, while their allies would reap the main political benefits. Suspicion of the French, and concern about growing American influence in the postwar world were important factors. This is ironic since suspicion of the British and the Americans was a major factor in deterring the French from pressing the war home to Berlin.[76] Woodrow Wilson of course had no intention of allowing anything of the kind.

If one of the least publicised of the succession of failures to get a proper hold of the German problem, the decision not to push what had become very much a total war to its logical conclusion, is one of the most intriguing. Whether a more comprehensive and, from the German public's point of view, more obvious allied victory would have significantly altered the course of postwar German history, can today only be a matter of guesswork. What is clear is that the unsatisfactory nature of the defeat, sufficient to destabilise Germany but insufficient to dissuade her from trying again, provided a poor basis for a stable peace. The real damage, however, was caused not as a result of the decisions of October 1918, but because of the prolonged and terrible delay in resolving the 'riddle of the trenches'. The advocates of attrition – stubborn, unimaginative and deeply callous, can have had little inkling of how their attempts to solve their immediate military problem which they had failed to foresee during the pre-war years, would destabilise the ensuing peace. The Great War's horrifically long rolls of honour would prove only an interim reckoning.

4 A Flawed Experiment

The end of the war, like the beginning, was marked by public celebrations. It was marked too by a brief, but tragically unwarranted outburst of optimism. The former Prime Minister, Herbert Asquith, believed that the war had 'cleansed and purged the whole atmosphere of the world'.[1] In fact it had done almost exactly the opposite. A bad war was about to result in a bad peace. Immense damage had been done to the fabric of European order. The balance of power had not been redressed. Russia had been defeated and had undergone a revolution which would disqualify her as an anti-German ally for 24 years. American involvement in Europe's Great War had been much too brief, and for many Americans also unwelcome, to persuade her of the need to take an active role in maintaining the balance of power. Britain and above all France had been materially and psychologically weakened. The very mechanism of the balance had been brought into disrepute. Instead of sober reassessment, there was emotive reaction – against Germany, against war, against power politics.

The full and very grave implications of this latter change took time to make themselves felt. All that was immediately clear was that international affairs were suddenly the subject of much wider interest than they had been. One example of this is the establishment of a new academic discipline – International Relations. The first university chairs in Britain were endowed by a well-known high street tailor, Montague Burton, in memory of his son who had been killed in the trenches. More generally the conduct of foreign policy was no longer something which the public was willing to leave to the professionals. The ideas, the jingoism which led up to the war, gave way to support for a new generation of writers and politicians who liked power politics as little as they seemed to understand it. The Great War had left an intellectual vacuum. The diplomats and statesmen who had conducted the secret diplomacy in the years prior to 1914 were, like the generals who presided over the bloodletting on the Western Front, discredited. The door was thus open for more idealistic, more unworldly men for whom war was an evil and peace a priority. 'If one word was repeated more often than any other during the years after the poignantly memorable Armistice,' writes Robert Farrell, 'that word was peace. Peace echoed through so many sermons, speeches and state papers that it drove itself into the consciousness of everyone.'[2]

It was a case of extreme to extreme, from the hubris of the prewar years to what soon degenerated into an exercise in escapism, a futile attempt to opt out of power politics. The naivety and short-sightedness of policies which relied on solemn declarations and pieces of paper in preference to hard military power, are today all too evident. Chamberlain's stubborn pursuit of appeasement in the face of all the evidence that Hitler was not a man with whom it was possible to do business, has become one of the set pieces of modern political folly. Yet however harsh the judgments, the sentiments which motivated policies which eventually contributed to a second world war were much more honorable and less foolhardy than those which had made possible the first. There is no doubting the sincerity, and indeed the sheer desperation which motivated the succession of initiatives and conferences which culminated in Munich. Chamberlain was speaking for much of the postwar generation when he told the House of Commons on the outbreak of war on 3 September 1939, that 'Everything that I have worked for, everything that I have hoped for, everything that I have believed in in my public life, has crashed into ruins.'[3]

Six figures stand out in the confused and unstable interlude between the armistice of 1918 and Germany's unconditional surrender in 1945. They divide into three contrasting pairs of men, each of whom had totally different attitudes to power and power politics. The starkest contrast is to be found in the 1930s between Neville Chamberlain and Adolf Hitler. Franklin Roosevelt and Josef Stalin constitute a more ambiguous, and also a better matched duo; they were after all allies. So too were Woodrow Wilson and Georges Clemenceau. It was these two who, along with Lloyd George, presided over the peace conference at Versailles. Versailles was a badly-organised and overambitious undertaking aimed at reaching a settlement comparable to the Treaty of Westphalia of 1648 and the 1815 Congress of Vienna. The British delegation took with it to Paris a specially-comissioned history of the Congress. But Versailles was not Vienna. This conference was held under highly unpropitious circumstances. Many of the participants were still, metaphorically speaking, shell-shocked. The atmosphere, heavily influenced by the continued 'fear-hatreds' of the war, boded ill for a rational or generous settlement of the German question, let alone for the establishment of a new European order. The scale of the agenda, the intractability of many of the problems, the differences not just of national interest but basic philosophy, would have taxed the capacity of the most rational and far-sighted statesmen. The situation became next to impossible when crucial issues were resolved piecemeal, to the point that when the overall terms of the peace with Germany were announced, they shocked many in the British and American delegations. As Harold Nicolson wrote in his classic account of the conference, 'We did not realise what we were doing. We did not realise how far we were drifting from our original basis. We were exhausted and overworked. We kept on mumbling our old formulas in the hope that they still bore some relation to our actions.'[4]

When, however, it came to their different views of power and power politics, Clemenceau and Wilson knew exactly what they did, and did not, want. The description of Versailles as a 'Carthaginian' peace is misleading. Punitive it most certainly was, but Clemenceau did not reflect the extremes of French thinking. He did not, unlike some of his compatriots, advocate the break-up of Germany; nor, in contrast to Marshal Foch and President Raymond Poincaré, did he support the annexation of the Rhineland. He did however articulate the French postwar obsession with security, and the country's deep-seated pessimism over the future. The 78-year-old premier had been mayor of Montmartre in 1871 when the capital had been occupied by the Germans during the Franco-Prussian War. He had become a symbol of French resistance to German aggression after 1914.

That conflict, which had been fought on French soil, had again brought the country close to defeat. France's main industrial area had been occupied and devastated. Although total French losses were similar to those of Germany, the fact that France's population was only two thirds that of its enemy, and that the French birth rate was static, weighed heavily on Clemenceau. As Keynes noted, France's future position remained precarious to one 'who took the view that European civil war is to be regarded as a normal, or at least a recurrent, state of affairs for the future'.[5] For Clemenceau, and this time the words are his own, the war was 'simply the continuation of the recrudescence of those never-ending acts of violence by which the first savage tribes carried out their depredation with all the resources of barbarism. The means improve with the ages. The ends remain the same.'[6] Defending the treaty in September 1919, Clemenceau reverted to the vocabulary of prewar Social Darwinism. 'Life,' he told the French Chamber of Deputies,

is a perpetual struggle in war, as in peace ... That struggle cannot be avoided. Yes, we must have vigilance, we must have a great deal of vigilance. I cannot say for how many years, perhaps I should say for how many centuries, the crisis which has begun will continue. Yes, this treaty will bring us burdens, troubles, miseries, difficulties and that will continue for long years.[7]

Easy as it is to criticise Clemenceau's bleak pessimism, Keynes exercised too much of the prerogative of the detached, Anglo-Saxon observer. The French President's policy cannot simply be dismissed as that of 'an old man, whose most vivid impression and most lively imaginations are of the past and not of the future'. Was it surprising after all that France had gone through, that Clemenceau should see the issue 'in terms of France and Germany, not of humanity and of European civilization struggling forwards to a new order'?[8] The risk of German *revanchism*, as later events would bear out, was indeed real. What is true is that Clemenceau, like the generals of the Western Front, lacked imagination. And Keynes is certainly right in arguing that Clemenceau's approach precluded any kind of new beginning. It made it impossible to devise a peace based on enlightened self-interest, one designed to encourage the emergence of a democratic, stable Germany which would see its future as a responsible European Power. What the French sought to do was to squeeze substantial short-term advantage out of the German defeat, treating Versailles as an extension of the war by diplomatic means. *Inter alia*, the Rhineland was temporarily detached and occupied. The German army, which had numbered some 2.2 million in 1913 was reduced to 100 000 men, its General Staff disbanded, the country forbidden to make tanks, military aircraft and heavy artillery. More politically damaging in terms of the longer-term effects of this *diktat* within a still immensely powerful state, Germany was saddled with formal responsibility for having caused the war, along with an impossibly large bill for reparations.[9]

'Eighteenth-century peacemakers', Henry Kissinger remarks, 'would have regarded "war guilt clauses" as absurd. For them, wars were amoral inevitabilities caused by clashing interests. In the treaties that concluded eighteenth-century wars, the losers paid a price without its being justified on moral grounds.'[10] But a new spirit was abroad at Versailles, a spirit deeply hostile to eighteenth-century power politics. The French obsession with security contrasts with the equally deeply-felt alternative conviction that the world, certainly the civilised world, for the term had not disappeared from the international vocabulary, could not afford 'to go on with

> The good old rule,
> The simple plan,
> That they should take who have the power
> And they should keep who can.'[11]

This was more than a populist cause. 'We were journeying to Paris', Nicholson later recalled, 'not merely to liquidate the war, but to found a new order in Europe. We were preparing not Peace only, but Eternal Peace. There was about us the halo of some divine mission.'[12] Lenin was by no means the only apostle of a new order. On the international front, Woodrow Wilson unfolded a more beguiling, if similarly flawed vision.

The United States was a new and quite different player. A reluctant Great Power with strong reformist instincts, the country had hitherto made a point of heeding Washington's famous warning against foreign entanglements. Protected by geography, and indirectly by the Royal Navy from the unpleasanter facts of international life, it had the opportunity to think harder than most European countries could have done, of the contradictions between democratic values and the operating norms of power politics. (Americans still debate the issue of idealism versus realism in international affairs in a way that Europeans outside the political left do not do.) The country founded on the proposition that all men had been created equal, and endowed with the inalienable rights of life, liberty and the pursuit of happiness had resisted being drawn into the maelstrom of great power rivalries. This despite the fact that it had developed a formidable industrial power, outstripping both Britain and Germany. America's share of world manufacturing output, which had stood at 14.7 per cent in 1880, had risen to 32 per cent in 1913, compared with 13.6 per cent for Britain and 14.8 per cent for Germany.[13]

Expansion had contributed to a brief flirtation with Imperialism in 1890s. But Americans rapidly decided to accept the advice of men like Charles Eliot, President of Harvard, who denounced navies and large standing armies as 'the abandonment of what is characteristically American ... The building of a navy and particularly of battleships is English and French policy. It should never be ours.'[14] The principle of American 'exceptionalism' was too deeply rooted to be permanently upset by Admiral Mahan, or any of the jingoists who gained brief prominence during the Spanish–American war. They wanted to go on living their lives in peace and quiet. They continued to believe that they had a mission to show the world an example of abstention from the quarrels and conquests which had characterised a Europe whose political mores they had so explicitly rejected, and still implicitly feared. They did not define their greatness in military terms.

Eventually, however, the wars of the old world intruded on the new. America could not be attacked as France had been. Making no claims to be a Great Power, it had, unlike Britain, nothing to prove by immediately joining a Continental war. But American ships began to be sunk in increasing numbers by German submarines in the Atlantic. And in 1917 the British intercepted and published a telegram from the German Foreign Secretary, Arthur Zimmerman, offering Mexico the three provinces she had lost in 1848, (Arizona, Texas and New Mexico), if she attacked the United States. America's entry into the First World War was therefore very different from that of its co-belligerents. The Americans were not propelled by the spirit of belligerent nationalism which had possessed Europe, but by what one American historian describes as 'an aroused sense of national honor combined with a missionary zeal to achieve world peace and democracy'.[15] That zeal was most fervently articulated by their President, Woodrow Wilson.

Wilson is one of the key figures in this story; he is also the most paradoxical, the most difficult to weigh up. The man who did more than anybody else to extol the idea of a just peace during the war, had only limited success in mitigating the punitive and most destabilising elements of the Versailles Treaty. The President who brought the US out into the world, also bears a good part of the responsibility for its rapid relapse into isolation. Having persuaded the Europeans to support the League of Nations, he could not persuade his own Congress to do the same. His critics feared that he was entangling the United States in perpetual conflict around the globe, allowing foreign powers to meddle in American domestic affairs and violate the Monroe Doctrine. Party politics explains part of this failure, but Wilson contributed much by his unwillingness to compromise.[16] For Wilson it was a matter of all or nothing, and in the end he got nothing. America did not join the League, while the crucial security guarantee which the US had offered France at Versailles was also voided.

Wilson was a Presbyterian with a highly developed conscience, a political scientist who had become President of Princeton. He had been a commentator on foreign policy since the 1890s, by which time he had already established the outlines of a theoretical rationale for an international community.[17] For much of the war, Wilson acted as the voice of international reason. As the war drew to its close, he became the leading proponent of international reform. It was Wilson who called for peace without victory in January 1917; it was Wilson, by now the leader of a belligerent power who a year later outlined a set of American war aims including open diplomacy, freedom of the seas, general disarmament, the removal of trade barriers, and the the impartial settlement of colonial claims. The last of his 14 points provided for the formation of 'a general association of nations ... for the purpose of affording mutual guarantees of political independence and territorial integrity to great and small States alike'. Power politics, the President was effectively saying, was a moral anachronism which had to be replaced by something better. When he visited Europe in

December 1918, the first American president to do so, he was received as a public hero.

Wilson was by no means the first person to start thinking about a League of Nations. The term was first introduced into diplomatic currency by a Cambridge classicist, Goldsworthy Lowes Dickinson, in an article, published in *The Atlantic Monthly* in December 1914.[18] Detailed study of how such a body might be organised was quickly undertaken by private individuals and organisations in both Britain and the United States. Indeed the key work for the draft of the Anglo-American Covenant had been done in Britain by a committee chaired by an an expert on international law, Sir Walter Phillimore, and later by Robert Cecil and General Smuts. Wilson went to Paris with only the vaguest idea of how the system would work.[19] But no other wartime leader invested anywhere near as much energy or political capital in seeking to tame the tiger of power politics. No other leader, with the exception of Lenin, whose attention was to be taken up by domestic concerns, had such a radical and compelling vision of the future.

Wilson, like Lenin, was an outsider in European politics. The contrast with men like Lloyd George and Clemenceau is striking, but it should not be seen simply in terms of an apparent idealism versus a weary cynicism. Wilson's ideas did not neglect American interests. On the contrary they coincided very neatly with them. The United States had a strong interest in encouraging a regime of international tranquility. It could afford to take a moral stand on territorial acquisition since it had no territorial ambitions of its own. It could, unlike France, advocate disarmament, and arbitration with complete safety.[20] The real difference lay in their respective concepts of international politics. Whereas Clemenceau saw the world in bleakly Hobbesian terms, Wilson sought to apply the principles of Lockean liberalism to a new world order.[21] His vision, drawn dangerously heavily from his academic analysis of American domestic politics, was that of a civilised international society, in which states while retaining their independence and sovereignty, 'would be governed in their conduct towards each other by the same principles of honour and respect for the community law of civilised society that govern the individual citizens of all modern states in their relations with one another'.[22] To this end he sought to liberate the old European world from its bad old militarist habits, 'making a society instead of a set of barbarians out of the governments of the world'. He sought a system which went beyond the balance of power, one which would end the arms races and secret diplomacy which had characterised the Europe Colonel House had visited in the summer of 1914.[23]

Not everybody was convinced. The response in high political circles, certainly in France, boiled down to a paraphrase of the famous comment on the charge of the Light Brigade – '*C'est magnifique, mais ce n'est pas la politique*'. Some of the Clemenceau's comments, and they are by no means entirely unreasonable, had a distinctly feline quality. The League would be a 'bridge leading to the New Jerusalem'. Wilson was complimented for his 'noble candeur', a phrase best translated as noble simple-mindedness. A writer in *The Herald* of 4 January 1919 described Wilson as 'the world's greatest Liberal'.[24] It was not a compliment. The liberal thinking on which Wilson drew so heavily, had never managed to come to grips with the problems posed by power in the international arena. For it began from the questionable assumption that man was naturally good. Mankind would live in a state of harmony were it not for the vested interests of princes and statesmen, of soldiers, diplomats and more recently, armaments manufacturers. If their power could only be brought under democratic control, disputes could be resolved through arbitration, and war would cease to be a problem. The fallacies of this philosophy, already clearly articulated in Thomas Paine's *The Rights of Man*, were compounded by a tendency to withdraw from difficulties and deny their existence. Liberal thinking on foreign affairs relied much too heavily on the power of goodwill and reason in an unreasonable world. As Lawrence Martin argues, it often seemed more at ease in criticism or in the advocacy of self-restraint than in coming up with practical solutions to the kind of problems facing the postwar world.[25]

Wilson failed to transcend these weaknesses. It was one thing to get states to say that they would respect one another's territorial integrity. Devising a workable system whereby they could always be held to their word was a very different proposition. It was not possible in 1919; it is still not possible in the 1990s. Wilson's mistake was to tackle the problem of power head-on rather than adopt a political version of what the British military writer, Basil Liddell Hart, was to describe as the strategy of the indirect approach. Wilson was simply too ambitious. A League might have worked had it proved possible to establish a European order whose legitimacy was accepted by all its main members, but this the Versailles settlement had conspicuously failed to do.

The importance of this task had not been lost on the cannier Lloyd George, who along with the early advocates of appeasement, recognised that the key to lasting peace lay in trying to turn Germany into a satisfied power. Nor was it lost on the Treasury's most brilliant representative at Versailles, John Maynard Keynes. One of the central planks of his attack on the treaty was that it provided nothing to make the defeated Central Empires into 'good neighbours, nothing to stabilise the new States of Europe'. Keynes believed that the perils of the future lay not in the traditional preoccupation with 'frontiers or sovereignties but in food, coal and transport'. The priority for Keynes was a revival of European economies through a resolution of the twin problem of reparations and war debt. Believing that the British and French would not have to worry so much about reparations, if the Americans stopped insisting on getting back the money they had lent the two countries during the war, he proposed that the German government and its defeated allies issue what would in effect be reparations bonds 'in payment of all indebtedness between any of the allied and associated governments'. European states would thus gain the means to pay for imports pending the revival of their export industries, while the long-term overhang of debt which had arisen from the war would be greatly reduced. In an accompanying memorandum intended for Wilson and Clemenceau, Keynes argued that:

> A proposal which unfolds future prospects and shows the peoples of Europe a road by which food and employment and orderly existence can come once again their way, will be a more powerful weapon than any other for the preservation from the dangers of Bolshevism of that order of human society which we believe to be the best starting point for future improvement and greater well-being.[26]

Whether, as Robert Skidelsky suggests, adoption of Keynes's plan would have prevented the Depression and thus avoided Hitler's accession to power, is again one of those historical might-have-beens, which in T. S. Eliot's phrase can remain a possibility 'only in a world of speculation'.[27] What is indisputable is that Keynes's ideas were well ahead of his time. The notion that the peace had economic consequences, or that international relations had acquired a crucial economic dimension which could be fashioned into a potent weapon for stability, was not then part of the conventional wisdom. Americans, who thirty years later would finance Europe's economic recovery from another war through the Marshall Plan, were still in an ungenerous mood. Wilson himself did believe that free trade was a precondition of a world without wars. So too were self-determination and the reduction of armaments. His broad thinking was far from unsophisticated. He recognised that the League would have to evolve and develop over time. The Covenant was 'not a straitjacket, but a vehicle for life'.[28] That said however, his immediate focus was on determining rules and structures for the maintenance of international order, rather on creating the stability essential to underpin it. There was far too little attention to providing incentives for good international behaviour.

This was a critical misjudgment because Wilson simply did not have the tools for the job he had set himself. Too much was expected of arbitration, which could never hope to cope with the more intractable and dangerous international disputes. And when it came to the crucial question of enforcement, far too much store was set by economic sanctions and by that new and untested factor in international affairs, the force of public opinion. The role of public opinion as a force for peace was a central tenet of liberal thinking. Indeed according to Wilson, the Covenant, depended chiefly on 'the moral force of the public opinion of the world and the cleansing and clarifying influence of publicity'.[29] Chiefly, but not entirely, because he went on to add the qualification that force remained in the background. But where would that force come from? The British and Americans had rejected French proposals that the League should have its own armed forces, along with its own military staff. Wilson would not countenance the substitution of international militarism for national militarism. The British could not envisage putting part of the British army 'under the command of a general who was not a British subject'.[30] (The United States is today similarly unfavourably disposed to American forces serving under foreign commanders in UN peacekeeping operations.)

The League therefore would have to depend on members really meaning what they said when they had subscribed to the doctrine of collective security, that they would regard an attack on one member as an attack on all. That may have appeared reasonable in 1919 when the idea that peace was indivisible, and that all nations would be willing to identify their national interests with the military support of the larger international order seemed axiomatic.[31] When however three years later the League debated a Draft Treaty of Mutual Assistance, which would have obliged members to come to the aid of a victim of aggression, the motion was blocked, even though military action would only have been required from states from the same Continent.

In a letter to Wilson written in July 1918, House admitted that solving the problems of a League of Nations in a way which would satisfy the hopes of the people 'and yet satisfy a practical mind' would be extremely difficult. But, he went on to argue, because the world 'will be so weary of war and the thought of it ... it will seize upon any intelligent way out'.[32] And that is partly, but only partly, what happened. For all that has just been said, at the time Wilson's ideas seemed to have a great deal going for them. Relatively little new thinking had been done about ways of reforming or reorganising power. Other than Keynes', Wilson's were the only radical ideas on the postwar agenda. They had the added attraction of being advanced by the President of the strongest power on earth. Last, but by no means least as House had suggested, people wanted to believe in them. They wanted to believe that this *had* been the war to end all wars, and that reason and goodwill would now prevail. They bridled when Clemenceau declared that 'if the balance, which was produced spontaneously during the war, had existed earlier, if for example Britain, America, France and Italy had agreed to say that whoever attacked one of them attacked all of them, the war would never have taken place'.[33] And for a nearly a decade, events appeared to prove the optimists right.

The 1920s was a uniquely favourable time to try and operate an organisation like the League. No other decade in the twentieth century was as free of major crises, tensions or wars. Down and out in the immediate postwar years, Germany under Gustav Stresemann's stewardship, sought international rehabilitation. The French, deprived of British and American support, quickly discovered that Clemenceau's German strategy was unsustainable. The result was a *rapprochement* within the framework of the Locarno Pact of 1925. There was even some, albeit rather vague, talk from the French side of a European federation. With power politics seemingly in abeyance and no major challenges to face, the League notched up a number of modest successes. It enjoyed immense public support in Britain. It was used by the Powers, even if a good deal of the most important business was conducted outside its auspices. Two vital absentees, Germany and Russia eventually joined, but not the United States.[34]

In the memoirs he published in the 1970s, Jean Monnet, a member of the League's Secretariat, recalled that

> We got results. We overcame crises that were no less serious than those of Berlin or Northern Ireland today; we administered territories by new methods; we put a stop to epidemics. We developed methods of cooperation among nations which hitherto had known only relationships based on power. We placed great hopes in the development of the League, and the difficulties we encountered acted as a stimulus. It was only later that I realized how we had underestimated them, or rather how we had failed to dig deep enough.[35]

For appearances were misleading. This was a shallow and fundamentally unstable peace which immediately began to disintegrate with the onset of the Depression. The first international repercussions of the great crisis of modern capitalism made themselves felt in the Far East, with the Japanese attack on Manchuria in 1931. The League took no action – and failed its first major test. It failed again, and much more damagingly in the face of Mussolini's Abyssinian adventure in 1936. When it came to containing Hitler's ambitions, it was more or less irrelevant.

The 1930s also witnessed the end of that other great postwar quest which occupied more of the League's time and energy than had any other issue, the quest for disarmament. Before the First World War, disarmament had not been very high on the international agenda. Fear of being unable to stand up to the economic pace of the arms race had motivated the Tsar's call to the Hague Conference in 1899. It was fear of war which brought disarmament to the fore in the 1920s. Arms had become firmly associated with war. Arms races, which had become such a prominent feature of the pre 1914 world, were widely believed to cause war. The increase in armaments, as Grey argued, produced

> a consciousness of the strength of other nations and a sense of fear. Fear begets suspicions and distrust and evil imaginings of all sorts, till each Government feels it would be criminal and a betrayal of its country not to take every precaution, while every Government regards the precautions of every other Government as evidence of hostile intent.

A world with fewer arms was seen as a safer one.[36] This however, was to confuse the symptom with the disease. It was, in the words of the Spanish diplomat, Salvador de Madariaga, who headed the League's disarmament division, to tackle the problem of war 'upside down and at the wrong end ... Nations don't distrust each other because they are armed: they are armed because they distrust each other. And therefore to want disarmament before a minimum of common agreement on fundamentals is as absurd as to want people to go undressed in winter.'[37]

Given that the underlying political tensions remained unresolved, the prospects were not encouraging. Nevertheless the end of the war had brought its own process of disarmament, enforced in the case of Germany, and there were some early successes starting with the 1922 Washington Naval Treaty whereby Britain, Japan and the United States established an agreed ratio of capital ships and aircraft. The world's three greatest naval powers actually had to scrap tonnage in order to meet the agreed limits. These were subsequently also extended to cruisers and submarines. In 1925 38 states signed the Geneva protocol prohibiting the use of poison gas. Three years later came another, more revealing agreement. Generally known as the Kellogg–Briand Pact, its formal title was self-explanatory – *The International Treaty for the Renunciation of War as an Instrument of National Policy*. With the exception of Argentina, Bolivia, El Salvador and Yemen, everybody signed. Again, it was much easier said than done. The signatories themselves attached a series of reservations to the agreement, and did nothing by way of providing enforcement mechanism. An enthusiastic public acutely anxious that war might somehow be wished away, did not appear to notice.[38]

When it came to comprehensive disarmament, the negotiators got nowhere. By Article 8, which Wilson had written into the Covenant, members of the League had recognised that the maintenance of peace required 'the reduction of national armaments to the lowest point consistent with national safety'. It was only in 1932, after a host of impractical or unacceptable proposals had already been discussed and discarded, that a disarmament conference was finally convened in Geneva. Here the problems all came to a head. The continuing French obsession with security clashed with the determination of the Germans to achieve the military equality denied them under the Versailles Treaty. Britain and the United States might have been able to resolve this issue by offering France guarantees, but were unwilling to do so. Then there were the technical difficulties. What in practice was 'the lowest point consistent with national safety'? What allowance should be made for 'the geographical situation and circumstances of each state', another point referred to in the Covenant? Who would decide whether a weapon is 'offensive', in which case it should be banned as likely to facilitate attack, or permitted on the grounds that it was only 'defensive'? Certainly not the parties involved, all of whom were naturally inclined to view their own armaments as 'defensive', and those of their potential adversaries as 'offensive'. The issue is neatly encapsulated by the description of one American delegate, Senator Swanson, sitting in the Sea Commission, 'blowing great clouds of smoke from his cigar and demonstrating in fervid Southern eloquence that battleships were the most defensive weapons; they became a symbol of the American home and family, they could be given to children to play with as toys, so harmless was their use and purpose.'[39] And finally, had agreements eventually been reached, there would have been the question, so familar from the arms control negotiations of the Cold War years, of how they should be verified and enforced.

In fact the question was to prove academic. In October 1933, nine months after Hitler came to power, Germany withdrew from Geneva. The conference was adjourned *sine die* in June 1934. This was the time for a complete change of course. Wilson's attempt to 'Lockeanise' or 'deHobbeseanise' international politics had proved impossibly ambitious. Although the mood in 1919 had been such that people wanted to believe that it could be done, the hard facts are that Wilson had neither the necessary political clout nor a workable blueprint. If Clemenceau can be accused of being excessively cyncial, Wilson was insufficiently so. His understanding of the nature of international politics had been too liberal, and too parochially American. Wilson would have done much better had he concentrated on trying to create a stable Germany which could then work out its role in Europe in negotiation with the other Powers, rather than on setting his sights on a scheme buoyed up by moral rectitude and hope rather than hard-headed analysis. Put at its harshest, Wilson paid the price for forgetting that while radical change does indeed require vision, politics remains the art of the possible.

Yet however open Wilson is to criticism it is impossible to dismiss him. Unlike Clemenceau, Wilson left a long-term legacy. More than any other major international figure, Wilson began the process of delegitimising power politics. His stress on self-determination undermined the legitimacy of empire and domination. Before the establishment of the League, war was seen as a normal and acceptable instrument of national policy, a matter in which only the nations most immediately concerned had any interest or right of say. With the formulation of the Covenant of the League of Nations, this ceased to be the case. Nations did not stop attacking each other, but war, except for purposes of self-defence, had lost the international legitimacy which had placed it at the heart of *Realpolitik*. And Wilson provided the political impetus for a new kind of international organisation. The League and its successor, the United Nations, were based soundly on the principle of national voluntarism. It could not do more than its members authorised. But, and we have this on Jean Monnet's testimony, the League prefigured also the notion of supranationality which was to become central to the first really successful experiments in taming power politics in western Europe after the Second World War.[40]

The real case against Wilson's ideas, and the case which has to be set against these achievements, is not the fact that League was fundamentally flawed, and thus inevitably failed its key tests. Given more propitious circumstances, given indeed American participation, it might have proved itself more useful just as the United Nations, for all its similar inherent faults, has proved itself useful. Rather it is that by its very existence it encouraged the development of unrealistic expectations. Once Europe did revert to the old game of power politics, governments found it impossible to adapt quickly enough. When the idea of a League of Nations had first been discussed in Britain during the First World War, one of the most influential officials in government, Maurice Hankey had argued that the scheme was dangerous on the grounds that it would only create a fictitious sense of security. It would 'put a very strong lever into the hands of the well-meaning idealists, who are to be found in almost every Government who deprecate expenditure on armaments, and, in the course of time, it will almost certainly result in this country being caught at a disadvantage'.[41]

The failures of the 1930s cannot of course all be placed at the door of the League. The Depression was for more important. But the League was both expression and cause of a state of mind which made a return of power politics particularly difficult to cope with and which ensured that the brief window of opportunity in the immediate aftermath of Hitler's accession to power, would be lost. Germany, as Hitler well knew, was dangerously vulnerable during the early stages of its rearmament. 'That will show whether or not France has *statesmen*', he told his generals as early as 3 February 1933. 'If so, she will not leave us time but will attack us, presumably with eastern satellites.'[42] The Poles, well aware that Germany had never accepted its eastern frontiers, did indeed want to attack. The French too were worried. 'We shall have to fight them again', Edouard Herriot told an American visitor in April.[43] But when three years later Hitler, with a minimum of reserves, reoccupied the Rhineland in contravention of both the Versailles Treaty and the Locarno Pact, the French took no action. It was a gross miscalculation. As Hitler himself later admitted, had the French marched in, the Germans would have had to withdraw with their tails between their legs, since the forces then available to them would have been inadequate for even moderate resistance.[44] The failure was symptomatic. France was lapsing from long-standing weakness into the state of demoralisation which gave rise to appeasement and contributed to the collapse of 1940.

The French, however, were not alone. None of the Powers were in a mood for bold action. They were reluctant even to rearm. A report produced for the British government in 1934 referred to the 'moral disarmament' of the population as one of Britain's worst defence deficiencies.[45] Even when that deficiency was overcome, politicians and their electorates remained unwilling to face up to the inevitable. The result was first appeasement, then a war of unprecedented proportions and profound consequences.

5 The Remastery of Power

The 1930s and first half of the 1940s witnessed the second of the three great twentieth-century hegemonial challenges. Fascist, racist and nationalist in character, it was by far the most far-reaching and destructive. The estimated *European* death toll in the Second World War is more than five times that for the First World War.[1] By November 1942 Hitler's forces controlled Continental Europe from the Atlantic to a line in Russia which ran east of Leningrad in the north down to the Black Sea and the Caucasus. In the Far East the Japanese who had begun their process of expansionism in Manchuria in 1931, controlled much of north east China and south east Asia. The Second World War represents the the high-water mark of power politics. This would be the last great war of conquest. For in fighting as long and hard as their overweening ambitions drove them to do, the Axis Powers brought about a new technological stalemate which would prove much more difficult to break than the stalemate on the Western Front. New tactics and new weapons had eventually solved the 'riddle of the trenches'. The nuclear riddle has, so far at least, proved insoluble.

The immediate origins of the remastery of power lie in a combination of technological opportunity and political and economic crisis. What made Hitler such a formidable figure was the fact that he came to power before the ghost of trench warfare had been exorcised, but when mobile warfare and decisive victory were once again possible. The 1930s witnessed a very unequal contest between diametrically opposed views of power. There was, for the first time, a deep divide between those states, revisionist, unstable and authoritarian, intent on reviving the practice of power politics, and the *status quo* democracies desperately anxious to convince themselves that they had indeed said 'good-bye to all that'. The latter were reluctant to accept the fact that the most unscrupulous members of the system would inevitably set its rules. The polarisation between power and fear, as later towards the end of the Second World War, between power and idealism, was stark and destructive.

Appeasement was not originally an attempt to gain peace at any price, but rather to re-establish a rational and ethical basis for the resolution of international problems in the tradition of Gladstone. It began from the not unreasonable assumption that one way of avoiding war was by admitting and satisfying 'legitimate' – and thus by implication also limited –

grievances through negotiation and compromise.[2] It was a matter, in Chamberlain's words, of substituting 'the method of discussion for the method of force in the settlement of differences'.[3] This approach had gained immense appeal in a Britain where, under the influence of Keynes's *Economic Consequences of the Peace*, the Versailles settlement had been comprehensively discredited. Once passions had had a chance to cool, a much more sober, if not necessarily realistic assessment of the origins of the conflict emerged. The mood of August 1914, along with the scale of German war aims, were forgotten. According to this new historical revisionism, two countries which had no real clash of interest had unwittingly drifted into conflict. Both the war and the peace settlement had been a mistake.[4] The German problem, and here the argument moved onto much stronger ground, should be solved not by the kind of punitive peace sought by Clemenceau. Rather, as C. P. Scott, the influential editor of the *Manchester Guardian*, put it, Germany should be seen not 'as an enemy to be feared and destroyed, but as a part of the Europe of which we ourselves form an integral part, and which for many a long year will need all our help and all our care to save it from ruin'.[5]

Some progress in this direction was made in the mid- and late-1920s. Following their abortive attempt to occupy the Ruhr in 1923, the French finally recognised that they lacked the strength and support to keep Germany within the straitjacket which Clemenceau had sought to fashion at Versailles. The result was a period of Franco-German rapprochement, beginning with the Locarno Mutual Security Pact of 1925 intended in the words of its preamble, to 'contribute greatly to bring about a moral relaxation of tension between nations'. Most of the restrictions of the Versailles Treaty now began to be removed, and in his advocacy of a European union, Briand urged not only economic association but also a degree of political and social federation. Although the ideas were never clearly spelled out, this was essentially an expression of French weakness in the face of German economic and future political power, 'a plea for help – for German help – in managing that power'.[6]

All hope of such help disappeared with the advent of Hitler. While the French no longer knew what to do about the German problem, the British, and in particular Neville Chamberlain, who became Prime Minister in 1936, thought that they did. Chamberlain was a man with a mission. In a speech he gave in April 1938, Chamberlain outlined what sounds less a diplomatic programme than a dream. Noting that neither Fascism nor Communism were in harmony with 'our temper and creed', Chamberlain went on to exhort his listeners not to:

forget that we are all members of the human race, and subject to the like passions and affections, and fears and desires. There must be something in common between us, if only we can find it, and perhaps by our very aloofness from the rest of Europe we may have some special part to play as conciliator and mediator. An ancient historian once wrote of the Greeks, that they had made gentle the life of the world ... I can imagine no nobler ambition for an English statesman than to win the same tribute for his own country.[7]

What the Prime Minister sought, as he had made clear in a private letter written the previous autumn, was nothing less than the 'appeasement of Europe and Asia and ... the ultimate check to the mad armaments race'. To Chamberlain, a man with a strong belief in rationality as the foundation of human behaviour, war 'wins nothing, cures nothing, ends nothing'.[8]

This was a generally-shared view which, if anything, had gained strength with the passage of time. Britain in the 1930s was living under what was widely – and wrongly – perceived to be a dual threat. The popular image of war was shaped on the one hand by memories of a trench warfare which was now obsolete, and on the other by the much exaggerated threat of a new weapon which had first appeared during the First World War – the bomber. Reporting to the Cabinet after his return from the first of his visits to Hitler in 1938, Chamberlain remarked how

that morning he had flown up the river over London. He had imagined a German bomber flying the same course. He had asked himself what degree of protection they could afford for the thousands of homes which he had seen stretched out below him, and he had felt we were in no position to justify waging a war today, in order to prevent a war hereafter.[9]

In fact the Germans did not subscribe to the theory of strategic bombing. Hitler had a much more realistic view of the limitations of the bomber than did the British; the 'knock-out blow' against London which both the military and the public feared, was not in fact then feasible.[10] But this was a world in which people tended to reason from fear. Like Sarah Burton, the heroine of Winifred Holtby's novel, *South Riding*, published in 1936, they were 'haunted by the menace of another war. Constantly, when she least expected it, that spectre threatened her, undermining her confidence in her work, her faith, her future. A joke, a picture, a tune, could trap her into a blinding waste of misery and helplessness.' The shape of things to come, the title of one of H. G. Wells' novels, was not inviting.[11]

Appeasement cannot therefore simply be dismissed as bad policy, the classic way of how not to handle a bully. In its later forms at least it must be seen as the last most desperate phase of the flight from power politics, which had begun with the support for Wilson and the League. The soldiers had stood and fought; postwar British and French society tried to flee from war. They were in no psychological, and in the specific case of France, in no political condition to face up to a revival of the German threat. Fear paralysed policy. As Alexis Leger, Secretary-General at the *Quai d'Orsay*, remarked in March 1938, 'France could only react to events, she could not take the initiative.'[12] Even at the very last moment, when Germany had attacked Poland in defiance of the Anglo-French guarantee given a few months earlier, the French hesitated.

Yet at the official level at least the French had far fewer illusions about Hitler's ambitions than the British. The active policy of appeasement which the latter sought, was sustainable only on the basis of the view, which the French did not share, that Hitler had limited objectives, that he was a man whom Chamberlain believed it was possible, to 'do business' with. According to R. A. C. Parker, the most recent student of Chamberlain's policy, Chamberlain quite genuinely believed this. But Parker also notes the Prime Minister's 'enviable capacity for self-satisfaction', his overconfidence in his ability to 'persuade colleagues, foreigners, and most difficult of all, excitable dictators to be reasonable in their conduct,' as well as his reluctance to change his mind.[13] One must also suspect, for there is plenty in what Chamberlain said and wrote after his meetings with Hitler to show that he has also recognised the more sinister sides of his character, that he repressed or discounted such evidence that did not concur with what he wanted to believe. (The British Prime Minister was by no means the only one to do this. 'I think' Albert Speer remarked long after the war, 'that we saw only what we wanted to see and knew only what we wanted to know.') Unlike the Foreign Secretary, Lord Halifax who had earlier declared that Hitler did not have Napoleonic ambitions, Chamberlain never revised his view.[14]

Few in the late summer of 1938 wanted to question these optimistic judgements. When Daladier returned to Le Bourget airport from Munich, he was greeted not by the vengeful mob he expected, but by an enthusiastic crowd. Some twenty thousand letters and telegrams were delivered to Number 10 Downing Street in late September and early October, as well as gifts in what Chamberlain privately described as 'embarrassing profusion'. Chamberlain, to quote one MP, had done 'something that the mass of the common people of the world wanted done'.[15]

Recording the events of September 1938 nearly 30 years later, Harold Macmillan summed up the prevailing mood of the time:

> My son would stay at school and go to Oxford in the autumn. My home and children, like all the other homes throughout the country, would be spared ... It was as if we had come to the edge of a precipice and then – by some miracle – had been pulled back to safety. Yet when we met to discuss the true situation and hear the reflections of those whose judgements we trusted, we began to see beyond the fragile screen of complacency and self-deception, skillfully designed to delude a whole people and lull them into a fictitious sense of security.[16]

For September 1938, like August 1914, quickly proved to have been an act of collective self-delusion. Munich really was the end, albeit by contemporary standards a very remarkable end of the road. The term 'Summit' had not yet entered the international vocabulary. The 69-year-old prime minister had never flow in an aeroplane before. But unconventional diplomacy could not save the day. What Chamberlain did not, and could not recognise, was the incongruous, if not grotesque nature of these encounters between a man described by one of his biographers as a 'sensitive and highminded product of the Victorian peace',[17] and the former inhabitant of a Vienna doss-house who had called his political testament *Mein Kampf* (My Struggle). A starker contrast of personalities and values would have been difficult to imagine. While Chamberlain sought peace in his time, Hitler was more than content to take power politics into the realm of the demonic. The war that he would fight in the East, in what was explicitly conceived as a *Vernichtungskrieg*, a war of annihilation, against a racially inferior people, surpasses all the horror of the Western Front – 'the longest, most intensive and brutal conflict between two nations in history'.[18]

In marked contrast to 1914, public pressure played no part in this process. Foreign policy was a relatively secondary factor in Hitler's path to power. Hitler had certainly been helped by the general anger against Versailles – in the election campaign of September 1930 which marks the beginning of the Nazis' electoral success, all of the competing 24 parties placed treaty revision on their programmes. Germans sought the restoration of their country's own sense of greatness and power. But the idea of a Thousand Year Reich was not to the forefront of the electorate's concerns. What they wanted was a leader to rescue a country which had lost hope. The Great Power which had failed to achieve domestic stability before the First World War, had after 1918 moved from crisis to crisis – from revolution and near civil war in the aftermath of defeat, through the psychologically deeply destructive hyperinflation of 1923, to the Depression with its bankruptcies, salary cut-backs and six million unemployed.

However enthusiastic the response to Hitler's hypnotic speeches and the power rituals of the Nuremburg rallies, the public at large had no taste for war. Although there had been some revival of bellicism on the political Right in the late-1920s, its prewar popular manifestation was gone. Munich was greeted with enthusiasm and relief not just in Britain and France, but also in Germany. Efforts by the German press and radio to whip up war fever in late September failed. An armoured division moving ostentatiously through Berlin was greeted with complete indifference. The outbreak of war a year later was again met with apathy. One *Gauleiter* who travelled around the country in September 1939 noted that nothing on the journey had reminded him of 1914 – 'no enthusiasm, no joy, no cheering. Wherever you went there was an uncanny quiet, not to say depression. The whole German people seemed to be gripped by a paralytic fear which made it incapable either of applauding or of expressing discontent.'[19]

The mood changed once the German army started winning victories. This was partly a function of success, partly also of the fact that the country did have unfinished business and unsatisfied ambitions. Although Stresemann had relied on patience, compromise and something approaching a European consensus, the ultimate goals of this calculating practitioner of *Realpolitik*, were far from modest. As later outlined by an aide, they included the freeing of the Rhineland, recovery of Eupen-Malmedy and the Saar, the perfection of Austria's *Anschluss* and the acquisition, whether under mandate or otherwise, of 'an African colony where essential tropical raw materials could be secured and an outlet created for the surplus energy of the younger generation'.[20] Military leaders meanwhile hoped for the recovery of lands lost to Poland. And while never a major public issues, there was the question of settling accounts with France. A German lieutenant who wrote home after the 1940 campaign, referred to the end of a great battle which 'lasted twenty-six years'. In Berlin the American journalist William Shirer noted that the capture of Paris had stirred something 'very deep in the hearts of most Germans. It was always a wish-dream of millions here'.[21]

While another war was bound to be on a large scale given that Germany's territorial and economic power base remained intact, the extremes to which Germany went in her second hegemonial bid could not have been reasonably anticipated. There is a sense in which Germany and Europe were unlucky. The risks of a resurgence of power politics had been inherent in the outcome of the First World War. They had been increased by the unsatisfactory and contradictory nature of the peace. But the odds against the emergence of the one man who would marshall German power with such grandiose and ruthless daring, were substantial. The Second World War was very much Hitler's war. As Alan Bullock remarks of the Russian campaign, which lies at the heart of Hitler's strategy, nobody else in the Nazi leadership or of the wider circle of German nationalist politicians 'combined the imagination to conceive so fantastic an undertaking with the sorcerer's ability to persuade so many others with much greater practical experience of soldiering, business, industry and administration to engage in the attempt to carry it out'.[22]

Hitler's path from corporal to warlord, far from being foreordained, had a strong element of the fortuitous about it. The very fact that he had survived four years of trench warfare as a despatch runner, a group which had a particularly high casualty rate, is in itself remarkable. Few in 1924, following the failure of the Munich *Putsch*, would have expected Hitler to make a come-back. That he did so was the result not just of the Depression, without which he would not have got his critical electoral base, but also the mistakes and miscalculations of his political opponents. Had fog not caused him to cut short his speech on 8 November 1939 at the Munich Beer House on the anniversary of the *Putsch* attempt, Georg Elser's assassination attempt might have succeeded. In A. C. Grayling's words, Hitler had 'an evil inviolability' about him.[23]

One of the most pathologically predatory figures ever to have trodden the European stage, Hitler sought not empire in the traditional sense of the term, but a demographic reordering of the Eurasian landmass. To understand the ideological, as well as some part of the psychological framework of his aggressiveness, we have to go back to his political education in the more unsalubrious parts of pre-1914 Vienna. His experience of life in the house for men – that school for meanness where he spent three and a half years, went a long way to shape the philosophy of struggle which became the basis of his *Weltanschauung*. It was here that, along with anti-Semitism and Social Darwinism, the young Hitler absorbed many of the worst traits of late nineteenth-century European thinking – extreme nationalism, a scepticism about humanity and reason, the romantic glorification of blood and instinct, and an oversimplified interpretations of Nietzsche's concept of the 'strength and radiant amorality' of the superman.[24]

Hitler's political arrival sees the final infection of the twentieth century with the malignancies spawned by the great industrial and intellectual upheavals of the second half of the nineteenth century. While the synthesis was new, Hitler was, in Joachim Fest's words, 'a profoundly anachronistic phenomenon. In his naive imperialism, in his magnitude complex, in his conviction of the inescapable choice between the ascent to world power or doom, he was a leftover of the nineteenth century.'[25] His obsession with *Lebensraum* in the east combined thoroughly old-fashioned notions of a war of plunder with a Malthusian fear of the potential inability of an increasing German population to feed itself, which had been a stock in trade of right wing German thinking since the end of the last century.

Hitler also shared the view of the geopoliticians of the earlier era, that no stable solution of Germany's problems was possible until Germany had control over Europe. 'We cannot, like Bismarck, limit ourselves to national aims. We must rule Europe or fall apart as a nation, fall back into the chaos of small states.'[26] What was new, at least in the in the mainstream of international thinking, was his preoccupation with race and and *Volk*. Again the ideas go back to the nineteenth century, to the writings of Gobineau and Houston Stuart Chamberlain. For Hitler the question of race was an obsession. He saw race and *Volk* rather than nations as the fundamental historical unit of growth and decay. Races were linked with the soil; they depended on territory which must expand in order to provide their populations with living space. *Lebensraum* is very much at the centre of Hitler's thinking. Germany needed space to accommodate a population which he had claimed in *Mein Kampf* was increasing by some 900 000 per year. Hitler shared the view widespread in Germany that, in contrast to the other powers, Germany was, to use the title of a contemporary novel, 'a nation without space'. Birth control and internal colonisation were no answers, since they would weaken the race in both numbers and quality and encourage what he and many on the Right saw as the undesirable increase in urbanisation. (History, he claimed, taught that while a nation could live without cities, it could not live without farmers.)

This was a recipe not just for conquest, but world conquest. The search for living space was a continuous process. Each conquest would allow a further expansion of the population, which in turn would facilitate further expansion. 'Wherever our success may end,' Hitler remarked in 1928, 'that will always be only the starting point of a new fight.'[27] And Hitler wanted to fight. War for him was was not simply a means, as in the final analysis it had been for Wilhemine Germany. It was as much an end in itself – 'the ultimate goal of politics.' 'War', said this consummate Social Darwinist, 'is the most natural, the most ordinary thing. War is a constant; war is everywhere. There is no beginning, there is no conclusion of peace. War is life. All struggle is war. War is the primal condition.'[28]

Hitler spoke from experience. Although at one point in *Mein Kampf* he describes the Western Front as 'hell' there is no doubt that the war left an overwhelmingly positive impression on him. It was he went on to write, 'the greatest and most unforgettable time of my earthly experience'. He refused to take leave, and begged to be sent back to the Front immediately after recovering from wounds. Trench life provided him with the community and comradeship he had previously lacked. For him, as for a significant number of Germans who later gravitated to the Right, the experience of this *Frontserlebnis* (front experience) easily outweighed the horrors of the war. Hitler relished this education in hardness and manliness, not least because he glorified in war itself. In contrast to the vast majority of soldiers who felt a revulsion against the violence and destruction, Hitler was drawn to and fascinated by it. It is this perversion, it is difficult to use any other term, which distinguishes this 'new' bellicism from the naive form evident in the years leading up to the First World War.[29] War was not simply an abstraction to men like Hitler – unlike the generation of 1914, they knew exactly what they were calling for.

Addressing his generals on the eve of the war, Hitler described German strength as lying in 'our quickness and our brutality; Genghis Khan has sent millions of women and children into death knowingly with a light heart. History sees in him only the great founder of states.'[30] The brutality was in Hitler's nature; the speed was a function of the maturing of the technology of industrialised warfare. Unlike his adversaries, Hitler, who had a remarkable technical grasp of new weaponry, had realised that the crisis in land warfare was over. Decisive military action was again a possibility; states were recovering their coercive potential. This was not because of any single new weapon, such as the tank or bomber, but rather because of the combination of new weapons and technologies which had emerged in the wake of the great battles of attrition, opening the prospect of an offensive revolution based on the principle of 'speed of attack through speed of communication'.

Most of the basic elements for the *Blitzkrieg* were already in place by the end of the First World War. Indeed during the last months of the war the British High Command tentatively approved a plan for 1919 which would have inaugurated the tactics which the Germans used against Poland 20 years later. Although slow to recognise the importance of the tank during the First World War, in the 1920s the German army took considerable interest in the weapon. They studied, wrote about and even trained for armoured warfare using, ironically enough given what was later to happen, a Russian training and testing centre at Kazan. By the time rearmament began the *Reichswehr* air staff had developed a comprehensive air doctrine which emphasised the tactical role of aircraft in support of ground forces.[31]

'The next war', Hitler remarked shortly after his accession to power, 'will be quite different from the last world war. Infantry attacks and mass formations are obsolete. Interlocked frontal struggles lasting for years on petrified fronts will not return ... They were a degenerate form of war.'[32] There were, however, still several things to be done. New aircraft, notably the Stuka divebomber, technical advances in the field of radio communication, as well as the logistical experience gained during the Spanish Civil War were still needed before the full promise of mobile warfare could be realised. It was only in the late 1930s that it finally became possible for entire divisions of tanks to break through enemy defences and surge through the gaps to overwhlem the nerve centre in the rear. Hitler also had to provide the the necessary daring which was so essential to the success of *Blitzkrieg*, and which many of his generals lacked. Mindful of the bitterly hard fighting between 1914 and 1918, the German General Staff seriously overrated the French army. They continued to see France as the leading military power on the Continent, with a military tradition which no other state could equal. Hitler had a shrewder sense of French weakness. 'Every army is a mirror of its people. The French people think only of peace and good living, and they are torn apart in Parliamentary strife ... After the first setback it [the army] will swiftly crack up.'[33] When the Germans launched Operation *Sichelschnitt* in May 1940, a French army, which had failed to make comparable advances after the First World War, found itself facing a thoroughly modern *Wehrmacht*. Surprised and outclassed, the French surrendered within the six weeks originally allowed for in the Schlieffen Plan. German casualties amounted to 'only' 27 000 dead and 111 000 wounded.[34] The contrast with the last round could hardly be starker.

Bismarck would have stopped there. For Hitler, however, France had been a secondary objective. The real target, as he had already made clear in *Mein Kampf*, was Russia. And with the attack on Russia, the second, the real Hitler finally emerges. The first Hitler was a master of power politics. This was the man who had so skilfully manipulated his adversaries fears of war during the crises of the late-1930s – the reoccupation of the Rhineland, the *Anschluss* with Austria, and Munich. It was the man who in August 1939 snatched a diplomatic pact with the Soviet Union from under the noses of the British and French, thereby ensuring that he could pick his main victims off at will and avoid the exigencies of a two-front war. The Hitler of Operation Barbarossa by contrast was the fanatic and fantasist who had declared he would never survive the defeat of his people. The Russian campaign marks the fusion of material and ideological motives. Russia would provide Germany with raw materials, manpower and of course the living space Hitler was so obsessed by. Over and above that, however, its conquest would demonstrate the superiority of the German master race over the Slavic *Untermenschen* and save Europe from the plague of Jewish Bolshevism. And it would place Germany in a position to defeat the Anglo-Saxon nations in the final struggle for world power.[35]

In the run-up to Operation Barbarossa, an army 3 200 000 men strong, with 3350 tanks and 600 motor vehicles, including armoured cars, was assembled. It was not enough. Hitler gambled on the impossible, the ability to finish the campaign before the onset of the Russian winter. He fielded an immensely effective army against an enemy demoralised by political purges and deprived of vital intelligence by Stalin's stubborn refusal to look the facts in the face and recognise that an attack was imminent. By any military standards except that required by Barbarossa, the achievement of the German army in Russia was incomparable.[36]

By the end of November the cold weather set in, interfering with machinery and reducing combat effectiveness. On 5 December the German offensive ended and the Russian counteroffensive began. Two days later Japanese bombers attacked Pearl Harbor. The attack had not been coordinated with Berlin, though the Japanese had certainly been encouraged to take on the United States by the German successes in Europe. Hitler was not however perturbed. He had long underestimated the economic and military potential of the United States. He expected, or perhaps more accurately hoped, to have defeated Russia by the time America could effectively intervene in Europe. At the same time his sense of historic destiny appears to have been stimulated by the prospect of a conflict between continents and he immediately declared war on the United States, announcing that 'a historical revision on a unique scale has been imposed on us by the Creator'.[37] Long and bitter fighting lay ahead before Germany was finally and conclusively defeated. But this was the point where the old curse of German power – its fatal lack of proportion – reasserted itself with a vengeance. The country was once more up against a stronger coalition. In purely military terms the Germans again retained a considerable advantage over all of their enemies. In material terms, and this would more eventually become a *Materialschlacht*, they were at a fatal disadvantage. In 1940 the armaments production of the Allied combatants (the figures are in 1944 dollars), amounted to 3.5 billion, compared with 6.75 billion for the Axis. In 1943 the Allied combatants produced 62.5 billion dollars worth of armaments – the Axis Powers 18.3 billion.[38]

What was important here however was not simply the power of the new alliance which Hitler had succeeded in forging against himself, but the fact that it was determined to take Hitler on on his own terms of all or nothing. The *second* World War was to be a fight to the finish. Allied war aims became the 'total elimination' of German and Japanese war power. It had not started out that way. The lack of clear objectives during the early phase of the war is neatly reflected in a limerick then circulating in the Foreign Office:

> An elderly statesman with gout,
> When asked what the war was about,
> In a Written Reply
> Said, 'My Colleagues and I
> Are doing our best to find out.[39]

When however, in August 1940, by which time Churchill was prime minister, the first British bombers attacked Berlin, they dropped leaflets warning that the 'war which Hitler started will go on, and it will last as long as Hitler does'.[40] By the time the policy of unconditional surrender was publicly announced by Roosevelt at Casablanca in January 1943, it was already something of a formality, the basic decision as Eric Larrabee puts it, having been taken 'long before and at some deeper level in many, many minds'.[41] Unconditional surrender may have reflected a certain element of democratic crusading on the part of the United States. It was certainly intended to ensure that in contrast to 1918, once the war had been won, it would stay won. Above all it reflected the fact that this war was in a different class from the traditional pre-twentieth-century European conflict fought for limited ends and terminated by negotiation between victor and vanquished. Churchill had not simply been engaging in rhetoric when in one of his most famous wartime speeches, he described the enemy as 'a monstrous tyranny, never surpassed in the dark, lamentable catalogue of human crime'.

The implications of unconditional surrender had not however been thought through. Nobody knew at this stage what was to be done with Germany once it had been defeated. More immediately important, the American political leadership, unlike it should be said to the Chiefs of Staff, had not considered the implications in terms of increased Soviet power. For if Germany was to be totally defeated, Soviet forces who bore the brunt of the fighting and fielded the brunt of the manpower, would move deep into Europe. It was this prospect which came increasingly to preoccupy Churchill. At a cabinet meeting held in autumn 1943, Churchill warned that it would be wrong 'to weaken Germany too much – we may need her against Russia'.[42] The Prime Minister, deeply attuned to the traditional British need to maintain a balance of power on the Continent, made a series of attempts to try and limit the extent of the Soviet advance into eastern Europe. Only one of these, the famous or infamous 'spheres of influence' agreement of October 1944, whereby Britain gained a predominant voice in Greece in exchange for Soviet predominance in Romania, was successful. In 1943 and 1944 Churchill championed an Allied expedition up the Danube to try and reach Vienna and Budapest before Soviet forces. In the Spring of 1945 he advocated an Anglo-American dash to take Berlin, arguing that it was 'highly important that we should shake hands with the Russians as far east as possible'.[43] Similar arguments were advanced for American forces to take Prague.

The Americans would have none of this. While there were genuine military objections to a Danubian expedition, the predominant reason for American resistance was political. This, as Washington saw it, was America's second chance to right the world. The United States had returned to Europe in Wilsonian mood. There had been no great debate about who had 'lost' the preceding peace. No attempt had been made in the interwar years to rethink American attitudes towards power politics. Isolationism had remained a potent force until almost the very moment when the Japanese attacked Pearl Harbor. Churchill was faced with an ally who, while willing to mobilise resources on a massive scale to defeat the enemy, was nevertheless determined to try and shun power politics afterwards. This was particularly true of the Secretary of State, Cordell Hull, who in Charles Bohlen's words 'rejected the concept of power in world affairs'.[44] It was true of the most senior general like Eisenhower and Omar Bradley. 'As soldiers,' Bradley later wrote, 'we looked naively on this British inclination to complicate the war with political foresight and non-military objectives'.[45] And it was true above all of the President, Franklin Roosevelt.

Roosevelt had served as Assistant Secretary of the Navy under Wilson and was heir to the liberal American tradition which was as hostile to power politics, as to its European practitioners, whose international role he wanted to see radically reduced. One historian writes of Roosevelt's desire to preside over Europe's retirement 'from the international scene'.[46] His more explicit aim was to replace the old balance of power with a cooperative international order based upon a continuation of the wartime collaboration of the allies. To this end he was, as Henry Kissinger writes:

> impatient with truisms claiming to embody the lessons of history. He rejected the idea that a total defeat of Germany might create a vacuum, which a victorious Soviet Union might then try to fill. He refused to countenance safeguards against possible postwar rivalry among the

victors, because these implied the reestablishment of the balance of power which he in fact wanted to destroy.[47]

Since there would be no equilibrium to maintain, the US would have no need to maintain forces in Europe after the war.

That this immensely ambitious project failed was first and foremost Stalin's responsibility. Roosevelt was making him an offer which it was very much in Stalin's long-term interests to accept. Taking Eastern Europe would mean isolation and high military expenditure. 'When I was young,' Hull once told Molotov, 'I knew a bully in Tenessee. He used to get a few things his way by being a bully and bluffing other fellows. But he ended up by not having a friend in the world.'[48] Stalin refused this offer, not just because he was greedy, insecure, or indeed unimaginative, but because it was couched in a political language he did not understand. Stalin's *Weltanschauung* was conceived in terms of power. The larger patterns of international life had no meaning for him other than how they bore on his immediate strategic and domestic problems. The reform of the international system was simply not on his agenda.

All this Roosevelt could not and would not recognise. He badly needed Stalin's long-term support, and went out of his way to convince himself that he would get it. In the process he misread Stalin almost as fundamentally as Chamberlain misread Hitler. 'I really think the Russians will go along with me about having no spheres of influence,' he remarked after the 1943 Tehran Summit.[49] Of one thing I am certain,' he is quoted as saying at the time of Yalta, 'Stalin is not an imperialist.'[50] Roosevelt's thinking suffered from the traditional liberal combination of rationalism and overoptimism, reinforced by legacy of isolationism. Roosevelt had spent his life managing men, and believed that, at bottom, Stalin could not be so different from other people. A country as vast as the Soviet Union could not have further territorial ambitions. Stalin, he remarked in the context of a discussion of Soviet ambitions in Manchuria, 'doesn't want any more ground. He's got enough.'[50] The Soviet leader would cooperate with Roosevelt's ideas of postwar peacekeeping because it was so obviously to his advantage to do so. Above all there was was the old liberal assumption that men were fundamentally good. People behaved well if they were treated well, and if Stalin was given everything Roosevelt possibly could, and Roosevelt asked for nothing in return, '*noblesse oblige*, he won't try to annex anything and will work with me for a world of democracy and peace'.[52]

Reality could not however be conjured out of existence in this fashion. Like others who had sought to wish power politics away, Roosevelt only succeeded in making its next manifestation more difficult to deal with. In refusing to seek the territorial advantage which Churchill urged, as in his earlier refusal to negotiate postwar borders when Stalin was still much weaker, he allowed the lines of division to be drawn further east than was militarily necessary. The result was to give Stalin a larger empire than he might otherwise have had.[53]

Roosevelt had overestimated American power. The United States was not strong enough to change the world and take power out of international politics. Roosevelt's America, like Wilson's before it, would have done better to have accepted the rules of the existing game, and then played them for all they were worth. That these were cynical and reactionary was beyond dispute. The 'parceling out of the Balkans' in the spheres of influences agreement reached by Stalin and Churchill in October 1944, was, in Lloyd Gardner's phrase, 'reminiscent of the treatment of the Ottoman Empire after World War 1, except that the stakes were oil rather than people'.[54] The US was by no means the only state seeking alternatives. In the western half of Europe some people were looking for even more radical options. Already in 1942 the Belgian Foreign Minister, Paul-Henri Spaak had noted the need to reconcile the rebirth of nationalism with internationalism. The principle of national sovereignty would have to be modified 'not only where the small countries are concerned but also in regard to the great ones'.[55] But by his reluctance to the moment of his death in April 1945 to take a more realistic and more pragmatic view of power in a war in which the US had fought hard and, as the firebombings of German and Japanese cities showed, ruthlessly, Roosevelt did more harm than good.

In the final analysis it was Hitler rather than Roosevelt who foresaw the future. On 2 April 1945, ten days before Roosevelt's death and a month before his own suicide Hitler wrote:

With the defeat of the Reich and pending the emergence of the Asiatic, the African and perhaps the South American nationalisms, there will remain in the world only two Great Powers capable of confronting each other – the United States and Soviet Russia. The laws of both history and geography will compel these two powers to a trial of strength, either military or in the fields of economics and ideology. These same laws make it inevitable that both Powers should become enemies of Europe. And it is equally certain that both these Powers will sooner or later find it desirable to seek the support of the surviving great nation in Europe, the German people.[56]

What Hitler did not foresee was the way in which this new conflict would be shaped by a weapon in which he had never shown particular interest, yet which was to prove his most portentous, and ambiguous legacy.

Although German scientists had been responsible for the crucial discovery that by the beginning of 1939 had opened the way for the development of an atomic bomb, they never produced the quality and quantity of analysis which made the British and American programmes possible. Perhaps they did not choose to; they certainly were under no strong political pressure to do so. As Albert Speer later wrote, the idea of the atomic bomb strained Hitler's intellectual capacity. He was unable to grasp the revolutionary nature of nuclear physics, which was tainted in his eyes by the number of Jewish scientists associated with it. In 1942 therefore, on the assumption that the war would be over before a bomb could be developed, the decision was taken that nuclear physics were irrelevant to the war effort. The Germans had no fears that the Allies would develop a nuclear bomb first; they saw no advantage in making the huge investment which a nuclear programme would require.[57]

None of this however was known to the Allies. They began with the very different belief that the war would be a long drawn-out affair, and that given the kind of investment eventually seen in the Manhattan Project, it would be possible to produce what would, quite literally, be a war-winning weapon. Indeed on the assumption that the Germans (who were working from roughly the same scientific base) had reached the same conclusions, an all-out effort to get the bomb first was an imperative. With better intelligence they might have come to a different conclusion. Although they did not know it, the world's first nuclear arms race was a one-horse affair. And by the time the first bomb was ready, the war in Europe was over. The two bombs dropped on Japan simply hastened the inevitable; the Japanese were already close to surrender before Hiroshima and Nagasaki.

But if the new weapon had little direct effect on the war, it certainly shaped the peace. In notes he made in May 1945, the American Secretary of War, Henry Stimson, laid out the implications in stark terms:

May destroy or *perfect* International Civilization
May (be) *Frankenstein* or means for World Peace.[58]

In fact the alternatives would not turn out to be quite so simple. The real choice was more complex and ambiguous. The new superpowers which emerged from the Second World War could accept the need for radical change in the conduct of international affairs and abandon power politics, precisely what Roosevelt wanted to do. Alternatively they could try to continue the game but change the rules, by excluding the final recourse to major war. That was not, however, how things were perceived at the time. Roosevelt does not appear to have taken the nuclear factor into account in his thinking about a new world order. And for all his concern about postwar cooperation with Stalin, he refused, under pressure from Churchill, to share the nuclear secret with his Soviet ally. In so doing he contributed to a gamble of momentous proportions. Once cast, the nuclear spell would prove impossible to break. The brief and terrible remastery of power might be over, but the possibility of what now would quite literally be a suicidal war could never be ruled out. It was a high price to pay for the failure to recognise that power politics had already become a deadly anachronism fifty years before.

6 A Nuclear Education

With the defeat of Germany and Japan the cast changed. Britain had been permanently weakened and reduced to a secondary role; France was, for the time being, down and out. Although the German problem had not been removed from the agenda, the new lead actors had a much broader set of preoccupations. They also had to fashion a new set of rules for a rivalry which was to last longer than the Peloponnesian War, the First and Second Punic Wars, and the Napoleonic Wars.[1] A rivalry of both states and ideologies, it was heavily militarised, punctuated by recurrent crises, but always kept, however uneasily, under control.

Like the two world wars, the shape of the Cold War was very much a function of military technology. Nuclear weapons neither caused nor ended the conflict. They do not of themselves explain why there was no direct clash of arms between the protagonists. Yet without them US–Soviet rivalry would have taken a very different form. Nuclear weapons are at the heart of this 'experiment in conflict without war'.[2] They are a key determinant of its peculiar combination of restraints and intensities – the proxy wars in the Third World, the arms race and the ritual tests of nerve and will which culminated in the Cuban missile crisis. While Cold War was certainly a misnomer to those involved in the fighting in Korea, Vietnam or Afghanistan, this was a conflict which did not generally impinge on the norms of daily life. It did not impair enjoyment of what in the West was a real and prosperous peace. Preparing for war was an activity which the more affluent protagonists could comparmentalise, not least because it was no longer primarily seen as prelude, but as prevention.

But only just. The scale of the preparations, which are at the heart of the Cold War, were such that they often tended to overshadow the political and ideological substance of the rivalry. They also served to obscure another, equally important game, which had come into play even before the first use of nuclear weapons at Hiroshima and Nagasaki. For behind the constant manoeuvrings for political and strategic advantage which substituted for any more conclusive engagement, lay the larger historical issue of whether power politics could continue in the nuclear age. Could a weapon which was too powerful to use, nevertheless effectively intimidate? If so, would this entail more risk than the new rivals were prepared to run? Was nuclear power 'fungible'? The answers to these questions would only emerge as a result of trial and error. It would take time for the protagonists to accept that while they were indeed superpowers (although the terms had first been used before the advent of nuclear weapons, it quickly came to take on specifically nuclear connotation),[3] they were hobbled rather than strengthened by the fact. Like the armies on the Western Front they found themselves locked into a long stalemate. Coming to terms with this situation provided a hard and expensive education in the realities of nuclear power. But the remastery of power was already over.

The Cold War, like the atomic bomb, was very much Hitler's legacy. Hitler had set out to crush Soviet power at a time when it was weak. Instead he had conjured up a superpower which occupied half of Europe and divided Germany. But while Stalin, who in the war years, had shown himself a consummate player of *Realpolitik*, now held a very strong hand, it was one which it was very easy to overplay. Stalin wanted, to use a Russian proverb, to kill two hares with one shot. He sought extensive unilateral advantage, but also hoped for a continuation of cooperation with his wartime allies. The Soviet Union had won an immense, and an immensely costly victory. It had borne the bulk of the fighting against Germany and the bulk of the casualties. Between 1941 and 1945 Soviet forces destroyed or disabled an estimated 607 Axis divisions. Their casualties were no less than 50 times those of the United States.[4] Not unnaturally, Stalin, who had frequently bemoaned the fact that while tsarist Russia had won wars, it did not know how to exploit the fruits of victory, now looked for some very substantial rewards.

Something of the scope of Stalin's ambitions is suggested by his Foreign Minister's assertion that the Soviet Union, 'now stands in the ranks of the most authoritative of world Powers. Now it is impossible to resolve the important issues of international relations without the participation of the Soviet Union.'[5] More specifically Stalin sought to regain territory ceded to Turkey in 1921, as well as revision of the Montreux Convention governing the access of ships through the Straits. He sought trusteeship of one of Italy's former colonies, preferably Tripolitania. The US and Britain had bases all over the world, Stalin complained to Bevin in 1946. 'Why should not Soviet interests be taken into account?' He sought to regain the Russian sphere of influence in Xinjiang, Outer Mongolia, Manchuria and Korea. According to Molotov's later account, Stalin even played with the idea of regaining Alaska.[6] And of great importance to this obsessively insecure man in control of an obsessively insecure state, he sought territorial security against the resurgence of German power.

At the same time up until 1947 or even 1948, he wanted to maintain cooperation with Britain and the United States. Even during the Berlin blockade Stalin still referred them as 'allies'.[7] The war had taken a heavy toll of Soviet assets as well as lives. The country had lost perhaps as many as 27 million of its people, and some 30 per cent of its economic wealth.[8] As well as time to recover, it needed economic aid, possibly from the United States, certainly from Germany in the form of reparations. On the diplomatic front cooperation with the United States offered influence not just in the postwar world as a whole, but also more immediately over the future of Germany, which was now under Four Power occupation.

But there was a hefty price, and this Stalin was not prepared to pay. He instinctively preferred, in Maxim Litvinov's words, to grab all he could while the going was good, rather than try and cash in the accumulated goodwill which he had gained in the West during the war.[9] Stalin had in any case no great expectations of how far cooperation could be taken, or indeed how long it would last. He expected a crisis within the capitalist system, that would provide him with ample room for geopolitical manoeuvring in Europe and Asia, eventually allowing him to sweep the old world away.[10] At the same time his deep-seated suspicions of the West, which had not been allayed by the brief, and never very easy period of wartime cooperation, were intensified first by the atomic bomb, and then by the increasingly hostile response to his pursuit of unilateral advantage. Within little more than a year after the end of the war, a report from the Soviet ambassador in Washington, which was in fact inspired and 'coauthored' by Molotov, declared that the United States was 'striving for world supremacy'. The US government was portrayed as completely under the sway of monopoly capital and bent on limiting the Soviet Union's postwar role. Broad plans for American expansion had been developed and were being implemented by the establishment of a system of bases 'stretching far beyond the boundaries of the United States' as well as an an arms race and the 'creation of ever new types of weapons.[11]

Such fears quickly became self-fulfilling prophecies. The more suspicious the two sides grew of each other, the more urgent their perceived needs to prevent one another filling the power vacuum which the war had left in the heart of Europe. The result, as *The Times* had warned in April 1946, was 'the division of the world into spheres of influence and eventually into hostile blocs'.[12] This was a far cry from the new world order which Roosevelt had sought. Americans had no hidden desires for hegemony. Their secret dream in the first postwar years was rather, in Kissinger's ironic words, 'to play the role that India's first Prime Minister,

Nehru later arrogated to himself; we would have liked some other country, say Britain, to maintain the balance of power while we nobly mediated its conflicts with the Soviet Union'.[13] The option, however, was no longer there. The British were too weak to cope with the Soviet Union single handed, and isolationism, like appeasement, was both morally and strategically discredited. The Second World War had made the men who now shaped American policy acutely conscious of the relationship between the control of resources and international power. The United States could not allow the Soviet Union to emulate Germany or Japan by gaining control of Europe's economic wealth and population.[14] Communist control of Europe would isolate the US from its friends and sources of supply, forcing it into defence measures which might 'bankrupt our economy, and change our way of life so that we couldn't recognize it as American any longer'.[15]

As this new conflict gained momentum, it quickly became clear that it would be very different from its predecessors. For the first time in history alliances were set up with with very large standing forces and complex command structures. Europe rapidly became a vast, if discreetly armed camp. At the same time there was a surreal element in all these military preparations. Hundreds of thousands of men had been permanently mobilised to fight a war which, to use Ivan Bloch's 1899 phrase, was 'impossible, except at the price of suicide'.[16] The *impasse* which strategy, if not yet power politics had reached even before the advent of Mutual Assured Destruction, is conveyed in comments made by Eisenhower to the Joint Chiefs of Staff in 1954. At the time the US was considering the use of nuclear weapons in the context of a very different conflict – that between France and the Vietminh in Indochina. The US, Eisenhower warned, might end up by having to launch nuclear attacks against first China and then Russia. But then what?

> Gain such a victory, and what do you do with it? Here would be a great area from the Elbe to Vladivostok ... torn up and destroyed, without government, without its communications, just an area of starvation and disaster. I ask you what would the civilised world do about it?[17]

None of this however prevented the two sides deploying some tens of thousands of nuclear warheads or developing big, costly and increasingly dysfunctional weapons systems which, in the words of one critic, shared with the baroque a grandeur 'that may portend degeneration'.[18] It was a recipe for stalemate.

The scale and intensity of the Cold War was a function of the character of the protagonists as much as of the technology at their disposal. These were immensely powerful, proud and self-righteous states; world powers with global ambitions for which they were willing to pay a high price. Both were given to an ideological absolutism more akin to the earlier wars of religion than the recent clashes of nationalisms. The resultant tendency to overreact was accentuated by the difficulties which, for very different reasons, both had in a managing power.

On the surface the United States adapted quickly and easily to its new and unsought strategic responsibilities. By 1948 the British embassy in Washington was reporting that while only a year earlier power politics was a term which still 'bore a sinister connotation in the American mind' it had now come to be accepted as a 'normal technical term'.[19] But if they now proceeded to embrace power politics, they did so with something of the fervour of the new, if not entirely convinced convert. Americans were still uncomfortable with the notion of national interest and needed a larger, more universal cause to justify their actions. The Truman Doctrine, America's Cold War manifesto, said nothing about the real immediate issue – the need to take on Britain's role in the eastern Mediterranean. Instead it was couched in the language of high moral principle, of a great struggle between freedom and tyranny in which the United States should 'support *free* peoples who are resisting attempted subjugation by armed minorities or by outside pressures' (emphasis added).[20]

This was of more than rhetorical import. It complicated the inherently difficult tasks of establishing the limits of America's new security perimeter, and of distinguishing between those countries and conflicts where its vital interests were and were not involved. Knowing relatively little about what was actually happening in obscure places like Vietnam or the Ogaden, Washington tended to see events through the distorting prism of East–West rivalry, making too much of Soviet or Chinese involvement and too little of the the underlying indigenous causes of conflict.

The United States had made the mistake of demonising its adversaries. The Soviet Union was not just a rival; it was an evil empire promoting an evil ideology. This, as George Kennan had already warned in 1946, was bad policy. 'We need to study the Soviet Union,' he wrote, with the 'same courage, detachment, objectivity, and the same determination not to be emotionally provoked or unseated by it, with which a doctor studies unruly and unreasonable individuals.'[21] They never did so. The spectre of Communism may indeed have been a real threat in Europe in the immediate aftermath of the Second World War when, as the Director of the OSS, William Donovan noted, the Soviet Union had a 'strong drawing card in the proletarian philosophy of Communism,' while the US had 'no political or social philosophy equally dynamic or alluring'.[22] But Washington continued to credit its adversary with the capacity of fomenting world revolution long after its ideological drawing-power had waned.

The United States was not of course the first state to have miscalculated Soviet power. The Germans had exaggerated Russian strength in 1914; the British underestimated it in 1939, when Churchill first referred to it as a 'riddle wrapped in a mystery inside an enigma'.[23] Here was an aggressive, and indeed an aggressively insecure state. Its leaders interpreted events beyond their borders within an ideological framework which made it next to impossible for them to establish a realistic sense of what was actually going on. Soviet rhetoric, with its inheritance of Social-Darwinism, was uncompromisingly militant. Socialism was the wave of the future; it would in Khrushchev's infamous phrase, 'bury' its capitalist rival. At the same time Soviet leaders could not forget their historical vulnerability. Khrushchev speaks of Stalin having 'lived in terror of enemy attack. For him foreign policy meant keeping the air defence units around Moscow on a 24-hour alert.'[24] Such fears were not easily assuaged. Soviet security policy remained heavily militarised long after Stalin's death, with concepts of offence and defence inextricably interlinked. The Soviet Union did nothing to modify the large potentially offensive presence in Eastern Europe originally established as a counter to the American nuclear monopoly in the late 1940s.[25]

It also retained the obsession with secrecy of what had historically been a closed, authoritarian state, anxious to hide its weaknesses from the outside world. This was a double-edged sword. It did create an illusion of strength, which must have been worth quite a number of rockets and divisions. But in a heavily militarised, technologically dynamic world it bred dangerously counterproductive suspicions. Precisely because nobody in the United States could read Soviet political purposes or be sure of its military strength, and because Moscow cultivated an impression of menace, Americans tended to fear the worst. They constantly exaggerated Soviet strength. The Americans worried about a succession of bomber and missile 'gaps' and about what later became known as 'windows of vulnerability'.[26] Just as at the end of the Second World War, the US had raced a German nuclear programme which no longer posed a threat, so the US repeatedly sought to forestall possible Soviet developments, which its weaker adversary was only then forced to match. The superpowers never succeeded in reaching a strategic plateau on which they were both willing to rest.

The cost for unnecessarily extending and inflating the rivalry, was very heavy. The US paid not just in dollars, but also in political coin. Vietnam did much domestic damage; the activities of the CIA, notably in Third

World countries, proved discreditable and indeed morally debilitating. But it was the Soviet Union which suffered most. It was poorly equipped for a long-term competetion with a technologically more dynamic rival which could easily afford both guns and butter. Just after Sputnik 2 went into orbit the British Ambassador, driving some 30 miles outside Moscow, observed two women shouldering ox yokes with dangling buckets, trudging five hundred yards to a river where they broke the ice to draw their household water.[27] The later jibe that the Soviet Union was 'Upper Volta with missiles' was dangerously near the bone.

The Soviet Union was also unlucky. The Red Army had fought and won the last great war of conquest, establishing itself on the Elbe from where it overshadowed the rest of the Continent. No sooner had it got there however, then it found itself within a nuclear straitjacket. While it could try to overawe and threaten, to play on Western fears and weaknesses, it could never afford to implement its threats, and was thus always vulnerable to having its bluff called. Nuclear diplomacy – blackmail is a more emotive term – was a test of wills requiring a demanding combination of good judgement and steely nerves. The analogies used at the time were with childrens games. One of these in which teenagers drove cars at each other at high speed, the loser being the first to swerve, went under the unflattering name of 'Chicken'. Dean Rusk's remark during the Cuban missile crisis that 'We are eyeball to eyeball, and the other fellow just blinked' derived from a game in his native Georgia where 'we would stand about two feet apart and stare into each others eyes. Whoever blinked first lost the game. It was not an easy game to win.'[28]

Nuclear diplomacy had been pioneered by the United States. But although the Americans enjoyed an effective nuclear monopoly well into the 1950s, they had little politically to show for this. Once hostilities ended in August 1945, the new weapon proved unuseable even under the most apparently favourable conditions. The National Security Council (NSC) records of March 1953 record Eisenhower and Dulles agreeing that 'somehow or other the taboo which surrounds the use of atomic weapons would have to be destroyed'. But every time the question was considered – during the Korean War, at the time of Dienbienphu and later during the crises over the two small islands off Taiwan, Quemoy and Matsu, it became evident that this would be not just militarily and politically impractical, but also morally impossible.[29]

Threats were another matter. Eisenhower abandoned Truman's 'abstemious approach' to the role of nuclear weapons, establishing them as 'a standard tactic in confrontation'.[30] To what effect in the succession of Asian crises of the 1950s is unclear. What is clear is that the American nuclear monopoly, and the implicit threat it represented, failed to overawe Moscow. The initial assumption among the very few Americans who knew about the atomic bomb, had been that nuclear weapons could provide the United States with influence and leverage against the Soviet Union. The Secretary of War, Henry Stimson, had even speculated that it might induce a transformation in the character of the Soviet system. And Stalin was certainly worried. 'Hiroshima', he is reported to have said in mid-August 1945, 'has shaken the whole world. The balance has been destroyed.' He feared that the United States would try and use its nuclear monopoly to impose a postwar settlement.[31] Indeed when the Secretary of State, James Byrnes, attended the London Council of Foreign Ministers in September 1945, he was confident that the atomic bomb would strengthen his hand. But he deliberately abstained from any direct threat or indeed mention of the weapon in the hope that the reality of the bomb would make the Soviet Union more tractable. It did not. Molotov conspicuously ignored the implicit American threat showing the Russians, in Byrnes' words, 'stubborn, obstinate, and they don't scare'.[32]

This last point is telling. Molotov's stance may have been partly a matter of bluff and bravado, partly a calculation that the American arsenal was still very small and that the American nuclear monopoly would not last for ever. But there was also Stalin's early realisation that nuclear intimidation was only effective against 'those with weak nerves'.[33] While the atomic bomb may have given the Americans confidence to do things they might not otherwise have done, the assumption of American officials prior to the first Soviet atomic explosion in 1949, that the Soviet Union would back down provided it was not directly challenged, is not easy to verify. Nuclear weapons may have contributed to the considerable caution with which Stalin handled the 1948 Berlin crisis; the Soviet Union never interfered with the Western airlift. It had not however prevented him from imposing the blockade in the first place. What is certain is that once their monopoly was broken, and in particular once the Soviet Union exploded its first H-bomb, American officials began worrying about an enhanced Soviet disposition to take risks.[34]

These fears proved premature. Stalin was generally a cautious leader who only moved when he believed himself, in the case of Korea wrongly, certain of success.[35] His immediate priority was to rectify the balance of power and protect himself against blackmail. 'Do you realise,' he asked his military leaders and scientists in 1947 when he was already pressing for development of intercontinental missiles, 'the tremendous strategic importance of machines of this sort? They would be an effective straitjacket for that noisy shopkeeper Harry Truman. We must go ahead with it, comrades. The problem of the creation of transatlantic rockets is of extreme importance to us.'[36] The policy paid off. As Dean Rusk notes, the ability which the Soviet Union gained in the 1950s to strike against the United States changed the basis of American foreign policy, injecting more caution and prudence into US policy.[37] What it failed to do was to provide the Soviet Union with substantial new leverage against the West. This was not for want of trying, indeed it was the attempts by the the much noisier Nikita Khrushchev to gain nuclear advantage *vis-à-vis* the United States which made the late 1950s and early 1960s the most critical period of the Cold War. These were years of high anxiety and danger, when the *impasse* into which power politics had run began to become clear, and when the first and most difficult part of the superpowers' nuclear education was completed.

Khrushchev embodies the contradictions which characterised the early phase of nuclear diplomacy – the desire to exploit this extraordinary new form of power, combined with a real but imperfect recognition that there was a point, as yet undefined, beyond which one could not safely go. Publicly, Khrushchev was much more realistic about the revolutionary nature of nuclear war than Stalin had been. It was Khrushchev, following on from ideas developed by his immediate predecessor, Malenkov, and indeed also Beria who had supervised the Soviet nuclear programme, who declared that nuclear weapons did not recognise class principles and proclaimed the doctrine of 'peaceful coexistence', of competition short of war. It was Khrushchev who said, or is alleged to have said, that when he was appointed First Secretary of the Central Committee and learned all the facts about nuclear power, 'I couldn't sleep for several days. Then I became convinced that we could never possibly use these weapons, and when I realized that I was able to sleep again.'[38] And yet it was Khrushchev who brought the world closer to nuclear war than any man before or since.

Khrushchev was an uneasy mixture of the self-confident and the insecure. A self-made man determined to be honoured as the leader of a world power and ready to throw his weight around if he was not; a Russian who demanded respect for his country's achievements but feared contempt.[39] Of peasant background and poorly educated, he had much curiosity about the outside world, but little knowledge of it. The sharp political skills which had allowed him to survive under Stalin and later succeed him, were countered by an emotional streak, an ability to get carried away. Immensely energetic, he was attracted to things novel – such as nuclear rockets, about which he sometimes spoke in incongruously homely language. Russian factories were turning out rockets like sausages. Rockets were not like cucumber. Above all perhaps, and this had been seen most dramatically in his famous 'secret' speech denoucing Stalin to the Twentieth Party Congress the large majority of whose members were opposed to his views, he was something of a gambler. One of his aides would later describe as *azartnyi* – an adventurer, a 'risky' man.[40] It was this which made him dangerous. Khrushchev was no chess player; he did not think his moves through. When an idea gripped him, he was 'inclined to see in its implementation an easy solution to a particular problem, a sort of cure-all'.[41]

These traits went with an ideological optimism and aggressiveness quite foreign to Stalin. Khrushchev had never freed himself from what an assistant later described as the old 'black and white' formula acquired in his youth, which divided the world into two hostile capitalist and socialist camps, one of which would eventually bury the other. Influenced to a large degree by Soviet technological successes such as Sputnik and the first ICBM test carried out in 1957, Khrushchev believed that the correlation of forces was now shifting decisively in favour of the Soviet Union. The West had lost its former superiority in power, and knew it. The process of decolonisation in Africa and Asia, which was then gathering pace, greatly improved the prospects for the spread of socialism, and Moscow could now provide an atomic umbrella under which anticolonial movements could operate.[42] Khrushchev had learned something about atomic bluff from John Foster Dulles and his much publicised notion of brinkmanship. Dulles, he told colleagues in 1961, 'knew where the brink was (that the Americans) should not overstep, and behaved in a prudent way, taking our resistance into account and seeing that, with sheer force and extortion, they could not get what they wanted'.[43]

But, though it took him time to realise this, nor could Khrushchev. At first sight nuclear intimidation seemed perfectly suited to his style and temperament. He had considerable dramatic gifts and used his tongue to good effect. He worked instinctively, exploiting his rhetorical abilities to try and frighten the West, giving an impression of much greater nuclear power than he in fact had. Consciously or otherwise, he played on his reputation for unpredictability. As a public performance the results were effective, if crude. But the approach had had the makings of trouble; eventually he overstepped the mark.

The beginnings, however, were suitably cautious. His first exercise in nuclear diplomacy was at the time of Suez when veiled threats of some unspecified nuclear action caused anxiety in both London and Paris, though without affecting the outcome of the crisis. It was sheer bluff. As the then Foreign Minister, D. T. Shepilov, later admitted, there was 'a firm decision not to bring the matter to the point of armed conflict ... we always kept in mind that we would avert war by any means'.[44] The same was true of the succession of Soviet nuclear threats during the prolonged Berlin crisis of the late 1950s and early 1960s. But while Suez had been very much a target of opportunity, Berlin was deliberately chosen.

The five-year long Berlin crisis lacks the drama and intensity of Cuba's 'thirteen days'. But it is important both as a case study in the potential of nuclear diplomacy, and as one of the key stages in the long-running postwar struggle over the future of Germany, which the Soviet Union would eventually lose. Berlin was one of the few places where the Soviet Union chose directly to challenge the West, rather than relying on proxies as it had done in Korea and would do later do in the Third World. But then Berlin was very much the Soviet Union's own problem. It had occupation rights as well as forces on the ground. Berlin was unfinished business. The 'solution' to the German problem which had emerged over the preceding years had come about by default. Unable to agree about Germany, the Four Powers had ended up partitioning it along the lines of temporary occupation agreed during the war. Soviet officials as one historian notes, proceeded to bolshevise the eastern zone of Germany, 'not because there was a plan to do so, but because that was the only way they knew how to organise society'.[45] As division consolidated in the early 1950s with the emergence of West Germany as an independent state, and the subsequent incorporation of both Germanies into NATO and the Warsaw Pact, the Four Power occupation of the former German capital, now well 'behind' the Cold War lines, came to be seen by the Soviet Union as best as an irritant, at worst a danger.

Berlin, however, was not the main issue. Khrushchev used it as a lever to try and gain formal Western recognition of, and hence legitimacy for, his half of Germany. Personally strongly committed to the building of socialism in the German Democratic Republic (GDR) he was worried about the internal stability of a country which lagged economically so obviously behind its Western counterpart. He was also deeply concerned about the prospect which seemed to loom in the mid- and late-1950s, that West Germany might gain access to nuclear weapons. The absence of a formal peace settlement more than a decade after the Second World War made everything seem dangerously temporary. A settlement of the German question would, in Khrushchev's view, remove the chief obstacle to the negotiation of a long truce between the Soviet and Western blocs and a peaceful transformation of the world from capitalism to socialism.[46]

These were by no means entirely unrealistic goals, indeed Berlin was one place where nuclear diplomacy might have worked. The political situation, in Eisenhower's private words, was 'abnormal'.[47] The city was militarily indefensible by conventional means, and the West knew it. Any renewed Soviet moves to cut communications would place the *onus* of escalation, which could all too easily mean nuclear escalation, on the West, an option which was neither politically acceptable nor strategically credible. Berlin, as Khrushchev kept trying to convince both politicians and public opinion in Europe, was not worth a nuclear war. Eisenhower, who worked from the premise that there was 'nothing in the world that the Communists want badly enough to risk losing the Kremlin', was not unduly worried by such threats.[48] Kennedy by contrast was much less at ease with the simple and by 1961 obsolescent doctrine of massive retaliation. He worried that if Khrushchev believed that 'all we have is the atomic bomb, he is going to feel that we are … somewhat unlikely to use it'.[49]

The most dangerous phase of the crisis therefore occurred in the summer of 1961 when Khrushchev tried to bully a new and inexperienced president into concessions. Acutely conscious that his credibility was at stake, Kennedy responded with a measured series of military responses. What then eased tensions was, paradoxically enough, the Wall, which exposed the underlying weakness of the Soviet position. With the flow of refugees gathering pace, the Soviet leader, as Kennedy had told an aide at the end of July was in danger of 'losing East Germany. He cannot let that happen. If East Germany goes, so will Poland and all of Eastern Europe. He will have to do something to stop the flow of refugees. Perhaps a wall. And we won't be able to prevent it. I can hold the Alliance together to defend West Berlin, but I cannot act to keep East Berlin open'.[50] There was a brief and momentarily dangerous confrontation between American and Soviet tanks at Checkpoint Charlie when the two sides behaved, in Khrushchev's words, like 'rams with horns interlocking', and likely to pull each other off a cliff.[51] But by the autumn of 1961, the worst was over.

Khrushchev was from start to finish bluffing. At no stage during the crisis was there any kind of Soviet military alert, or attempt to interfere with the traffic routes. He did not want war and was clearly shocked by Kennedy's July military measures. 'Let us not create a war psychosis', he pleaded two weeks later.[52] When people stood up to his bloodcurdling threats, he quickly backed down. The British mbassador to Moscow, Sir Frank Roberts, recounts an incident shortly before the building of the Berlin Wall when the Soviet leader lost his temper and declared that he could destroy Britain with eight nuclear bombs. When Roberts responded that the RAF would then retaliate destroying Moscow and many other Soviet cities, Khrushchev suddenly, but typically 'changed his mood, and said, 'Well, maybe you are right. Let's have a drink.' Averill Harriman, the wartime American envoy to Moscow, had had a similar experience during a conversation with Khrushchev in 1959.[53]

Crude as they may have been, Khrushchev's tactics were not without potential. As he once rightly remarked, if he went to church to pray nobody would listen to him, but if he took a couple of bombs with him 'people will listen'.[54] Nuclear threats could not simply be ignored. Dean Rusk recounts an exchange which occurred in August 1963 following the signing ceremonies for the limited test ban treaty. Khrushchev invited the American Secretary of State for private discussions at his *dacha*. As Rusk later told the story, Khrushchev drew him aside and

> told me something that still chills my blood. Adenauer, he said, had told him that Germany would not fight a nuclear war over Berlin; de Gaulle and Macmillan had made the same points.
> Why should I believe that you Americans would fight a nuclear war over Berlin?
> That was quite a question, with Khrushchev staring at me with his little pig eyes ... I stared back at him and said, 'Mr Chairman, you will have to take into account the possibility that we Americans are just goddamn fools.' We glared at each other, unblinking, and then he changed the subject and gave me three gold watches to take home to my children.[55]

And yet at the end of the day all Khrushchev personally achieved was the Wall. If what Anne Tusa describes as 'an assertion of sovereignty by an unrecognised state',[56] it was also a very poor advertisement for either East Germany or the Soviet system. It certainly fell well short of Khrushchev's aims. This is surprising because the Americans, as indeed the British, were willing to make concessions. The United States was prepared to consider diplomatic compromise over the access regime and the status of Berlin. An internal White House memorandum of late August 1961 indicated a willingness to 'shift substantially toward acceptance of the GDR, the Oder-Neisse line, a non-aggression pact and even the idea of two peace treaties'.[57]

That nothing ever came of these ideas is partly to be explained by German and French opposition. The US could not afford to impose a settlement on its allies, if only because the ensuing crisis of confidence would so obviously be in Moscow's interests. At the same time the Soviet Union was oddly unskilful in keeping up the pressure. Soviet diplomacy swung back and forth, sometimes conciliatory, sometimes overbearing. Conciliation let the West off the hook; overbearance turned Berlin into a prestige issue and caused the United States to dig in its heels. Khrushchev lacked his Foreign Minister's relentless persistence. The golden rules of superpower diplomacy as privately outlined at this time by Gromyko to some of his officials, were to demand the maximum, to use threats while offering a way out, and once the talks had started, never to give ground.

Your partners will then offer you as a compromise part of what you asked for, even though this never belonged to you. But the negotiations were never pressed home in this fashion.[58]

If the Berlin crisis shows Khrushchev playing a reasonably strong hand, his attempt to deploy missiles in Cuba was fundamentally misconceived. In Khrushchev's defence it might be argued that nuclear diplomacy was still in its tentative stage. There were as yet no accepted ground rules; nothing had so far happened to create the consciousness of danger necessary to provide an effective brake on brinkmanship. The fact remains however that Cuba revealed Khrushchev as a man with a deeply flawed sense of what this new form of power politics could effectively, let alone safely, achieve. It betrays something of the misjudgement which led the Kaiser to issue his 'blank cheque' to the Austrians. Along with July 1914 and Munich, Cuba ranks as one of the three key crises of the century. It was certainly *the* crisis of the Cold War, the one occasion when both sides recognised that the lines of prudent competition had been unambiguously crossed. If the superpowers did not actually come to the brink, they came disconcertingly close to it.

Cuba is in many respects the rogue crisis of the Cold War. It was the only crisis in which a significant number of nuclear weapons were moved or in which a superpower beat a public retreat under the direct threat of nuclear war. It was the only crisis in which either superpower trespassed blatantly into the other's sphere of influence; it was one of the only crises in which domestic politics were a significant factor. But it was also, or rather it could also have been, a pointer of things to come. While Berlin had been an attempt to consolidate the *status quo* in the wake of the Second World War, Cuba went to the heart of the wider conflict which had since developed between the two blocs. It reflected a new Soviet agenda which was bound to place the superpowers on a collision course. This had already been evident at the Vienna Summit where Kennedy complained that the Soviet Union 'wished to destroy the influence of my country where it has traditionally been present. You wish to liquidate the free system in other countries'. While the Soviet leader disputed this formulation, he demanded that the West recognise that 'Communism exists and has won the right to develop. Such recognition should be *de facto* and not *de jure*.' 'The United States,' he complained at one point,' is so rich and powerful that it believes it has special rights and can afford not to recognise the rights of others.'[59] The missile crisis represented a continuation of this dialogue by more menacing means.

Cuba had a direct bearing on both American security and domestic politics, which other contemporary troublespots, such as Laos or the Congo, did not. It was unfortunate, though perhaps not entirely coincidental there-fore, that the revolution which had brought Fidel Castro to power in 1959, one of the few Communist revolutions which had occurred without the aid of the Red Army, should have had such emotional appeal to Khrushchev.[60] By 1962 he had become convinced – wrongly – that the Americans, who had indeed tried more indirect ways of disposing of Castro, were now intent on a full-scale invasion. The loss of Cuba would, as he wrote in his memoirs, be a terrible blow to Marxism–Leninsm, gravely diminishing Soviet stature throughout the world, but especially in Latin America. Since a conventional Soviet defence was more or less impossible, only an extra-ordinary measure, such as the deployment of nuclear weapons, could ensure the defence of the island.[61]

It is tempting, and not entirely flippant, to say that missiles were fashion-able, a new and dangerous toy for a First Secretary to play with. They cer-tainly made Khrushchev, who had long laboured under a military inferiority complex *vis à vis* the United States, unduly bold. During the Berlin crisis he had merely evoked them; now he proceeded to deploy the actual hardware. Khrushchev successfully hid the fact that he was operating from weakness by a determined policy of bluff and deception. He was helped by the successes of the Soviet space programme – Sputnik had taken the world by surprise in 1957, and, until the advent of the U2 reconnaissance aircraft, by poor American intelligence. But it was a dangerous game. The Soviet Union, as one Central Committee member pointed out during a meeting on strategic arms policy in 1959, was provoking an arms race in which they 'would be the big losers given American technological prowess'.[62] The initial American reaction had already taken the the form of the deployment of medium range missiles in Europe, including Turkey. Then came a substantial build-up in American intercontinental missile forces which tipped the strategic balance even further against the Soviet Union. Worried during the tense autumn of 1961 about the impact of Khrushchev's strategic boasting on opinion in Western Europe, the Third World and indeed the United States, the Americans decided to spell out the actual military balance in public.[63]

Seen against this background, the strategic rationale for the deployment of Khrushchev's attempted nuclear *coup de main* in Cuba, comes into clearer focus. By 1962 the US had some three thousand warheads; the Soviet Union by contrast – the figure is probably still best regarded in terms of an order of magnitude rather than an exact total – had around two hundred and fifty. There were only around twenty or twenty-five ICBMs capable of reaching the United States from Soviet territory. Nor was there any likelihood of an early shift in the balance, since technical problems had delayed deployment of the first generation of Soviet long range missiles.[64]

The detailed evidence is still lacking, but the assumption remains that the deployment of the more generally available IRBMs on Cuba, represented a strategic short-cut. By deploying medium-range missiles so that they could now threaten the American homeland, Khrushchev sought a means of redressing what by any standards must be regarded as a gross imbalance. As Khrushchev's son, Sergei, later remarked, his father worried about the prospect that somebody in the United States might think that 'a first strike was possible ... Our inferior position was impossible for us.'[65] Anatoly Dobrynin writes of Khrushchev's fear that nuclear superiority might make the US 'particularly arrogant'.[66]

This was Khrushchev at his most audacious, and outrageously impudent. The plan was to deploy the missiles secretly in September and October. Then, after the November mid-term American Congressional elections, Khrushchev would travel to Havana where he and Castro would sign a treaty and publicly announce the presence of the weapons.[67] The announcement, it must be assumed, would have given him immense pleasure. For it would not simply have been a remarkable coup, it would also have evened the score. Khrushchev would have paid the US back in its own coin for stationing missiles so close to its own border – the Jupiters in Turkey, while of relatively little military significance, rankled Khrushchev disproportionately. (Though it is worth noting that Eisenhower had been concerned about the deployment of IRBMs in Greece, remarking that if Mexico or Cuba obtained similar weapons, the US would have to take 'positive action, even offensive military action'.)[68] The Soviet Union would have been shown to be a real equal of the United States. And from this publicly declaimed position of strength, Khrushchev could hope to renew his Berlin campaign, and begin negotiating a *detente* which would release scarce resources from the arms race into the domestic economy. Last, but by no means necessarily least, Khrushchev could also look forward to strengthening his position against an increasingly vocal Chinese challenge for leadership of the Communist world.[69] One additional consideration which takes on particular significance in the light of the Chinese rivalry, was concern that Castro might be moving away from Moscow.[70]

The scheme was quite simply too good to be true. If not actually 'harebrained', it had certainly not been properly thought out or subjected to anywhere near sufficient staff work. Remarkably, or perhaps not remarkably in view of his personality, Khrushchev had committed himself to the deployment without consulting his intelligence or foreign policy advisers in Moscow, or his embassy in Washington. When some of his senior associates, including Gromyko, did cast doubt on its feasibility and warned of the likely strong American reaction, their views were either dismissed or discouraged.[71] Despite his knowledge of American reconnaissance overflights of Cuba, Khruchchev had initially managed to convince himself that it would be possible to deploy the weapons, along with some 42 000 Soviet forces, without being detected.[72] Later, when he came to accept the fact that the Americans were likely to discover the missiles before they became operational, he assumed that Kennedy, who was believed to be more concerned with Berlin and the forthcoming Congressional elections, would accept a *fait accompli*, just as he had accepted the the presence of the hated Jupiters in Turkey.[73]

This was a major error of political judgement which would not have been committed by a leader with a better understanding of American domestic politics. But one needs to be cautious before putting too much of the blame on Khrushchev. His belief that, if Kennedy *did* find out about the missiles, he would conceal the information from the American public ahead of the mid-term Congressional elections, was not entirely unreasonable. As Michael Beschloss points out, Kennedy was in the habit of witholding from the public information which might prove politically embarassing.[74] The Kennedy Administration had also failed to spell out, if only because nobody in Washington ever imagined that Khrushchev would commit what from America's point of view was such an intolerably provocative act, the implications of direct Soviet interference in the Western Hemisphere.[75] It did, however, finally issue a tough warning in early September, leading Khrushchev to add tactical nuclear weapons to the expeditionary force.[76]

When discovered in mid October, the surreptitious deployment of missiles ninety miles off the coast of Florida was seen by Washington not simply a threat, but an affront. There was no question that the weapons would have to go, and the Administration proceeded to combine skill and determination in what turned out to be the single most effective exercise of nuclear diplomacy of the Cold War. Their most immediate advantage was time and intelligence. Because the missiles had been spotted before becoming operational, Washington had a few vital days in which to get over its initial anger and think through its tactics. The conditions of absolute secrecy in which Excomm operated created an environment in which the crisis could be 'managed' in something approaching a rational atmosphere. The implications of all the options could be thoroughly examined. The idea of a private letter to Khrushchev was rejected, since as McGeorge Bundy told Soviet officials many years later, 'We couldn't imagine your obviously adventurous leader backing off from a move of this seriousness if we merely confronted him privately.'[77] The more dangerous extremes, invasion or an airstrike against the missile sites, which Kennedy had initially favoured, were, for the time being at least, rejected in favour of blockade which would buy time, and involve significantly less risk.[78] These decisions, it should be noted, were made without knowledge of the presence of the Soviet tactical nuclear weapons. How the US would have responded had they known of this additional nuclear presence, is a question as unanswerable as it is intriguing.

Good intelligence gave the Americans a second advantage. For the first time in many years Washington was able to take the initiative. Kennedy's surprise announcement on Monday 22 October clearly wrong-footed Khrushchev. From now on the Soviet leader was on the defensive and without a fall-back position.[79] Unwilling to challenge the blockade, or otherwise up the *ante*, he had ultimately no alternative but to back down. Although the Americans eased his path by long-term assurances not to invade Cuba, and by private promises to remove the obsolete Jupiters from Turkey, they also took full advantage of the growing momentum of by the crisis to ratchet up the pressure. On 27 October an American U2 reconnaissance aircraft was shot down over Cuba. That evening, in a remarkable exchange with the Soviet ambassador, Robert Kennedy, warned that 'we had to have a commitment by at least tomorrow that those bases would be removed. *This was not an ultimatum, I said, but just a statement of fact.*'[80]

In fact Khrushchev had already decided on Thursday, 25 October, only three days after Kennedy had initiated the public phase of the crisis with his radio broadcast announcing the blockade, to look for a diplomatic solution. According to Aleksandr Fursenko and Timothy Naftali, the primary influence was

> a general sense of the military inferiority of the Soviet Union. He could not go to war in the Caribbean with any hope of prevailing. He had tried to achieve some measure of parity with the United States to defend Soviet interests in that region: but clearly he had failed. John Kennedy's actions since Monday showed that he was not deterred by the missiles that the Soviet Union had managed to deliver to Cuba. Khrushchev had witnessed the courage of the Soviet people in staving off defeat at the hands of the Nazis; but a head-to-head struggle in the nuclear era could only bring defeat and devastation to the Soviet Union.[81]

It was thus the timing rather than the substance of the final decision on the withdrawal, announced by Moscow Radio three days later, which was precipitated by the heightened sense of crisis produced by the downing of the U2. The Soviet military in Cuba had been specifically ordered not to shoot down reconnaissance aircraft without prior authorization, but fearing that an American air attack was imminent, and unable to reach their force commander, had nevertheless done so.[82] News the next day of a forthcoming Kennedy television broadcast raised fears that the Americans were about to announce the invasion of Cuba. According to Sergo Mikoyan, son of one of Khrushchev's closest associates, 'there was a feeling that we were just on the eve of a Third World War ... There was confusion and, in the very last hours, even panic. Khrushchev actually became very much afraid that he had led the country into a catastrophe.'[83] The American president cannot be seriously faulted for hyperbole when he told a group of congressional leaders that 'We have won a great victory ... We have resolved one of the great crises of mankind.'[84]

7 'Great in What?'

There was little question as to who the immediate winner and loser of the Cuban missile crisis had been. Kennedy had achieved a very public success. Khrushchev by contrast had gained at best part of what he wanted and suffered a public humiliation. He had, as the British ambassador in Moscow, Sir Frank Roberts noted, 'unquestionably backed off when the chips were seen to be down. We know this, Khrushchev knows it; and a large part of effective world opinion, in neutral and bloc areas, as well as in the West, also noted it.'[1] But a nuclear crisis was not a a zero-sum game. Both sides had had an overriding common interest in avoiding catastrophe. Both sides had learned a salutary and necessary lesson. Cuba had brought the two leaderships face to face with the nature of nuclear risk, and if it did not finally discredit brinkmanship, it forced them to look again at a range of issues from arrangements for the command and control of nuclear weapons to the totally inadequate communication arrangements between the two capitals.[2] The direct forms of nuclear intimidation practised by Khrushchev were never repeated. Cuba thus completed the first and most important part of their nuclear education. Having tested the limits of rivalry, they now proceeded to explore the limits of accommodation.

Cuba left an immediate legacy in the form of the the Partial Test Ban Treaty, the first arms control agreement of the Cold War, and the 'hotline' between Moscow and Washington. It laid a good part of the groundwork for *detente*. But it was not until the very end of the decade that the two sides were ready to begin serious negotiation. The Soviet Union had first to gain the nuclear parity which had been so conspicuosly lacking in 1962. For the key lesson which Soviet leaders had derived from the crisis was the need to catch up with the United States. Nuclear parity was essential for the Soviet Union to gain respect, as well as the self-confidence which would allow Brezhnev and his colleagues to eschew the shrill tones adopted by their predecessor. Or, to use Alexander Bessmertnykh's formulation, 'without parity we couldn't do well in foreign affairs'.

Although the build-up had begun before Cuba, it was the steady and continuous increase under Khrushchev's successors, averaging perhaps 4 per cent a year, which brought about the qualitative change in Soviet military strength which was to dominate the superpower relationship from the late 1960s to the early 1980s.[3] There was a new emphasis on conventional power, including naval and airlift capability which would allow the

Soviet Union to intervene in the Third World. At the same time strategic nuclear weapons remained what the novelist Vasilii Grossman called 'the sceptres of power', surrogates for the war which the superpowers could no longer fight. The side which surged ahead in terms of quality or numbers believed it was entitled to geopolitical gains.[4] By the end of the 1960s the Soviet Union had effectively been promoted from the status of a Eurasian Power to a global superpower. It now felt itself in a position to capitalise on its strength, and to try and convert arms into influence.

Its path was greatly eased by the Vietnam War. This was a self-inflicted American wound, a product of a serious overestimation of the threat posed by Communism in Asia, as also of America's power to counter it. It caused a major breach in the consensus which had underpinned American foreign policy since the Second World War. Faced with the most serious crisis of American self-confidence of the Cold War, policy-makers were even more than usually sensitive to the growth of Soviet power. At the same time Vietnam or rather the domestic reaction against it, helped bring to power a new administration run by men with strongly pragmatic instincts, and a quite unusually well-honed feel for geopolitical realities. In contrast to their predecessors, Nixon and his National Security Adviser, Henry Kissinger, explicitly based their policy on those very European concepts of the national interest and the balance of power. The fact that their adversaries were Communists was a secondary consideration. Gone was the ideological rhetoric of the earlier Cold War years. For Kissinger and Nixon, the internal order of the Soviet Union was neither an object of policy, nor a bar to dealing with it. Human rights would not feature in their thinking. American policy was based on Soviet *international* behaviour. At no previous, or indeed subsequent, stage of American foreign policy, was the ghost of Woodrow Wilson so firmly banished.

This new American flexibility was however by no means entirely advantageous to the Soviet Union. The first major initiative of the Nixon–Kissinger team was to break the bilateral framework of the superpower relationship through a long overdue *rapprochement* with China. The US had been slow to recognise that China was too large, and potentially too powerful a state to be left indefinitely outside the international community, there as Nixon wrote in 1967, 'to nurture its fantasies, cherish its hates and threaten its neighbours'. 'Unless China is cultivated while it is still developing its strength', he later wrote, 'we will one day be confronted with the most formidable enemy that has ever existed in the history of the world.'[5]

Rapprochement with China also served a more immediate purpose. By the late 1960s Sino-Soviet relations had deteriorated to a degree that war seemed possible. In the wake of the Warsaw Pact intervention in

Czechoslovakia, the Chinese feared that they might become victims of the 'Brezhnev doctrine' by which the Soviet Union claimed the right to intervene in the affairs of socialist states. In March 1969 fighting broke out along the Ussuri river on the Sino-Soviet border and the Soviet Union began to drop some very public hints that it might be considering a strike against Chinese nuclear facilities. This in turn deeply worried the United States which feared a possible restoration of the old, apparently monolithic Sino-Soviet bloc. 'Whether the Soviet Union was capable of realizing so vast a project', Kissinger writes, 'remained far from clear. What was obvious, however – especially to an administration basing its foreign policy on a geopolitical conception – was that the risk could not be run.' In what Kissinger goes on to describe as 'perhaps the most daring step' of Nixon's presidency and clear evidence of America's 'return to the world of *Realpolitik*', Nixon warned that the United States would not be indifferent to a Soviet attack on China.[6]

The Americans moved rapidly to exploit the unprecedented opportunities of a situation in which the two giants of the Communist world were more afraid of each other than they were of the United States. 'Triangular diplomacy' was an exercise in tightrope-walking premised on the assumption that the US bargaining position would be strongest if it remained closer to both China and the Soviet Union than either was to the other. The US must 'never lean to one side or the other'. Soviet fear of closer ties between Washington and Beijing could thus be exploited to encourage Moscow to be more accommodating towards Washington. China, in turn, which still had its own capacity for upsetting the Asian equilibrium, would be restrained by the need for American goodwill in setting limits on Soviet adventurism.[7]

The literal translation of *detente* is relaxation of tension. A rather better definition as applied to superpower relations from the late 1960s to the mid 1970s is Cyrus Vance's 'a policy of regulated competition coupled with reciprocity'.[8] Certainly it had from the beginning as much to do with the pursuit of national advantage by less dangerous and costly means, than with maximising common interests. The Strategic Arms Limitation Talks which became the centrepiece of *detente*, made at best a very modest contribution to reducing the risks of the arms race. Negotiation allowed each side to get a handle over some of the other side's programmes. SALT 1, which was signed in 1971, was a classic trade-off. The Americans capped their anti-ballistic missile capability which worried the Soviet Union; they in turn froze the deployment of offensive weapons in which they had an advantage, which the Americans believed would probably have increased in the absence of an agreement. But while both sides abided by the agreement, they nevertheless went ahead, as Nixon and Brezhnev had specifically told one another that they would do, with strategic programmes which were not specifically restricted. The actual totals of weapons increased substantially.[9]

The fundamentally competitive nature of *detente* was by no means confined to SALT. Each side expected it to limit the other's capacity to make advances. The Americans sought to prevent the Soviet Union exploiting nuclear parity. They hoped to enmesh the Soviet Union in a web of interdependent relations which would create both incentives for moderation and penalties for intransigence. More ambitiously, Kissinger, the student of Metternich and the Congress of Vienna, sought to create a system in which the Soviet Union would have an established and accepted role, a system to which it felt it could 'belong' and to whose stability it would therefore be committed.[10] The Soviet Union for its part saw in *detente* a framework within which to limit America's future capacity for the nuclear blackmail it felt itself to have been subjected to during the Cuban missile crisis. Thus while Washington sought a means of 'managing' or neutralising the growth of Soviet power, Moscow sought to manage a shrinkage of America's role in the world.[11]

Neither succeeded. But the Soviet Union did make short-term gains, most notably in terms of prestige. Simply by entering into serious negotiations, it gained recognition of its co-equal status with the United States. The superpowers were finally on a par. The arrogance of which Khrushchev had complained at the Vienna Summit now seemed a thing of the past. Anatoly Dobrynin describes the ceremonial reception on the White House lawn at the time of the 1973 Washington Summit, as 'the supreme act of recognition by the international community [*sic*]' of Soviet power and influence. It was the moment of Brezhnev's 'highest triumph. What could be greater than his being placed on a footing equal to the American president, with the Soviet Union equal to the United States – of all powers – in its nuclear might, its missiles and their warheads?'[12]

How great a contribution those additional missiles made to the eventual recognition of Soviet wartime gains in Europe which Khrushchev had originally sought, must be more questionable. Despite his own failures Khrushchev had in fact laid a good deal of the groundwork. Western acceptance of the division of Europe was a matter of time. Eastern Europe had long been accepted as a *de facto* Soviet sphere of influence. The West, as de Gaulle remarked in 1969 to Nixon, had really no choice. Unless they were prepared to knock down the Berlin Wall, 'there is no alternative that is acceptable. To work toward *detente* is a matter of good sense; if you are not ready to make war, make peace.'[13] A similar view had been expressed six years earlier by Egon Bahr, who was to play a central in the formulation of West Germany's *Ostpolitik*. '*Detente*' he noted to Willy Brandt, 'is compelled by the nuclear stalemate.'[14]

Brandt acted on this advice once he became Chancellor in 1969. The new socialist government believed that the time had come to draw a final line under the past. This was in part a moral imperative, a matter of healing and seeking to make good past damage. Men like Brandt, along with Helmut Schmidt and the future President, Richard von Weizsaecker who had both fought on the Eastern front, sought reconciliation with the East.[15] But there was also the recognition, which previous governments had been unready or unwilling to acknowledge, that the country could not go on indefinitely ignoring reality. They had to accept their wartime losses and recognise the postwar borders, as indeed the GDR itself. It was in their interests to accommodate the Soviet Union when in Brezhenev's words, it sought West Germany as 'an ally against the past'.[16]

Yet what the Soviet Union had gained was no more than a semblance of permanency. Moscow was well aware that the two sides had diametrically opposed objectives. Bonn was recognising the GDR, not because it had abandoned the prospect of unification, but because it saw acceptance of the *status quo* as the precondition for eventually changing it. 'To be sure,' Brezhnev told Honecker at a meeting in July 1970, 'Brandt also expects advantages. He wants to penetrate you. But with time he will find that ever harder.'[17] What Brezhnev failed to take into account was that international recognition did not, and could not, buy the domestic legitimacy essential to the long-term stability of East Germany or any other East European client. Opponents of these regimes had in fact gained a powerful new weapon from the Final Act of the 35 nation Conference on Security and Cooperation in Europe, which inscribed the subversively dangerous question of human rights onto the European agenda. Senior Soviet politicians and diplomats had been uneasy, but Gromkyo had managed to persuade his colleagues on the Politburo that human rights questions, certainly as they might apply to the Soviet Union itself, could be sidestepped. In its anxiety to gain the widest possible support for what appeared to be a postwar settlement highly favourable to the Soviet Union, Moscow had thus contributed to the eventual break-up of its European empire.[18]

The agreements reached on Europe, while by no means as final as the Soviet Union hoped, were at least specific. The same cannot be said of the 1972 Basic Principles of Relations between the United States and the Union of Soviet Socialist Republics, to give it its formal name, and the 1973 Prevention of Nuclear War (PNW) agreement. While couched in general terms, they were in practice concerned with behaviour in the Third

World, where nuclear diplomacy, albeit now in more restrained, stylised form, continued to be practised. Both sides were genuinely commited to the general proposition that that they had no alternative in the nuclear age but to conduct their relations on the basis of mutual coexistence. But they retained very different ideas about what this meant in practice, which the two agreements did little to clarify. The Soviet preoccupation was primarily with those phrases which recognised superpower equality, the references to 'reciprocity, mutual concessions and mutual benefit'.[19] The Americans, by contrast, who had been much more reserved about these agreements, were more interested in getting Soviet acknowledgement of the need for restraint. No attempts were made to elucidate the statement that 'efforts to establish unilateral advantage at the expense of the other, directly or indirectly' were 'inconsistent with these objectives' or to agree at what point the superpowers should, as they had just agreed, consult 'to defuse political tensions before crises arose'.[20]

It is in the Third World that the contradictions at the heart of *detente* are at their starkest. Each side, as Raymond Garthoff notes, 'saw an agreement which might be used to curb the other, but neither considered how the Basic Principles or PNW Agreement would restrain its *own* options and restrain its own behaviour'.[21] Although Moscow and Washington talked to each other more than they had done – Kissinger actually travelled to Moscow to negotiate a ceasefire during the Yom Kippur War – competition in the Third World remained intense. In contrast to Europe, there were no lines of occupation or accepted spheres of influence. At stake on what was literally and metaphorically the last battlefield of the Cold War, was the struggle for the ideological and strategic alignment of the large number of states which had come into being since the beginning of the conflict.

The Soviet ambition of establishing itself once and for all as a global superpower, is reflected in a remark made at the Twenty-Fourth Party Congress in 1971. Echoing almost exactly Molotov's comments in the immediate aftermath of the Second World War, Gromyko declared that there was today 'no question of any importance which can be decided without the Soviet Union or in opposition to it'.[22] This however was precisely what the United States was unwilling to concede. Washington's great fear was that the Soviet Union would accumulate seemingly marginal geopolitical gains – in Egypt and Angola, Yemen and Ethiopia – which over time would allow it to overturn the larger balance of East–West power. There would therefore be no American-approved hunting licence in the Third World. On the contrary, Washington was determined to reverse Soviet gains. Kissinger made no secret of his intention to try and expel the Soviet Union from Egypt. Indeed he saw *detente* as 'partly a tranquilizer for Moscow as we sought to draw the Middle East into closer relations with us at the Soviet expense'.[23]

At the time it seemed a highly ambitious undertaking. By the early 1970s the Soviet Union had established itself as a regional Middle Eastern Power with a Mediterranean fleet and on-shore military facilities in Egypt and Syria. But the Soviet position was less strong than it looked. Conventional arms did not buy easy or lasting influence in the post-colonial world, any more than nuclear weapons provided an easy means of intimidation. For all its ideological rhetoric, the Soviet Union was an Imperial Power operating in a world in which the principles of self-determination originally propounded by Woodrow Wilson had become a powerful force. Although it was initially able to exploit anti-Western nationalism, the parallels between Soviet and the old British and French Imperialisms gradually became rather too obvious. There were complaints from Egypt and Syria of interference in their domestic affairs. There was resentment over a Soviet military presence intended to serve Soviet rather than than Arab interests. A Treaty of Friendship and Cooperation signed in 1971 raised memories of the hated Anglo-Egyptian treaty of 1936. Cannier Arab leaders, such as President Assad of Syria, knew how to keep their new ally at a distance, taking, as one Soviet ambassador was reputed to have complained, everything from them except advice.[24] In Egypt, which became militarily overdependent on Moscow, the reaction came in 1972 when Sadat suddenly expelled some 20 000 Soviet military advisers from the country.[25]

The Soviet Union fared little better when it tried a more indirect approach. Proxies were the obvious, and generally the only realistic means of exerting power in this new world of independent states in which direct control or intervention, as both the Vietnamese and later Afghan exceptions underscored, carried a politically prohibitive price. But they were by no means problem-free. The armies of developing countries tended to make poor use of the sophisticated weaponry with which they insisted on being supplied. The Arabs, who faced an unusually competent Israeli adversary, proved particularly bad, and were repeatedly outclassed. This was not necessarily a disaster. The Soviet Union was able to capitalise on the Arab defeat in the Six Day War to gain military facilities. But the defeat of Soviet arms was bad for prestige, and put a serious strain on superpower relations at a time when Moscow was anxious to promote *detente*.

It was also dangerous. The major crises of the period, when recourse was again made to nuclear diplomacy, were occasioned by the need to protect Arab states against decisive Israeli defeats. The first use of the 'hotline' occurred at the end of the Six Day War, when Moscow threatened intervention to forestall an Israeli move against Damascus.[26] There was a second and much more famous incident at the end of the Yom Kippur War when Israeli forces threatened the Egyptian Third Army. Victor Israelyan, who was involved in decision-making during the crisis, wrote:

> With the situation hopeless for Sadat, and not wanting to become a party to the war, the Kremlin leaders concluded that the only way out of the deadlock was to exert effective pressure on Washington and force the Americans to pressure Israel. Therefore it was decided to hint to the Americans that in case the United States was not ready for joint action the Kremlin would not exclude the possibility of unilateral action in the Middle East. The participants (of the Politburo meeting) were convinced that even a reference to such an eventuality would frighten Washington and force it to take appropriate measures with Israel.[27]

This the Americans would seem to have done, although they also put their forces on nuclear alert.

In addition to military problems, proxy relationships also created political ones. All too often the tail seemed to wag the dog. Military dependence could rarely be exploited for Soviet political ends for fear that the proxy might as Egypt, and later Somalia did, switch alliances. Moscow was at a particular disadvantage in the Arab–Israeli conflict. Having broken relations at the time of the Six Day War, it had no diplomatic influence with Israel. Nor however could it force the Israelis to the negotiating table without precipitating a major confrontation with the United States. Washington would not tolerate a substantial Israeli defeat. The obvious danger, which was to materialise in 1973, was that the Americans would use their leverage with Israel to provide the peace settlement which Moscow could not deliver. Sadat manipulated the Soviet Union into providing the necessary offensive weapons for a war it did not want, but could not politically afford to prevent. The Americans then controlled the resupply of military equipment to Israel to bring about a final outcome which would allow an American brokered peace. The Soviet Union was co-chairman of the Geneva peace conference which convened in December 1973. But the conference adjourned almost immediately. Thereafter the Americans took over the peace process, the Egyptians switched alliances and the Soviet Union found itself on the sidelines of Middle East politics.[28]

The Yom Kippur War is one of the milestones of the Cold War – both the last direct military confrontation between the superpowers, and the first major public indicator of the limititations of of *detente*. A relationship in which cooperation and competition were so finely balanced was inherently fragile. It assumed a capacity to compartmentalise issues which never existed. The Strategic Arms Limitation Talks, which were the cornerstone if not quite the flagship of *detente*, simply could not be insulated from the political competition and the distrust it generated. It assumed too a continuation of the original pragmatism shown by the Kissinger–Nixon team. But *detente* had never gained real support in the United States. Even without Watergate there would have been opposition from liberals as well as those on the political Right, who had not been, or were not willing to be convinced that that in certain limited but vital respects, the Soviet Union might be an American partner.[29] Once Carter assumed the presidency in 1977, the new and highly sensitive issue of human rights moved centre stage. Perhaps most important, *detente* assumed a willingness on both sides to accept that there were limits beyond which competition could not be pressed without endangering the whole relationship.

Had Brezhnev not fallen ill in 1974 and lost his capacity to give impetus to a relationship by which he set great personal store, more might have been done to promote the cooperative dimension. But there is little reason to believe that he would have resolved the contradiction between an apparently sincere belief in the promotion of better Soviet–American relations on the one hand, and of continued support for anti-American movements and forces all over the world on the other. Unlike Gorbachev, he was not the man to rethink his very traditional Marxist–Leninist class approach to foreign policy. For all his apparent *rapport* with American leaders, he continued to see the United States as an opponent striving to undermine the socialist order. Neither he nor his colleagues had any inhibitions about exploiting the opportunities which arose in the mid 1970s in Angola and other parts of Africa. On the contrary, they were proud of assisting national liberation struggles and directing them towards Socialism, not least because here was a means of bringing about the eventual triumph of communism without war, not to mention reasserting their revolutionary credentials against the Chinese. Some in the Soviet military may also have enjoyed the prospect of defying the US by showing the Soviet flag in remote parts of the world. And with the US seeking to consolidate its position in Egypt and Chile, the Soviet Union felt that it had a right to take its own initiatives. The US had no legitimate concerns in places like Angola, Ethiopia or Somalia.[30]

There was one other reason why the Brezhnev Politburo now overplayed its hand. Nuclear parity, as the Americans had feared, along with a misreading of the larger international situation in the light of Vietnam, bred overconfidence. An article by Oleg Bykov, published in 1976, reflected a prevailing view in Moscow. It declared:

> The defeat in Vietnam clearly reflects the unalterable fact that no reinforcement of imperialism in our time can lead to a change in its favour in the correlation of forces on the international scene, or even to an interruption of the people's liberation struggle in one or another region of the globe.[31]

The Soviet Union believed that the United States was a superpower in decline, that modest support for radical movements could now yield substantial political dividends, and that regional conflicts could be disconnected, as Vietnam had effectively been, from the central superpower rivalry. Moscow could thus have its cake and eat it. It could maintain *detente* while continuing the very expansion the Americans were so anxious to prevent.

These were serious misjudgements. As Georgi Arbatov later observed, 'You cannot play such games with a great power. A great power will recover and then it will take its revenge.'[32] Well before the Soviet invasion of Afghanistan in December 1979, Americans had concluded that *detente* had been a one way street. The result was that a still very powerful United States first stepped up its defence expenditure, which it already began to do in Carter's time, and then proceeded to elect a militantly anti-Communist president who believed that Communism should not just be contained but defeated. The rhetoric was accompanied by covert action against left wing governments and movements.[33]

With the failure to establish a *modus vivendi* between the nuclear rivals, there was an ominous darkening of mood. US–Soviet relations again became angry and polarised. Concern about the increased risk of war extended deep into Soviet, as also into Western Europe society. But though few realised it at the time, the early 1980s were a turning point in the Cold War, and in the history of power politics. These were the years when the strains really began to tell, and when people on both sides started to think that things could not go indefinitely the way they had done for the last three and half decades. For the first time since the 1950s, large segments of Western public opinion began to revolt against the nuclear arms race. Contrary to official American fears at the beginning of the Cold War, public opinion had generally supported deterrence and acquiesced in the balance of terror. Despite occasional outbreaks of public *angst* there was no return to the mood of the 1920s and 1930s. Although the British government was keen in the 1950s and early 1960s to promote East–West summits and to enter into negotiations over Berlin, at no stage did the

British or any other Western governments feel compelled to act against their better judgement. There was no nuclear version of appeasement.

There were however intermittent reactions against nuclear weapons. Last seen in the 1950s, they re-emerged 20 years later in response to the proposed deployment in Europe of American Cruise and Pershing missiles as a counter to a build-up of Soviet SS20s. These weapons however were as much occasion as cause. The underlying protests were against the erosion of *detente* and the rekindling of the Cold War. What worried the protesters was not the decline of the credibility of the American nuclear guarantee to Europe, but the rhetorical belligerence of the Reagan administration, and its loose talk about the possibility of nuclear war. Theirs was a long-delayed protest against the nuclear condition, against the obscenity of overkill, against an apparently unending arms race. It may also, the point is necessarily hypothetical, have been a warning that public fear of nuclear weapons could not be indefinitely repressed, and that at a psychological level the Cold War was becoming increasingly difficult for societies to sustain.[34]

What is so striking about the nuclear reaction of the late 1970s and early 1980s is that it was not just the ordinary citizen who was becoming alarmed. The spectrum of concern included the Catholic Bishops in the United States, who for the first time began to question the morality of deterrence, as well as doctors, scientists and others with direct experience of nuclear affairs who increasingly spoke out about the dangers and weaknesses of deterrence. Strategists worried that the equation of security with the threat of massive nuclear devastation was becoming unsustainable. The prospect of apocalyptic casualties deprived the threat of credibility. In such circumstances, Kissinger warned, 'democratic publics will sooner or later retreat to pacifism and unilateral disarmament'.[35]

This was not President Reagan's view, but though few recognised it at the time, nuclear doubt reached into the very highest levels of government. The women who camped outside the missile bases in Europe did not think of the man who had spoken of the Soviet Union as an evil empire as an obvious ally. Ronald Reagan was a man who people tended to take by his rhetoric. Since his attitude was confrontational, it was assumed, wrongly, that he was also disposed to take confrontational courses of action with the Soviet Union.[36] Since he was strongly anti-Communist and pro-defence, it was assumed he was also pro-nuclear. In fact he was the very opposite. Reagan had come to office with a strong prejudice against the prevailing strategy of mutual assured destruction. As he wrote in his memoirs, 'Somehow this didn't seem to me to be something that would send you to bed feeling safe. It was like having two westerners standing in a saloon

aiming their guns at each other's head – permanently. There had to be a
better way.'[37] He had made the same point when told during a briefing at
NORAD headquarters in the 1970s, that there was nothing the US could do
to stop incoming Soviet missiles. 'Wouldn't it be better' he asked his
audience in the televised address in 1983 in which he announced his Strategic
Defense Initiative (SDI), 'to save lives ratter than to avenge them?'[38]

Phrased in these terms there was only one answer. It was the way the
question had been formulated which immediately became a matter of
dispute. Few issues say more about the paradoxes of the nuclear age than
the controversy raised by the idea of defence. SDI threatened, quite literally, to take the arms race into space – hence the term 'Star Wars'. It
threatened a completely new round in the arms race, one which the Soviet
Union feared it would no longer be technologically able to run.[39] But if, as
its supporters argue, SDI proved the ultimate Cold War bargaining chip
which the Americans played for all it was worth, it did not offer a way out.
Like the protesters, Reagan was tilting against the windmills of the nuclear
world. And yet if he did not the answers, he did at least ask important
questions. He challenged the accepted orthodoxies in a way that few
others could have done. George Shultz writes of Reagan's ability to break
through the entrenched thinking of the moment. Most of his senior
officials unquestioningly accepted mutual vulnerability, just as they
accepted unquestioningly the view that nuclear weapons were both
inevitable and desirable. 'The loss of nuclear weapons', according to one
senior member of the State Department, 'would mean the loss of a special
American preeminence; it would change the way we walk down the
street.'[40]

This was emphatically not the president's view. He dreamed dreams
while others accepted the *status quo*. What is striking about this, in many
respects oddly unmodern president, is his peculiar combination of vision
and ignorance. His remarks on nuclear matters frequently have a decep-
tive, almost naive simplicity, but it is the simplicity of the little boy
exclaiming that the emperor has no clothes. His moral denunciations of
deterrence are unanswerable.

At the same time there was an unrealistic nostalgia in his desire to
return to some kind of pre-nuclear golden age of security, combined with a
complete absence of technical reality. Reagan's grasp of the details of
nuclear weaponry was almost shockingly scanty. The idea of SDI drew on
a combination of Hollywood and an extreme version of the American
belief in the technological 'fix'. A senior White House official describes
the President seeing himself as 'a romantic, heroic figure who believes in
the power of a hero to overcome Armageddon'.[41] His way out of the

nuclear dilemma had more to do with fantasy and wishful thinking than the politically or technically possible. Reagan was even weaker on the practicalities of a nuclear free world than Woodrow Wilson had been on the practicalities of of the League of Nations. But he had something of the same determination and persistence. It led him to talk quite seriously about the abolition of nuclear weapons with Mikhail Gorbachev at their summit in Reykjavik in 1986. And it was on Ronald Reagan's watch that the Cold War drew to its unexpected end.

The Soviet 'new thinking' which suddenly came to international prominence after the election of Mikhail Gorbachev as General Secretary in 1985, can can be traced back at least as far as the 1970s. It was then that a group of younger, more independently-minded, middle-ranking officials began to rethink the old stereotyped Soviet views of the world which took no account of the complex political reality of the Third World, of new notions of 'common security' or of economic interdependence. As the director of one of the more influential Soviet think-tanks wrote in 1977:

> When the productive forces, science and technology are developing with unprecedented rapidity, the interconnection and interdependence of countries and people increases sharply ... Mankind is increasingly contending with problems truly global in scale, the solution of which requires collective effort on the part of different states.[42]

Over the next few years the need for change was reinforced first by the *debacle* of Afghanistan, and then by the accident at Chernobyl. As with Cuba, it again took a specific incident to dramatise the hitherto abstract dangers of nuclear war. General Yazov, who became Defence Minister in 1987, is reported to have told visitors that Chernobyl not only changed his previous view that nuclear war could be fought and won, but showed him that a country could be devastated simply by concentrated bombing of its nuclear power plants.[43] George Shultz believed that Chernobyl had left a 'strong anti-nuclear streak in Gorbachev's thinking.' The arms race, the Soviet leader wrote in his book, *Perestroika*, was unwinnable. Mankind had 'lost its immortality'.[44]

But the immediate impetus behind one of the most radical reassessments of foreign policy ever carried out by a major power except under the duress of defeat, was internal. The 'new thinking' was an essential precondition for the political and economic reform which Gorbachev was determined to pursue. The defence budget *had* to come down. The second superpower was having increasing difficulty keeping up with a rival which all along had been able to afford both guns and butter. The economic situation had seriously deteriorated since the highpoint of Soviet power in the mid 1970s. One leading Soviet economist of the period speaks of a zero growth rate in the years between 1981 to 1985, although there is also evidence that the economy had actually begun to contract during Brezhnev's last years.[45] Whatever the exact figures, and the full extent of the economic crisis was not immediately realised by the new team, the Soviet Union could not go on devoting a substantially larger proportion of a substantially smaller GNP to defence. What is significant about Gorbachev is his willingness to pay the necessary political price and abandon Soviet ambitions. Here was a leader ready to acknowledge that the military cost of superpower status was beyond the reach of a country which had suddenly lost its sense of moral self-righteousness and ideological mission.

This latter point is important, for the 'new thinking' was more than a rationalisation for withdrawal from Afghanistan and an unprecedently radical set of arms control agreements in which the Soviet Union gave up more than the United States. It was the doctrine of an erstwhile revolutionary power which had come to realise that instead of changing the modern world, it must rather join it. The Soviet Union which Gorbachev sought to create had a very new set of values and ideas. The emphasis at home as much as abroad was no longer on power, but on the rights of the individual and the rule of law. With the adoption of a new political morality came a repudiation of the past. In a remarkable speech delivered in 1990, the Foreign Minister, Eduard Shevardnadze, declared that

> The belief that we are a great country and that we should be respected for this is deeply ingrained in me as in everyone. *But great in what?* Territory? Population? Quantity of arms? Or the people's troubles? The individual's lack of rights? Life's disorderliness? In what do we, who have virtually the highest infant mortality rate on our planet, take pride? It is not easy answering the questions; Who are you and who do you wish to be? A country which is feared or a country which is respected? A country of power or a country of kindness?[46]

For three crucial years, from 1986 to 1989, the initiative lay with Gorbachev. He took the major initatives of the penultimate stage of the Cold War, gaining a prestige and credit for the Soviet Union which missiles had never bought his predecessors. But when it came to the crucial endgame in Europe, he began to lose control over events. Gorbachev had not sought the collapse of Soviet power in Eastern Europe. What he wanted was reform. While Brezhnev was haunted by the memories of the Second World War and the need for security, Gorbachev's priority was the extension of *perestroika* to Eastern Europe. The old East European leaderships must seek domestic political legitimacy, rather than relying on the Soviet army to keep them in power. Military intervention, as Gorbachev very quickly made clear, was a thing of the past. Previous interventions had proved to be 'pyrrhic victories'; the use of force under the new regime was incompatible with domestic and foreign policy objectives. The Soviet Union 'had no right' to interfere in East European affairs.[47]

Gorbachev however had not appreciated the full implications of this position. He seriously overestimated the possibility of an orderly transition to more open Communist systems in Eastern Europe, as indeed in the Soviet Union. Once the prop of Soviet military power was withdrawn, the empire collapsed. And once the Berlin Wall came down in November 1989, Moscow suddenly found itself faced with the prospect of German unification. It was politically and mentally unprepared. There had been some discussion of the German question in Moscow during the late 1980s, and Gorbachev and Kohl had formally recognised the German right to self-determination in the summer of 1989. But the division of Germany was still seen as essential to Soviet security. No new ideas had emerged and in marked contrast to other areas of Soviet foreign policy, there were no Soviet initiatives.[48] This placed the Soviet Union at a considerable disadvantage once what the former American High Commissioner in Germany, John McCloy, once called 'the Big Game' of settling the postwar political geography of Europe, got under way.[49] Here at last was the resolution of the German question which had eluded European policy-makers since the beginning of the century, but on lines very different from the Carthaginian model which the Soviet Union had enforced for four and a half decades.

That this was achieved with such relative ease – the negotiations were completed within a matter of months and involved no major crises – is in the first place a tribute to the groundwork laid in the late 1940s and 1950s. The framework for German unification – the European Union, NATO, what Chancellor Kohl described as the 'iron law that there will be no going it alone in German policy' – had long been in place.[50] Germany, Gorbachev quotes Bush as telling him, had shown it could be trusted. It had 'paid its dues'.[51] It is a tribute secondly to American policy. Within days of the wall coming down, the Americans had recognised that unification was inevitable, and that considerable effort would be needed to steer the process through smoothly. The prize was tremendous – the consolidation of the democratic revolutions in Europe, the reduction of Soviet military power in Eastern Europe and the elimination of the Soviet military presence in Germany. But the window of opportunity, as became obvious in the first half of 1990 was narrow. Germany, in the words of General Scowcroft, President Bush's National Security Adviser, was like a 'pressure cooker'; the lid could easily blow off.[52] Moscow, which still had 380 000 troops in East Germany, might choose to play a spoiler's role; Germany and the Soviet Union might cut a private deal as they had done at Rapallo in 1922 and again in 1939.

Unification had therefore to be pressed through quickly, though it was crucial not to weaken Gorbachev domestically in the process, or to leave Moscow harbouring a lasting bitterness which would one day result in the overthrow of the European settlement.[53] The trick was to involve the Soviet Union in the diplomatic process, but without giving it the opportunity to exercise any kind of veto, and to provide a raft of assurances concerning future German policy and NATO membership. There would also be a generous German financial contribution to cement the deal. Where however, cajolement ceased to work, Washington was ready to take a tougher approach. When in June Shevardnadze appeared to backtrack on the Soviet agreement to NATO membership, he was was bluntly warned that the US would go ahead regardless.[54]

Soviet acquiesence in this process reflects weakness as much as wisdom. The basic outline of policy was set by Gorbachev's longstanding determination to rule out the use of force. As he told James Baker in February 1990, the Soviet Union had to adjust to new realities and there was 'nothing terrible in the prospect of a unified Germany'.[55] Since Moscow did not 'want to see a replay of Versailles, when the Germans were able to rearm themselves', Germany needed to be 'contained within European structures'.[56] But like all of his colleagues, he baulked at the prospect of Germany joining NATO. Moscow still saw the alliance as a potentially hostile military bloc, and feared that without far-reaching guarantees, membership of a united Germany would tip the balance of forces in Europe against the Soviet Union. But it worried too about what would happen if Germany suddenly decided to leave the alliance. Gorbachev and Shevardnadze were acutely aware of the domestic sensitivity of the issue at a time of growing opposition to other policies. The accusation of having 'lost' Germany was already in the air. NATO membership would create what Shevardnadze described as an 'imagery' problem. 'It would look as though you had won and we had lost.'[57]

It took, as Gorbachev later told Bush, 'enormous efforts … tremendous work and political will' to deal with the German question and overcome 'the old approaches which seemed unquestionable'.[58] But, as Gorbachev well knew, the Soviet Union had little real choice. It did not, as Shevardnadze privately admitted, 'know the answer to the problem'.[59]

Without alternative ideas of its own, it was in serious danger of being left behind by events. A showdown with the United States would endanger the whole thrust of Gorbachev's foreign policy, as well as jeopardising the country's long-term relations with the new Germany. NATO membership was the lesser of the two evils; with its assurance of a continued American military presence in Europe it was at least preferable to German neutrality.[60] And so, in the summer of 1990 the sentence of indefinite division imposed on Germany for the horrendous aggression committed half a century earlier, was finally, if reluctantly, lifted. While clearly not forgotten, the worst of the past was at last laid to rest.

The end of the Cold War marks a return of a long-absent rationality to the conduct of Great Power politics. It meant the end of a simmering conflict which, as we shall argue in more detail in Chapter 9, had entailed quite unjustifiable risks, as well as the drastic curtailment of an arms race which had never been under more than partial control. The result was to provide the Soviet Union with substantially more security than it had previously had, and at a much lower cost. Unlike his predecessors, Gorbachev was recognised as a world statesman. But if the end of the Cold War, as many in the former Soviet Union would argue, was a common victory, judged by its own previous objectives, Moscow had suffered a substantial defeat. It had been unable to sustain its hegemonial ambitions or even to retain its outer empire in Eastern Europe. Germany had been unified on Western terms, and when Soviet forces finally withdrew, they left nothing lasting behind. Whereas the West had been more than able to stay the economic and technological course in what in key respects had once again been a *Materialschlacht*, the Soviet Union had not.

This was first and foremost a reflection of economic and political failure – the Soviet Union had been defeated from within as much as from without. But the fact also remains that the Soviet Union had faced an unprecedentedly difficult task. It was the first revisionist power to try to operate in a world in which intimidation had to substitute for coercion. This would not necessarily have been a critical handicap if economic growth had continued or if it had retained its ideological drawing power. Missiles by contrast, in whatever numbers, were no real substitute. They were the weapons of the *status quo*, effective at deterring American attempts at 'rolling back' the Soviet empire in Eastern Europe or major Israeli threats against Egypt or Syria. Under certain circumstances they might bring about change – Kennedy succeeded in forcing Soviet missiles out of Cuba; had he played his hands more skilfully, Khrushchev might have gained more in Berlin.

These however were very much the exceptions. Intimidation, as Stalin had immediately realised, only worked against those with weak nerves, and throughout the Cold War, the Western nerve conspicuously held. This was not a foregone conclusion. The Eisenhower Administration had believed that long-term the West Europeans would not be able to stand up to Soviet nuclear power. Terrified by nuclear war they would drift away from the American policy of resistance to Soviet encroachments. In 1961 the British ambassador in Washington reported on a private conversation with Kennedy on the possibility of nuclear conflict.

> When I said to him that I thought it was inconceivable that a democratic nation would be prepared to got to the brink of nuclear war without there having been an attempt to talk the matter over with the Russians, he said that he was not sure that this was true of the United States. He personally felt they ought to think in this way, but the attitude of complete and total distrust of the Russians had been so effectively created by the press and radio that if he cared to tell the people that it was useless to negotiate they would probably agree with him.[61]

This was perhaps as well. Kennedy, like all American presidents, knew that he had no alternative but to stand his ground. The need to face down a bully had been drummed in by the lessons of Munich, which were then still very fresh in the mind. The task was made easier not just by the anti-Soviet state of public opinion, but the knowledge, if never of course the certainty, that the Soviet Union was bluffing. Hitler had been able to intimidate because it was believed, rightly, that the risk of war was real. The Soviet Union failed because recourse to nuclear war so clearly defied reason. This left Moscow with the alternatives of upping the *ante* and taking what, after 1962, were regarded as unacceptable levels of risk, or of relying on the indirect and ultimately not very effective influence of a more equitable strategic balance and the support of proxy forces which all too often seemed to prove political and military liabilities. In the final analysis therefore the Soviet failure was a failure of coercion in a world in which both ideas and technology increasingly militated against the exercise of traditional forms of power.

This, to his credit, Gorbachev had recognised, and it is this which gives the 'new thinking' its larger historical significance. At its heart was a reassessment of the role of power in international relations. Part of it related specifically to nuclear weapons which in his speech to the General Assembly of the United Nations of December 1988, Gorbachev described as revealing the 'absolute limits' of military power. The use or threat of force could no longer be an instrument of policy. The building up of military power made 'no country omnipotent'. 'All of us, and primarily the stronger of us, must exercise self-restraint.'[62] Mankind, Gorbachev continued, was on the threshold of a new era in which the traditional principles governing international relations, which had been based on the balance of power and rivalry, were being superseded by a much more cooperative form of politics based on the primacy of international law and human rights.[63] It was a powerful and an immensely welcome refutation of power politics. But it was hardly novel. Japan and West Germany had come to similar if less clearly articulated conclusions nearly four decades earlier. Moscow was discovering the alternative of accommodatory politics very late in the day.

8 Peace in Their Time

Gorbachev's choice of the United Nations to present his vision of a new world order was as natural as it was ironical. More than four decades previously, Roosevelt had predicted that the UN would spell 'the end of the system of unilateral action, exclusive alliances, and spheres of influence, and balance of power, and all the other expedients which have been tried for centuries and have always failed'.[1] Roosevelt had offered Stalin the role of one of the world's 'Four Policemen', who along with Britain, the United States and Nationalist China, would exercise paramount authority in a largely disarmed world. Stalin, as we have seen, had wanted more. But while he had doomed Roosevelt's grand vision, the Cold War had not prevented the emergence of a smaller, post-Hobbesian, post-heroic order in which the old warrior ethic with its emphasis on the fighting virtues of strength, courage and national glory was finally superseded. It consisted of a series of overlapping regimes – the IMF, the World Bank, GATT, the OECD, the EEC, the G-7 – whose primary aims were the promotion of the economic stability and prosperity on which something approaching perpetual peace could finally be based.

Western and liberal in terms of ideology (although not geography), its centres were Washington and Brussels. Here for the first time was a group of states which no longer measured relative strength in terms of their capacity for destructiveness. One of the key figures in the early days of European integration, Robert Marjolin, writes of 'European history, the history of warring nation-states' having come to an end. Nothing, neither territorial gain, nor superiority of power nor prestige, any longer seemed worth tearing each other apart for.[2] In their relations with one another, the members of this new order had replaced the old notion of right is might with an *accommodatory* culture whereby disputes were settled by negotiation and compromise, on the basis of a set of mutually accepted rules. Although the old struggle for the mastery of Europe might continue in the form of the Cold War, some of the main players had abandoned traditional 'high politics' in favour of the 'low detail' of fish quotas and agricultural subsidies.

The economic origins of the most important, and certainly most benign change in the conduct of international relations since the advent of the Congress system in 1815, go back to the dark days of the mid 1930s, to the 'New Deal' and Keynesian demand management which provided the basis for the postwar policies of growth and full employment. But it was the war which provided the main impetus to the decline of power politics, changing not just the balance of power, but the way a number of key states thought about power. Bellicism was dead, nationalism was now looked upon as a cancer. National sovereignty was for the first time coming under attack. In marked contrast to the mood prevailing after the First World War, West Europeans – those in the East had no choice in the matter – wanted to look forwards rather than back.

At the same time West Europeans were increasingly inclined to look inwards.[3] There was a deep desire to overcome the internal divisions of the 1930s and to create new, more just and more prosperous societies. The overwhelming sentiment in Western Europe was that of '*nie wieder*', 'never again'. 'Never again', writes Peter Henessy of the mood in Britain immediately after the war,

> would there be war; never again would the British people be housed in slums, living off a meagre diet thanks to low wages or no wages at all; never again would mass unemployment blunt the lives of millions; never again would natural abilities lie dormant in the absence of educational stimulus.[4]

What made this mood so politically potent, was the shift, which the war had accelerated, from authoritarian to democratic-welfare state, from the state which the citizen was expected to serve, to the state which would serve the individual. The former had embraced power politics; the latter shied away from it. Governments had no electoral alternative but to concentrate resources at home, whether on radical programmes of social reform and welfare, or later, on consumption and the good life. This did not of course mean that countries such as France or Britain had suddenly given up their preoccupation with status and prestige or were ready to abandon their erstwhile world roles. But the general Western tendency was for societies to define success, progress and even in some cases prestige, in economic terms. The *Deutschmark* rather than the *Wehrmacht*.[5]

This was a receptive environment for the return of the old liberal equation between peace and free trade. Commerce, John Stuart Mill had optimistically argued in 1848, was 'rapidly rendering war obsolete, by strengthening and multiplying the personal interests which act in natural opposition to it'. Five years earlier Richard Cobden had described the impact of free trade as a breaking down of 'the barriers that separate nations; those barriers behind which nestle the feelings of pride, revenge, hatred and jealousy which every now and then break their bonds and deluge whole countries with blood'.[6] This thinking was both premature and oversimplified. Very high levels of economic interdependence, higher in some cases than those achieved since the 1950s, did not prevent the First World War, although acute international economic instability did contribute to the second. This latter development served to give economists a new respectability as peacemakers. Keynes, who had resigned over the failure of the Versailles settlement to take account of the economic consequences of the peace, became the prime intellectual mover of the 1944 Bretton Woods negotiations, which established the first major international institutions of the postwar era, the International Monetary Fund and the International Bank for Reconstruction and Development (later known as the World Bank).

The main political impetus behind these innovations came however from across the Atlantic. While the Europeans had planned their own welfare states, it was the US which provided the original engine for the reform of their international relations. Planning for the postwar world began immediately after the outbreak of war in Europe, even though at this stage the United States had absolutely no intention of entering it. The American planners assumed, reasonably, that after a decade of protectionism and Depression, states would be more willing to act on the basis of common economic rather than political interest.[7] They also assumed, rather less reasonably, that the causes of war were essentially economic. Cordell Hull was a particularly fervent believer in the old doctrine that free trade and stable currencies could of themselves guarantee peace. In early 1945 the Treasury Secretary, Henry Morgenthau, warned that unless the Bretton Woods agreements were ratified, states would have little alternative but to seek solutions to problems 'on the old familiar lines, lines which will inexorably involve playing the old game of power politics with even greater intensity than before'.[8]

Shorn of their vital political complement of a powerful United Nations, the Bretton Woods institutions could have only limited effectiveness. The temple of the new world order, whose economic pillars they were intended to be, never materialised. But Bretton Woods provided a foundation stone of the more modest 'Western' accommodatory edifice, which arose over the next few years. It established precedents – permanent international institutions endowed with considerable power and resources to deal with mutual monetary and economic problems – and imposed a sense of direction. Bretton Woods helped ensure that the United States would not revert to its prewar policy of economic isolationism. It laid the groundwork for the series of early postwar initiatives culminating in the Marshall Plan.[9]

The thinking behind the European Recovery Programme, to give it its formal name, was outlined in a speech given by the Undersecretary of

State in May 1947. Warning that human beings and nations, along with human dignity, freedom and democratic institutions, were existing 'in narrow economic margins', Dean Acheson went on to declare that

> It is one of the principal aims of our foreign policy today to use our economic and financial resources to widen these margins. It is necessary if we are to preserve our own freedoms and our own democratic institutions. It is necessary for our national security. And it is our duty and privelege as human beings.[10]

More than Bretton Woods, the British dollar loan of 1946 and the merger of the British and American zones in Germany on 1 January 1947, Marshall's Harvard address of 5 June marks a point of departure. It was a departure in the practice of European statecraft, whereby victors were much more likely to extract reparations from the vanquished rather than seek their economic rehabilitation, and where there were few if any precedents for financing even friendly states in peacetime.[11] The contrast with the Versailles settlement could not have been more striking.

It was a moment of departure too in American foreign policy. It meant an end of that idealistic universalism which had characterised American foreign policy during both the world wars. In his memoirs Dean Acheson referred to the emergence of new American *corpus diplomaticum* which

> differed from Mr Hull's preconceptions by relegating to the future the attempt at universality in a sharply divided world ... It placed the strategic approach to practicable objectives, concretely and realistically conceived, ahead of generalizations, even those wearing the garb of idealism. It developed institutions and means to aid in achieving these more limited and, it was hoped, transitory means.[12]

America thus abandoned its traditional determination to avoid entanglement with the Old World and its bad old ways. Roosevelt had explicitly rejected any American responsibility for the economic reconstruction of Europe. He did 'not want the United States to have the postwar burden of reconstructing France, Italy and the Balkans. This is not our natural task at a distance of 3500 miles or more.'[13] That policy was no longer viable. The US could not, as it done from the time of lendlease devised in 1940 when it still hoped to keep out of the war, through Pearl Harbor, 'unconditional surrender', and on to the occupation of Germany, keep on reacting to events. With its forces in occupation of the devastated half of Europe which they had helped liberate, the US had little option but to make a long-term commitment. It did so with imagination and in a very traditionally American way. The Marshall Plan was as much an act of reconstruction as of reform, an attempt to establish a zone of order rather than to maintain the balance of power, as the Truman Doctrine had sought to do. As such it represented enlightened self-interest of a high order. Brian Atwood speaks of the United States pioneering the notion that 'a nation could do well by doing good'.[14] Don Cook praises George Kennan's report, which provided the basis for Marshall's Harvard address, for its combination of altruism, expediency and common sense.[15] Walter Isaacson and Evan Thomas in their study of six of the key figures who shaped American foreign policy during this period, describe this as their subjects 'purest and greatest achievement, *power used to its best end*'. The architects of the ERP, believed that the restoration of Europe was 'not only right, but natural, even obligatory … It was not just the United States they sought to serve but, in a broader sense, the culture and civilization of the West'. To this end they brought the 'right mixture of vision and practicality, aggressiveness and patience'.[16]

In retrospect the US may have overestimated the gravity of the economic situation in Europe in the Spring of 1947, but that was not how it seemed at the time. The economic recovery already evident the year after the war, had been followed by a sharp fall in production and trade as a result of the bitter winter in 1947. There was a huge balance of payments deficit with the outside world, especially the United States and raw material suppliers; existing relief programmes were ending. Washington feared that European states might be forced to resort to trade by government monopoly, forcing the US to follow suit. It feared too an economic disaster on which local Communist parties, especially in France and Italy, would capitalise.[17]

From the beginning American policy-makers rejected short-term measures. American aid for Europe should, as a State Department paper had argued, 'be directed not to the combatting of communism as such but to the restoration of the economic health and vigor of European society'.[18] The result was some 13.6 billion dollars of economic aid, plus a large technical assistance programme aimed not simply at the reconstruction but the modernisation of European industry. The actual money did not in the event make the difference between economic life and death for West European economies. But by allowing them to generate capital more freely than they would otherwise have done, Marshall Aid acted like the lubricant in an engine, 'allowing a machine to run that would otherwise buckle and bind'.[19] Michael Hogan points to Marshall Aid's contribution to 'gains in productivity, to improvements in trade, and to an era of social peace and prosperity more durable than any other in modern European history'.[20]

The European Recovery Programme (ERP) also did something else. It helped give impetus to the incipient process of European integration. US policy-makers had insisted not only that the initial request must come from Europe, but that it must come as a joint European initiative, not in the form of a series of isolated and individual appeals. The Americans, as Kennan later explained,

> had serious doubts about the success of any movement toward European recovery that rested merely on a series of uncoordinated European programmes; we considered that one of the long-term deficiencies of the European economy as a whole was its excessive fragmentation, the lack of competitive flexibility in commercial exchanges, the lack, in particular, of a large consumer's market. By insisting on a joint approach, we hoped to force the Europeans to begin to think like Europeans, and not like nationalists, in their approach to the economic problems of the continent.[21]

And this they began to do. Marshall's offer compelled European governments to do something new, namely to consider a problem from a common point of view. The tendency was institutionalised by the formation, at American behest, of the Organisation for European Economic Cooperation, forerunner of the OECD. This was the first collaborative European economic institution, and its initial and unprecedented task was the allocation of Marshall Aid on a supranational basis. According to both Marjolin and the Belgian Prime Minister, Paul-Henri Spaak, who also played a key role in the early process of European integration, the European Economic Community (EEC) was the direct descendent of the Marshall Plan.[22] But economics could not do everything. Before the Treaty of Rome could be signed in 1957, the old political problem of Germany had first to be tackled.

The 'Federal' solution – the term 'Western' is better applied to the final settlement of 1990 – amounted to a new beginning. The western and larger half of Germany was transformed into a stable democracy renouncing power politics in favour of integration with an Atlantic community and its more tightly-knit European core. Ironically however what was to become the great success story of the whole period from Tirpitz to Gorbachev was very much a result of the division of Europe. As Stalin had privately remarked to Djilas in April 1945, this war was different in that whoever occupied a territory also imposed their own social system.[23] In the absence of a wider agreement with the Soviet Union, the British and Americans instinctively and naturally sought democratisation and denazification of their occupation zones. Their decision to rebuild the West German economy came less automatically. But as soon became clear, the desire to disarm and neutralise the former Reich, which in the extreme form originally espoused by Henry Morgenthau would have meant trying to put the clock back to a preindustrial, agrarian past, was inconsistent with the growing postwar need to reconstruct German industry and integrate it within the larger west European economy. It was, as Kennan noted, nonsense to talk about the recovery of Europe and oppose the recovery of Germany. 'People can either have both or they can have neither.'[24]

In opting for recovery the Americans were throwing down a major challenge not only to the Soviet Union, but also to France. While Moscow responded by hardening the lines of division on the Continent, the French by contrast proved unprecedentedly flexible and imaginative, to the point indeed that only five years after the war the initiative in the development of a Western accommodatory system passed from the United States to Continental Europe. And it was in Old rather than the New World, albeit under American encouragement that a new set of ideas which went beyond the traditional liberal agenda, now emerged.

The change, when it came in the spring of 1950 was completely unexpected. The French Foreign Minister, Robert Schumann, described the proposal for a European Coal and Steel Community under which France and German's coal and steel communities would come under supranational authority, as a 'leap in the dark'.[25] Like the Soviet 'new thinking', it was born of weakness and necessity as much as of vision. The old French inferiority complex *vis-à-vis* Germany was beginning to reassert itself. George Ball describes how the previous year in Paris 'even an itinerant American could sense a resurgence of introspection, a slackening of vitality, and the insidious exhumation of old, dark rivalries, fears and complexes'.[26] French policy-makers had run out of ideas for containing the revival of German power. The draconian measures advocated immediately after the war, a throwback to the thinking of Versailles, had quickly proved politically untenable. By the spring of 1950 it was clear that the more moderate alternative approach of trying to dominate Germany through the key industrial areas of the Saar and the Ruhr, could not continue indefinitely. German steel production was bound to increase; French insistence on control of the coal-rich Saar, which had been a major source of contention after the First World War, was liable to reignite what has been described as the 'reciprocating engine' of Franco-German hostility.[27]

It is at this point that the figure of Jean Monnet comes to the fore. During the First World War when still in his twenties, Monnet had been appointed French representative to the Inter-Allied Supply committee in London. His subsequent career, which included a spell as deputy secretary-general of the League of Nations, investment banker and head of France's postwar modernisation plan, had provided him with an extraordinarily wide range of contacts on both sides of the Atlantic. Like Marshall three years earlier, Monnet in 1950 recognised the need for a radical change of course. Unlike Marshall, Monnet had from the outset a plan. Its basis was scarcely new, indeed its origins can be traced back nearly a quarter of a century. The International Steel Cartel established in 1926 had seemed at the time to provide a possible means of settling Franco-German differences.[28] Gustav Stresemann, Briand's German partner in the short-lived Franco-German *rapprochement* of the mid-1920s, once said of the Cartel that it been the object of his life 'to realise in the political field what has been accomplished by economics in this pact'.[29] Variations on this theme had been advanced from both sides of the Rhine in the years following the Second World War. In retrospect, as Monnet's biographer, Francois Duchene notes, 'the Schumann plan seems to have been launched on a thousand lips'.[30] But it was Jean Monnet who in April 1950 came up with a practical initiative which offered an increasingly desperate French government a way out of the *impasse* into which its relations with Germany had come.

Monnet, for all his pragmatism, is a man of whom myths are easily made. The great transformation of western European politics which flowed from the European Coal and Steel Community (ECSC) was not the work of one man. Indeed Monnet himself was at pains to give credit to those he consulted in working out the vital practical details of his plan. Etienne Hirsch and Pierre Uri, like the more prominent Konrad Adenauer, the Italian premier Alcide de Gasperi, Robert Schumann, the Dutch Foreign Minister, Johan Beyen and his Belgian counterpart Paul-Henri Spaak, all belonged to the immediate postwar generation which, like their counterparts in the United States, espoused new thinking about the management of power. They were among the most creative and innovative group of men ever to have have shaped the relations of European or indeed any states. Monnet stands out however for his combination of idealism and realism. He had ideas, and knew how to get them implemented. The account of the gestation of the ECSC in his memoirs provide a fascinating insight into how that very rare phenomeon, the workable new idea for the organisation of international relations, evolves.

It is this practical streak which distinguishes Monnet from Woodrow Wilson. Monnet had a much greater direct knowledge of the world than Wilson. He was driven by personal experience, not liberal ideology or Calvinist certitude. Born thirty-two years after Wilson in 1888, Monnet was of the European generation for whom war had become a constant preoccupation. Almost his whole adult life had been spent in either the conduct, expectation of, or recovery from war. In his account of the origins of ECSC, Monnet places great emphasis on the dangers created by the way in which yet another war was increasingly being seen as inevitable. 'War was in men's minds and it had to be opposed by imagination.'[31]

While both Wilson and Monnet sought to find a way of replacing power politics by civil order, the Frenchman made no claims for the universality of the ideas and institutions which he promoted. His was a European approach to a European problem. But if Monnet's ambition was more limited than Wilson's, his success was correspondingly greater, and may yet have a significance which goes beyond the geographical confines of Europe. Monnet did more than simply devise a framework for a lasting Franco-German rapprochement, he offered a working solution to the problem of international anarchy. The emphasis was on institutions which would provide the necessary framework within which states could transcend the exclusive, antagonistic form of nationalism which had gripped Europe since the late nineteenth century. While he did not succumb to the liberal temptation of assuming a natural harmony of interests, he put much emphasis on the concept of community, on what states and peoples had in common. Monnet emphasised 'the psychology of the private contact, with its assumption that all the parties will benefit. It was the language of business, but also of community and civil politics, the reverse of the Social Darwinism of states'. 'We are here,' he told the delegates at the outset of the conference called to establish the ECSC, 'to undertake a common task – not to negotiate for our own national advantage, but to seek it in the advantage of all.'[32]

It was a message he never tired of repeating to men trained to advance and defend purely national interests. Dogged in his advocacy, his approach to the problem of power had, unlike Wilson's, been indirect. His aim was not the control of power, with its attendant problem of policing and sanctions, but something more radical, and paradoxically also more practical; the establishment of contexts in which power would lose its salience. The German problem was too intractable to be tackled head on. Rather he sought to deal with it through one of its main politico-economic causes. He later wrote:

The joint resources of France and Germany lay essentially in their coal and steel, distributed unevenly but in complementary fashion over a triangular area artificially divided by historical frontiers. With the industrial revolution, which had coincided with the rise of doctrinal nationalism, these frontiers had become barriers to trade and then lines of confrontation. Neither country now felt secure unless it commanded all the resources – i.e., all the area. Their rival claims were decided by war, which solved the problem only for a time – the time to prepare for revenge. Coal and steel were at once the key to economic power and the raw materials for forging the weapons of war. This double role gave them an immense symbolic significance ... To pool them across frontiers would reduce their malign prestige and turn them instead into a guarantee of peace.[33]

Schumann put a slightly different gloss on this latter argument. Writing to Adenauer, the French Foreign Minister noted that rearmament had always shown first in increased coal, iron and steel production. The proposed Community would enable each state to detect the first signs of rearmament and have 'an extraordinarily calming effect in France'.[34] To the British Ambassador, Schumann spoke of binding France and Germany so close that neither side could draw back and hit the other.[31] France would thus gain security; West Germany in turn would make a giant stride on the road to political rehabilitation. Small wonder that Adenauer is reported to have privately described the offer as '*unser Durchbruch*' ('our breakthrough, beginning').[35]

It was a much more generous offer than he might have expected, with the tremendous attraction, so soon after the war, of being based on an acceptance of equal rights. It also provided this very new, very insecure state, with an anchor. Adenauer believed that West Germany had to join one of the two main power blocs if it was not to be ground up between them. In practical terms Adenauer may have had no real alternative than to ally with the occupying Powers. But for the man who described himself as a European as much as a German, the Catholic Rhinelander who felt closer to France than to Prussia, this was a matter of conviction as much as necessity.[36] There is little reason to doubt Adenauer's sincerity when, at their first meeting, he told Monnet that he had 'waited twenty-five years for a move like this ... In accepting it my Government and my country have no secret hankerings after hegemony. History since 1933 has taught us the folly of such ideas. Germany knows that its fate is bound up with that of Western Europe as a whole.'[37]

In the event the ECSC, which was to consist of Italy and the Benelux countries as well as France and Germany, was to prove an institution of transition. Its economic impact turned out to be slight; although few realised it in 1950, coal and steel were the core industries of the past rather than the future. But this did not undermine the ECSC's political importance as a stepping stone from the suspicion and hostility of the old Europe, the Europe of power politics, to the Europe of cooperation and accommo-dation. The Community, with its High Authority, Council of Ministers and Common Assembly, helped knit if not whole countries, than important parts of their leadership together. And if it did not provide a model for further integration, it established a precedent. It showed that the problem of sovereignty was not insurmountable. It put the idea of 'Europe' firmly on the political map, providing 'a certificate of roadworthiness' which helped it to survive the potentially traumatic collapse in 1954 of the European Defence Community which had been intended to provide a framework within which German rearmament would be acceptable to its European allies. Monnet was not involved in the negotiations which led to the establishment of the European Economic Community in 1957, but as his biographer argues, without him there would have been two chances in three that the European Community would never have come into exis-tence.[38]

With the signature of the Treaty of Rome, the institutional framework of the new Western accommodatory order was essentially in place. What fol-lowed was consolidation in a Community whose members had not only committed themselves to 'an ever closer union', but had also affirmed 'as the essential objective of their efforts the constant improvement of the living and working conditions of their peoples'.[39] The crucial subtext, the need to ensure that war within the western half of Europe would become unthinkable, would not however go away. To use a term which would gain currency twenty years later, the European Economic Community proved to be the world's most ambitious confidence-building measure, an open-ended exercise in seeking to dissipate the distrust which had accumulated over the centuries. Although Western Germany was smaller and infinitely more amenable than the old *Reich*, although it no longer had a General Staff and had renounced nuclear weapons, the under-lying suspicions and fears lingered. France in particular felt it necessary to supplement its multilateral links with Bonn with a Franco-German treaty which provided for a host of regular bilateral contacts, including twice-yearly summits between President and Chancellor. In addition to keeping as close to their new allies as possible, the French also provided them-selves with their own reinsurance policy in the form of the *Force de Frappe*.

Yet the Germans or rather the West Germans, the terms often seemed to be interchangeable, behaved impeccably. They went out of their way to avoid being seen to be throwing their increasing weight about. The Community's most economically powerful member was also its most strikingly unambitious. This 'civilian' Power had traded the 'jackboot for the felt slipper'. A former President of the European Commission, Roy Jenkins, puts it more diplomatically when he notes how Germany has 'tried to push power away'. Foreign policy became guided by the notion that the world expected nothing more from Germany than to keep a low profile in crises and remain peaceful.[40]

West Germany, like Japan, was a Great Power transformed and reformed. The two great losers of the Second World War had repudiated power politics with something of the same fervour with which they had once embraced it. In Peter Schwarz's phrase Germany turned from *Machtveressenheit*, obsession with power, to *Machtvergessenheit*, the neglect of power.[41] This swing from extreme to extreme, was not perhaps entirely healthy. Certainly the very intensity of Japanese pacifist sentiment betrayed an acknowledged element of self-distrust. As the deputy director general of the Japanese Self-Defence Agency remarked in 1990, 'The Japanese people do not trust the Self-Defence Forces because they cannot trust themselves as Japanese. This is why they need the constitution to block security efforts.'[42] Some German politicians, notably Adenauer and later Helmut Kohl, also admitted to a distrust of their fellow citizens. Nevertheless it was an understandable reaction, part emotional, part moral, part pragmatic, to conspicuous failure. The full brunt of modern warfare had recoiled on the two countries. They had been defeated and occupied, their cities had been heavily bombed and their leaders tried as war criminals. Small wonder if, after experiencing what became known as 'the hour zero' in 1945, the West Germans readily renounced the value system of nationalism which had taken them into two world wars, along with belief in any kind of German mission. What they could not do was to escape the lasting moral guilt for Auschwitz and the Holocaust, which played a crucial role in impeding the restoration of German self-confidence and self-esteem.[43]

This did not however mean *immobilisme* as it did in the case of the Japanese. The Germans put their reaction against power politics to good use, complementing politico-military self-restraint with active participation in the great experiment in international relations which Monnet initiated. Whether the Japanese would have accepted a similar opportunity had they been offered it, is perhaps questionable. Geography, cultural distinctness and the absence of the burden of division, suggest that they might not. The West Germans by contrast badly needed membership of a larger European Community. They needed it to rehabilitate themselves as a civilised European state and to underpin democracy in a country where it never previously taken firm root. They needed it to compensate for division. As Adenauer remarked to his cabinet, 'One has to give the people an ideal and that can only be a European one.'[44] They needed it to help establish a new sense of identity. The EEC was part of the complex insurance policy West Germans took out with the West against a recurrence of the pressures imposed by what had, if anything, become an even more difficult geographical position from the one which had led Bismarck to speak of his *'cauchemar des coalitions'*. It protected them from temptation, while providing their partners with a framework which enhanced the predictability and transparency of Bonn's policies.

The choice, and the whole-hearted way in which it was implemented, was crucial. West Germany was the lynchpin not just of the EEC, but indeed of the whole Western accommodatory order. It was the only member which might have been tempted by a different course. If West Germany had seriously toyed with neutralism or been open to Soviet offers, had it chosen to approach unification with anything other than unremitting patience, Europe would have proved a more dangerous place. As it was, West Germany made a major contribution to the stability of the Continent, and to the success of an institution whose *modus operandi* was unique. It would have been unrecognisable to an earlier generation of political leaders who rarely travelled, and when they did confined their contacts to matters of high policy. More than any other accommodatory institution, the European Community became a power in its own right with a capital rather than simply a headquarters, and an unusually powerful bureaucracy in the form of the Commission. But it was a benign form of power which ensured that the interests of smaller members were not overlooked, and which encouraged states to play by the rules.

The point should not be overstated; the Community was a vehicle for, rather than an alternative to the pursuit of national interests. The battles within the organisation were loud and frequent. But the officials and ministers who worked with the Community developed a capacity to accommodate the national with the larger Community interest, if only because this was the only way it could keep going, and because in the final analysis all accepted that their overriding national interests were bound up with its survival. The pre-eminent club of the accommodatory order had effectively institutionalised the principle of enlightened self-interest, while taking a major step towards the 'Lockeanising' of international politics which Wilson had sought. According to Francois Duchene:

> By introducing a rule of law into relations between Western European counties, it [the EEC] has cut off a whole dimension of destructive expectations in the minds of policy-makers. The need to think in terms of hostile intent among neighbours (and so, very often, to encour-

age the very behaviour feared) has been minimised and replaced by aspirations that come nearer to the 'rights' and responsibilities which reign in domestic politics. With all its imperfections, the Community domesticates the balance of power into something which, if not as 'democratic' as domestic norms, has made the international system in Europe take a huge step in their direction.[45]

This situation is sufficiently remarkable to require us to pause and take stock. Does Duchene perhaps overstate his case? Is it all too good to be true? If, as we shall suggest, the answer is a qualified no, some hard questions nevertheless need to be asked about the contemporary basis and durability of the accommodatory order. This is surprisingly unfamiliar territory. Much more is known about how accommodatory politics evolved, than of the dynamics which have kept it going. At its core is a mutually reinforcing matrix of affluence, democracy and community – the supranational element by which Monnet set so much store has never been substantial. But we know relatively little about exactly how these elements interact, or how dependent different forms of accommodatory order may be on reinforcement by traditional external threats.

To understand this we need to return for a moment to the circumstances which made the new ideas and institutions of accommodatory politics possible. They were a product not just of two world wars, and the political and psychological revolutions which they brought about, but also of technological and economic advance. By mid century power politics had lost its economic rationale. Advanced industrialised states no longer needed to exercise political control over their markets or sources of their raw material. They could generate increased wealth and prosperity much more efficiently by supporting free trade abroad, while investing in new capital, better education and more research and development at home.[46] The notion of *Lebensraum* which had dominated German thinking little more than a decade earlier, had become completely anachronistic.

If power politics had become economically unnecessary – and indeed dysfunctional, accommodatory politics was suddenly practical in a way it had not previously been. The immediate impetus was the speed and scale of economic recovery which while certainly facilitated by the new spirit of accommodation, was not fundamentally caused by it. The phenomenal economic boom which saw the world's gross national product quadruple between 1950 and 1980 from two to eight trillion dollars owed more to the double recovery from the effects of both the Depression and the war, the accelerating pace of technological advance, and the availability, at least until the early 1970s, of cheap oil.[47] This recovery was under way before the Marshall Plan and well before the formation of the EEC; indeed, it is doubtful whether the Six would otherwise have been willing to go ahead. The influence of the Bretton Woods institutions, and the much later trade liberalisation under the various GATT rounds, while important, seems in causal terms to be secondary. This in other words was not just a better managed, but a much more manageable order. The point needs to be emphasised, not to diminish the achievements of Monnet, Marshall and their colleagues, but to put them into perspective. Accommodatory politics had simply not been possible before the late 1940s and early 1950s.

What is indisputable is that economic prosperity and success predisposed states in the direction of contact and compromise, just as hardship and dislocation had provided a fertile breeding ground for power politics at their most dangerously reactionary. The point, fully recognised by the Marshall planners, is neatly summarised in the lines from *Julius Caesar* which appear in a note written in 1936 by the Head of the Economic Section of the Foreign Office:

> Let me have men about me that are fat;
> Sleek-headed men and such as sleep o'nights;
> Yon Cassius has a lean and hungry look;
> Such men are dangerous.[48]

The children of the new 'settled societies' of the 'golden age' came very clearly into the former category. They were the first generation to enjoy the full benefits of the Industrial Revolution – continuously high standards of living and social and job security, with almost none of its politically disruptive and destructive side-effects. They did not hesitate to take full advantage of the new opportunities for personal betterment, comfort and travel, developing life-styles in which war was not an escape, as it had been in 1914, but an irrelevency and a disruption. It was associated with things they feared or disliked – casualties, destruction, inflation and higher taxes. Occasionally, as during the Falkland and Gulf wars, the old warrior instincts resurfaced, in Britain if not Japan or West Germany. For the most part, however, these societies looked elsewhere for their excitement, to popular entertainment and sport.[47]

Nowhere was this transformation more striking than in West Germany, where peace quickly turned out to be much more profitable than the militarist policies pursued by the Kaiser and Hitler. West Germans were anxious to remake prosperous private lives after the deprivations and the disasters of the past, a process which quickly became all-absorbing. Once economic growth had taken off, there was little point asking asking whether the West Germans would have accommodated themselves so readily to the division of their country, without Ludwig Erhard's *Wirtschaftswunder*. The question simply did not arise. At the same time prosperity underpinned the country's democratic revival. Although the conditions for this were much favourable than before – the old *Junkers* and industrial barons had gone, the power of the military had been broken, the Right discredited – few in in the immediate postwar years had much conception of what democracy meant. Those West Germans old enough to have lived through the Weimar period associated democracy with defeat, humiliation, economic crisis and chaos. Economic success by contrast served to validate the new political system, buying the necessary time for it to take roots. The passive support which the new system initially enjoyed, could thus be gradually converted into something more durable. In Mary Fulbrook's somewhat sceptical phrase, the percentage supporting democracy as opposed to Nazism in the opinion polls, grew in close correlation in the increase of the average weight of 'ever more satiated West Germans'.[50]

In Germany, as elsewhere, democracy was very much the ideology of accommodation. States founded on the principles of respect for the rule of law and the rights of their own citizens, tend instinctively to have *more* respect – the matter is relative – for international law, and to be *more* inclined to see the solution to international problems in negotiation and compromise, than authoritarian states. While not exempt from the arrogance and *hubris* of power, democratic governments which veered too far or too overtly from their basic liberal precepts, quickly found themselves in trouble. Suez was widely regarded in Britain not just as misguided, but wrong; Vietnam cost Lyndon Johnson his job. The open and decentralised nature of the democratic system gives a country's partners reassurance about its long-term stability and predictability, and thus greatly facilitates the constant process of negotiation and compromise at the heart of accommodatory politics. Democracies, as John Ikenberry puts it, 'do not just sign agreements; they create political processes that reduce uncertainty and build confidence in mutual commitments'.[51] The sheer intensity, intimacy and extent of dealings within the European Community would have been impossible among a less homogeneous, tolerant and pacifically-inclined group of countries.

Whether however, this combination of affluence and democracy would on its own have been sufficient to faciltate an accommodatory system as sophisticated as the EEC, is another matter. For all its very real strengths and merits, the postwar accommodatory order was no more than a subsystem which evolved and survived in the shadow of power politics. Although Marshall's 1947 offer to help reconstruct the economies of

Europe had been open to all countries, it was made in the confident expectation that Moscow would refuse to participate. One of the factors which had impelled the Secretary of State to take the initiative in the spring of 1947 was precisely the belief that Moscow had a political interest in seeing Western European economies fail.[52] At least part of the subsequent impetus to European integration must be ascribed to the manner in which the American initiative served to hasten the process of division. As Paul-Henri Spaak notes, Stalin has a claim to rival Monnet or Schumann as the 'father of Europe'.[53] His successors from Khrushchev to Chernenko ensured that such differences as did arise, whether between the US and its new allies or even within the EEC, were resolved without undue difficulty.

The importance of the Soviet threat diminished over time as economic interdependence increased and the new order took more independent roots. The richer Western states became, the larger and more complicated their economies, the more they needed the accommodatory order. And the better the accommodatory order worked, the more it served to underpin Western economic success and political unity, the more important a factor it became in the Cold War. Western Europe became an advertisement for the success of the liberal-accommodatory model, just as Eastern Europe demonstrated the failure of Soviet system. Divison nevertheless required strong defences. The two systems might be physically separated by wall, barbed wire and watch towers; the two peaces – the products respectively of liberal affluence and nuclear deterrence – could not be. Having renounced power politics themselves the West Germans found that they had become host to the world's greatest concentration of military power – more than four decades after Hitler's defeat there were still some 400 000 foreign troops on its territory.[54] But the problem was not simply one of numbers or megatonnage – West Germany had become a veritable devil's cauldron of tactical nuclear weapons. Who provided the man and the firepower was as, if not more relevant. For when it came to dealing with residual issues of military power, the West Europeans could not, or would not, cope.

Once again the problem was Germany. The immediate issue of rearmament which became acute following the outbreak of the Korean War in 1950, proved less intractable than it initially seemed, even if this time there was to be no European solution. The French tried. The Defence Minister, René Pleven, proposed a European Defence Community, along the lines of ECSC. The Pleven plan has been described as an attempt to rearm the Germans without rearming Germany. In its original form it envisaged a 'complete merger ... of armed forces in one uniform, under common discipline, under single command and responsibility – not to individual governments but to all member governments'.[55] Four countries did in fact ratify the eventual treaty. In France however the EDC stirred up a degree of controversy not seen since the Dreyfus case half a century earlier.[56] When the National Assembly finally rejected the proposal, it was left to the off-shore Powers, Britain, and above all the United States, to provide the military might and no less important, the long-term guarantees which would make German rearmament acceptable within a NATO framework. Without these arrangements, and the crucial decisions on German rearmament were made in 1955 before the signature of Treaty of Rome, the risk of a regression within the Western alliance to the patterns of the interwar years, with the weak once again worrying about the strong, and the strong worrying about each other, would have been real.[57]

Western Europe's accommodatory order never fully outgrew its dependence on the United States. The Americans had created much of the environment in which the ECSC evolved; American diplomacy was crucial in resolving difficulties during the subsequent negotiations.[58] Forty years later the American diplomacy was needed to overcome West European, as much as Soviet reluctance in the face of German unification. At one point Mrs Thatcher proposed that Soviet troops should be allowed to stay indefinitely in a united Germany.[59] Small wonder if Chancellor Kohl was driven in frustration to ask the American Secretary of State, James Baker, why West Germany had failed to establish its credentials as a reliable partner. 'Why,' he asked, 'doesn't that help? Logic doesn't help.'[60]

It did as far as the Americans were concerned. Because they were so much more powerful, had suffered relatively much less than their other West European allies, and remained geographically more detached, the Americans could afford to take a cooler, more far-sighted view of the most profound change in European history for forty years. They were much more willing to accept that the time bought by division had been well spent and that, contrary to Mrs Thatcher's belief, Germany had genuinely changed since 1945. They had no truck with the British Prime Minister's view that the Germans would now 'get in peace what Hitler couldn't get in war'.[61] Five years later it was left to the Americans to provide the impetus for a NATO intervention in Yugoslavia after the European Union had conspicuously failed to provide a European solution to what they had insisted in identifying as a European problem. The ability to harmonise interests at the economic and social level had still not been translated into the military dimensions of foreign policy. It was a real, and troubling, failure.

That said, this was a limited and incomplete, rather than a flawed experiment. The 'wise men' of the Atlantic community had gone much further than any of their predecessors in terms of putting power politics behind them. They had done so by marrying a new division of sovereignty between national and international institutions, with elements of the more familiar but hitherto inadequate liberal prescription for peace, international cooperation, free trade and prosperity. In the process they had succeeded in bypassing the problems of enforcement which had defeated Wilson and the supporters of the League of Nations. Power had not of course been rendered obsolete. But the word had begun to lose its glorifying overtones, coming instead to be seen only as the capacity to act.[62]

9 No Other Choice?

The implications of the accommodatory peace are far-reaching. They point towards a rule-based alternative to power politics in which national interests are balanced against those of a larger international society, which could prove of much wider application in the aftermath of the Cold War. But before assessing this prospect, we need to look again at the peculiarly intractable form which the problem of power took for most of the twentieth century. States found themselves facing a dual threat – from war and technological advance, as well as from the more familiar dangers generated by mutual rivalries and the anarchical structure of the international system. Far from easing, these traditional political dangers intensified. While neither Germany nor the Soviet Union had ultimately the power to realise their hegemonial ambitions, the cost of defeating them was immense. Matters were made worse by a series of mistakes and miscalculations, beginning with the failure to recognise the potentially 'suicidal' nature of war before 1914. In 1918 the Allies failed either to press home the defeat of Germany or to establish a lasting settlement. When German power revived in the 1930s the British and French sought appeasement, the Americans retrated into isolationism. The Cold War, while more skilfully handled, was nevertheless characterised by an absence of a sense of political discrimination and military proportion.

Why was the record quite so bad? Were twentieth-century leaders particularly unskilful in the exercise of *Realpolitik*? Were the problems they faced so daunting that power could be said to be verging on the unmanagable? As Kurt Riesler, Bethmann Hollweg's secretary, lamented in mid July 1914, 'This damnably confused modern world has become so complex that it can neither be grasped nor predicted. There are too many factors at once.'[1] Or was it rather a failure, cultural as much as technical, to master that complexity? These questions are made more pertinent by the extraordinary nature of the nuclear risks which the superpowers chose to run, and the nagging suspicion that despite their protestations of the need to build yet more weapons, or go closer to the brink, political leaders may have had more alternatives than they chose to claim.

In so far as it is possible to identify a common determinant to this complex of problems, it lies in the impact of the Industrial Revolution first on the distribution of and disposition to use power, and second on the pace and direction of military change. The twentieth century saw the emergence

of a new international revisionism born of a combination of the energies
and frustrations of the earlier phases of industrialisation, and later in the
1930s of the worst failure of Capitalism. Ambitious and arrogant but at the
same time disturbed and devoid of the institutions necessary to counter
their inbuilt instinct for excess, the new revisionists had no sense of limits.
They simply did not know where to stop. They consistently defied the
wise admonition of the Huguenot statesman, the Duke of Rohan that 'one
must not let oneself be guided by disorderly appetites, which make us
often undertake tasks beyond our strength; nor by violent passions, which
agitate us in various ways as soon as they possess us ... but by our own
interest guided by reason alone, which must be the rule of our actions'.[2]
Instead they allowed their pursuit of power to corrupt and impair judgement, overstating their own strength, while underestimating the risks and
dangers which war or coercive diplomacy entailed.

Nowhere was this more persistently true than in Germany. 'Germany as
the All-Powerful will not keep her balance for long', Romain Rolland had
noted in 1899 after first hearing Richard Strauss's setting of *Also Sprach
Zarathustra*. 'Nietzsche, Strauss, the Kaiser – giddiness blows through her
brain. Neroism is in the air.' German policy prior to the First World War
showed 'a fatal unwisdom'.[3] The German leadership had made no attempt
either to define its diplomatic objectives or to weigh up the military alternatives. Its war aims, in the last part of the conflict, were totally unrealistic.[4] The succession of disasters which followed the Armistice brought to
power a man whose deep-seated psychological need for violence and
conquest took Germany to total defeat and division.

Germany, however, was by no means the only power whose untramelled
expansionist impulse took on a disastrous dynamic of its own. The
Japanese government was even less equipped to control national ambitions.
The early stages of expansion in Manchuria and China were precipitated by
officers in the field. The real danger point, however, came nearly ten years
later following Germany's defeat of France and the Netherlands. Having
ignored American and British warnings not to move against French
Indochina, the Japanese found themselves facing an oil embargo which
threatened their long-term survival. Withdrawal at this point would have
involved what the military regarded as unacceptable humiliation. Instead
the country decided to gamble on a knockout blow against Britain and the
United States, thereby manoeuvring themselves into a war which they
could not in the long term hope to win. Stalin was to commit a similar
error, albeit on a lesser scale in the wake of the Second World War, when
he embroiled the Soviet Union in a long-term rivalry with a power whose
per capita income in 1949 was nearly five times as great.

Arrogance was compounded by other factors – ignorance in the case of the Japanese, few of whom had any sense of the power which the United States would be able to marshall. Lack of foresight and wishful thinking are also important. They were crucial factors in Germany's policy in 1914, not least because of the failure of decision-making machinery to adopt to the complexities of the modern world. Power was much too heavily concentrated in the erratic hands of the Kaiser. Those who had access to him, had no means of coordinating or discussing information. In glaring contrast to the procedures of Excomm during the Cuban missile crisis, in July 1914 there was no forum in which options could be properly thought through. Here was a modern crisis 'communicated by means of electricity conducted using nineteenth-century cultural forms – royal protocol, ethnic honour and mystical cosmology'.[5]

Others too had failed to modernise. The leaders of all the Great Powers shared a basic unmodernity, a failure affecting the political as much as the military class, to keep up to date. Both the diplomatic record up until 3 August 1914 and the military record of the years of trench warfare, suggest men, who having failed to comprehend the forces of modernisation which spurred on so much of their political action, found themselves hopelessly out of their depth. Geoffrey Barraclough in his study of the Agadir crisis of 1911 writes of

men of narrow vision and limited ability, competent enough in the sense that they did a routine job (most of them at least) reasonably conscientiously, but incompetent in the sense that they were totally unfitted by character and upbringing to meet the challenges of a world in the throes of revolutionary change. Their minds were shaped by the assumptions and modes of thought of the late Victorian era, and they shared an intense distrust of the new forces struggling to find an outlet in their day.[6]

The First World War is the only point at which the Powers can be said to have lost control. Not during the July crisis. Bethman Hollweg's lament on 30 July that 'things are out of control (*es sei die Direktion verloren*) and the stone has started to roll)'[7] smacks of rationalisation. Germany, along with the other Powers had been prepared to risk war – the famous railway timetables were only important at the last stage of a crisis in which there was no overwhelming desire to draw back from the brink.[8] The real loss of control came on the great battlefields of the of the Western Front – Verdun, the Somme, Passchendaele – where the war took on a momentum of its own which neither the generals nor their political masters knew how to contain.

Yet if few had anticipated the course of the war, the underlying fear of living in a strategically unmanagable world had been there for some time. In his novel, *La Bête Humaine*, published in 1890, Emile Zola describes a driverless train bearing intoxicated soldiers to war. 'With no human hand to guide it through the night, it roared on and on, a blind and deaf beast let loose amidst death and destruction.'[9] The politicians, if more circumspect, told a similar story. 'Exceptional expenditure on armaments,' declared Sir Edward Grey only months before the outbreak of the First World War, 'carried to an extensive degree, must lead to a catastrophe and may even sink the ship of European prosperity and civilisation. What then is to be done? I am bound to say, at the present moment I can see very little to be done.'[10] This fatalism resurfaces during the Cold War when the sheer momentum of military modernisation, combined with the irrationality of continuing to pile ever more sophisticated and destructive weapon upon weapon, created a feeling not just of danger but also bewilderment among participants. In an impassioned letter written to Kennedy during the height of the Cuban missile crisis, Khrushchev declared that armaments 'bring only disasters ... they are a forced waste of human energy, spent, moreover on the destruction of man himself'.[11] Harold Macmillan described the arms race as 'so fantastic and retrograde, so sophisticated and so barbarous, as to be almost incredible ... sooner or later, and certainly I think by the end of this century either by error or folly, the great crime will be committed'.[12] Jimmy Carter wrote of the need to do everything possible to stop 'this mad race'.[13]

This picture of very powerful men trapped in a system which they feared to be fatally flawed, yet which they believed themselves unable to change or reform reinforces the tragic view of a century so heavily scarred by war and killing. For they had, or they felt they had, no alternative. They could not afford to risk unilateral gestures. 'The difficulty in regard of one state stepping out in advance of the others,' and again it is Grey speaking, this time in 1907, 'is this, that while there is a chance their courageous action may lead to reform, there is also a chance that it may lead to martyrdom'.[14] Truman put it much more tersely. In a seven-minute long meeting to decide on whether the US should go ahead with the H-bomb, the American President posed the question, '"Can the Russians do it?" All heads nodded, "Yes they can ..." "In that case", Truman said, "we have no choice. We'll go ahead."'[15]

Arms control pursued independently of a political settlement did not provide an answer. Obviously futuristic weapons, or weapons such as antiballistic missiles whose value and efficiency was very uncertain were one thing. Existing or promising new technology could not be controlled by a negotiating process whose hallmarks were suspicion and the desire to avoid closing off promising military advantages. Some more progress was made on the numerical front, but SALT (Strategic Arms Limitation Talks) did little more than prune and contain excess. The very different configuration of the respective Soviet and American arsenals made it extremely difficult to devise deals which both made strategic sense and looked equitable. Any hint of an unequal deal in which 'we' gave up more than 'they' did, and there would be big political trouble. Henry Kissinger records the way in which the disparity in the number of missiles, which long predated SALT 1, suddenly became an issue once the treaty had been signed:

> A force level which the United States had adopted voluntarily because it provided America with more warheads than it did the Soviet Union, and which the United States was in no position to change for the duration of the agreement, was suddenly termed as dangerous when it was reaffirmed as part of that agreement.
>
> Unfortunately for Nixon and his advisers, 'inequality' was one of those code words that create their own reality. By the time the Administration's rebuttal had compared launchers and warheads and planned and negotiated ceilings, eyes had glazed over leaving only the uncomfortable feeling that what the Administration was defending was a 'missile gap' disadvantageous to the United States.[16]

The leaders of the superpower thus remained the effective prisoner of the extraordinary disjuncture which had developed very early in the Cold War between the military and the political approach to nuclear weapons. The former accumulated seemingly indiscriminately. In the words of one senior American officer the US didn't buy 'weapons to cover targets, we buy weapons independent of targets – because they are symbols of strength, because the Air Force wants new missiles or the Navy wants new submarines – and then we look around to find targets to shoot at'.[17] The politicians who would actually have to make the decisions to use nuclear weapons, thought in very different terms. In 'To cap the Volcano', an article published in 1969, McGeorge Bundy, who had been National Security Adviser to both Kennedy and Johnson, and a member of Excomm, spoke of

> the enormous gulf between what political leaders really think about nuclear weapons and what is assumed in complex calculations of relative 'advantage' in simulated strategic warfare. Think-tank analysts can

set levels of 'acceptable' damage well up in the tens of millions of lives. They can assume that the loss of dozens of great cities is somehow a real choice for sane men. They are in an unreal world. In the real world of real political leaders – whether here or in the Soviet Union – a decision that would bring even one hydrogen bomb on one city of one's own country would be recognized in advance as a catastrophic blunder; ten bombs on ten cities would be a disaster beyond history; and a hundred bombs on a hundred cities are unthinkable.[18]

And yet this basic political reality was never effectively imposed on the procurement process. The man who should have been most qualified to do so, America's only soldier-president of the Cold War, was surprised and horrified by the number of warheads and the amount of redundant targeting revealed in the United States first Single Integrated Operational Plan. But Eisenhower never took any action to cut back on rates of production which saw the American nuclear stockpile grow from around 1000 weapons in 1953 to some 18 000 by the end of the decade. Military modernisation took on a dangerously routine quality. At worst successive generations of new weapons – the SS20 which was to create so much trouble for the Soviet Union in the 1980s is a prime example – were developed and deployed without consideration of their strategic and political consequences. When negotiated alternatives were considered the tendency, as Robert McNamara notes, was to exaggerate 'the risks associated with an agreement, while failing to recognise the consequences of proceeding with no constraints.[19] Right up until the end of the Cold War, it remained much easier for governments to say yes to a major new project than to say no.

The arms racers, especially in the Soviet Union where the military industrial complex was later described by Gorbachev as an 'insatiable Moloch',[20] had all the advantages. They had privileged access to information, which they sometimes manipulated so as to exaggerate the threat. The largely secret nature of much of the decision-making process made it difficult to challenge their claims and assumptions. They were generally viewed as part of the solution rather than the problem. Fears of where the arms race was leading in the long term, of what nasty and possibly unmanagable things might one day emerge from the research laboratories, were very much secondary. In a world in which threats were defined primarily in political terms, so that the machinations of the adversary were infinitely more dangerous than the momentum of technological advance, the critics were seriously handicapped. While they might be able to make a stand over a particular weapons system with obviously destabilising potential, they could never get a handle over the arms race as a whole; sooner rather than later they found themselves up against the 'we have no alternative' riposte; failure to deploy more or develop new weapons would give the adversary a dangerous advantage.

Few in fact tried, or at least tried with any persistence. Legislators did not present a sustained challenge to nuclear excess. Public opinion oscillated between long periods of acquiesence and indifference, and sudden concern which from the political viewpoint proved an uncertain instrument. Attention to nuclear matters never lasted long. Real change was dependent on a very small group of men. If a President, Prime Minister or General Secretary of the Communist Party was willing to think radically and invest substantial amounts of time and political capital in the pursuit of alternatives, then things could be achieved. But these were busy men who for the most part felt they had many other, more pressing and politically important issues on their agenda. None of them, prior to Gorbachev, could see a real way out. While they genuinely wanted the success of a test-ban treaty or a strategic arms limitation agreement, in the final analysis most assumed that the problem could be passed on to their successors.

The results are familiar – arms bills running annually into the thousands of millions of dollars, arsenals many times larger than were needed at the time or could be readily dismantled after the Cold War was over, increased tension – and on occasion major crisis. The most serious crisis of the Cold War was a crisis about missiles and the strategic balance. None of this, however, led, or indeed contributed, to war. This was a very different state of affairs to the one which had prevailed in the conventional era. Although the arms race had not actually caused the First World War, it was in David Stevenson words, 'a necessary precondition for the outbreak of hostilities'.[21] But it was only once hostilities had broken out, that the full implications of the technological imperative became evident.

This was the point at which the weaknesses of pre-war strategic thinking were exposed, weapons development speeded up, and long-term inhibitions and taboos subverted. Prior to 1914, it was still possible to believe that old decencies would be maintained. A paper written in 1913 by Admiral Fisher arguing that since submarines carried no prize crews to put aboard their captures, they would have to sink them, drew an indignant response from the First Lord of the Admirality. Like a number of admirals, Churchill did not

> believe that this would ever be done by a civilised Power. If there were a nation vile enough to adopt systematically such methods, it would be justifiable, and indeed necessary, to employ the extreme methods of

science against them: to spread pestilence, poison the water supply of great cities, and, if convenient proceed by the assassination of individuals. These are frankly unthinkable propositions and the excellence of your paper is, to some extent, marred by the prominence assigned to them.[22]

Less than two years later, merchant ships were being sunk in the Atlantic, chemical weapons were in use on the Western Front in defiance of the Hague Convention, and cities were experiencing their first taste of bombing. The next great war, a total war against an absolutely evil enemy, saw a quantum leap in the use of the 'extreme methods of science' The most important was in the field of strategic bombing where the two main Western democracies, one of which Churchill now led, showed no scruples in targetting the populations of enemy cities. The physical and psychological distance between those who planned and dropped the bombs on the one hand, and their victims on the other allowed a moral detachment to the problem of bombing which would never have been permitted in land warfare. A Western ground army, as Richard Overy argues, would never have run amok in Hamburg, murdering 40 000 people. The result looked very much like one of crude revenge, a 'lynch-law against those states that violated the world order'.[23]

The culmination is to be seen in Hiroshima and Nagasaki. Strategic bombing had created a climate in which the use of the new weapon was not seen as raising profound moral issues. In the wake of the firebombing raids on Tokyo and the attack on Dresden, it seemed nothing more than strategic bombing made easy.[24] The taboo which subsequently developed against further use of nuclear weapons, had no effect on those charged with the task of making contingency plans for such a cataclysm. By 1954 Strategic Air Command had developed a plan designed to leave the the Soviet Union 'a smoking radiating ruin at the end of two hours'.[25] Overkill and deterrence quickly institutionalised what Robert Lifton and Eric Markusen describe as a 'genocidal' mentality, about which most people preferred to maintain a discreet silence. The moral awfulness of the situation was a deterrent to soulsearching. Civilised states which placed a high premium on human life did not wish to dwell on the fact that their security had become dependent on holding their adversary's survival to ransom.

Individually the key decision-makers who came into contact with nuclear planning shuddered. Dean Rusk recalls Kennedy's reaction to a briefing on the total effects of nuclear war, held early on in the presidency. At the end he was asked by Kennedy to come back to the Oval Office 'and as we got to the door he looked at me with a strange little look on his face, and he said, "And we call ourselves the human race".'[26] Those in more regular or routine contact with the nuclear unthinkable got used to it. One Pentagon official engaged in nuclear targetting describes how he and his colleagues 'never experienced guilt or self-criticism. Our office behaviour was no different from that of men or women who might work for a bank or insurance company'.[27]

It is difficult, going back over the origins of nuclear weapons, to avoid a sense of inevitability. If the discovery of fission had occurred at some other time, when states were not under the imperative necessity of war and there was a chance for wider debate on the question, things perhaps *might* have been different. The development of atomic weapons might have proceeded more slowly – the prospects for international control of a weapon still on the drawing board, would have been better. As it was, nuclear weapons were developed under conditions highly unpropitious to any radical change in the conduct or culture of international relations. Some of those aware of the the Manhattan Project, though not including Churchill who took only a cursory interest in the atomic bomb, were deeply concerned about the long-term prospect of a nuclear arms race. Roosevelt once remarked that the whole thing 'worried him to death'.[28] But he appears to have done little systematic thinking about the long-terms implications of this, the most remarkable and revolutionary of all weapons and what it meant for his hopes of rendering power politics obsolete.

The most radical alternative of the crucial wartime years came from the Danish physicist Nils Bohr. Bohr, like Roosevelt, was an idealist. He sought to change the whole framework in which the nuclear problem would appear, 'early enough so that the problem would be altered by it'.[29] He believed that 'the very necessity of a concerted effort to forestall such ominous threats to civilisation would offer quite unique opportunities to bridge international divergencies'.[30] The Big Two did not. Their mental frame of reference – and here we see a much more conventional Roosevelt, was dominated by more traditional calculations. Roosevelt and Churchill preferred to keep their hard-won nuclear secrets; staying ahead, and they were grossly optimistic in their estimates of how long it would take the Russians to catch up, was less a matter of calculation than instinct.

After the war the Americans partially changed tack. The Baruch Plan, tabled in 1946, proposed the creation of an International Atomic Development Authority controlling all phases of the development and use of atomic energy, including raw materials. Now however it was the Soviet turn to say no. The Soviet Union was hypersensitive to suggestions of international inspection and control. But the more basic reason for Soviet opposition lay in Stalin's determination as the leader of a Great Power (a determination it should be stressed which also had its echoes in London), to get his own bomb. Any other response would have been out of character. The Soviet leader's decision to break the American nuclear monopoly had been immediate and unhesitating. A combination of xenophobia, the instinct for raw power and also a failure fully to appreciate the revolutionary nature of nuclear weapons made Stalin totally unresponsive to Bohr's view that the power of nature was now the real enemy.[31] At no time therefore did the Great Powers sit down to talk about 'the world they were separately determined to create – a world of major states with bombs'.[32]

The implications of this failure of statesmanship went well beyond the moral dilemmas already outlined. The stakes qualitatively changed. They were now, almost literally, supranational. It was no longer a question of winning or losing a war from which a Power would expect to recover. The superpowers had acquired what Henry Kissinger later described as a 'fiduciary responsibility for hundreds of millions of lives'.[33] Their record in discharging this awesome burden is still incompletely documented. It will be a long time before we know how dangerous the Cold War really was. The evidence we do have suggests that it is at best ambiguous. At the political level at least a certain pattern does emerge. Poor intelligence, miscalculation and lack of foresight brought the superpowers in sight of the brink. But as soon as a crisis was signalled, correcting mechanisms quickly came into effect.

In the final analysis it is the operation of these correcting measures which is critical. And yet we cannot ignore the fact that political leaders were willing to gamble on a questionable capacity to maintain their control over events under tense and unpredictable circumstances. In a famous interview which he gave in 1954, John Foster Dulles outlined the notion of 'brinkmanship' – 'the ability to get to the verge without getting into war'[34] in what seemed disconcertingly simple terms. Dulles however, never went through a major crisis. Kennedy, who did, took a much more sceptical view of the prospect of micro-managing superpower confrontation. Kennedy was much more aware that the danger lay in the detail. Having studied the origins of the First World War as a student at Harvard, Kennedy was a strong believer in the 'rolling stone' interpretation of the Sarajevo crisis. During the Vienna Summit, Khrushchev complained that all he ever heard 'from your people and your news correspondents and your friends in Europe and everyplace else is that damned word miscalculation ... We don't make mistakes. We will not make war by mistake.'[35] The risk however could not be so easily dismissed. With both sides bluffing, disaster, as Macmillan privately noted in August 1961, could come by mistake.[36] Kennedy felt himself under immense pressure to prove that he had the grit to hold to his position. The Soviet ambassador in Washington,

Mikhail Menshikov was openly saying that when the chips were down, the US would not fight over Berlin.[37] According to one of his aides Arthur Schlesinger, the President worried that

> the time might come when he would have to run the supreme risk to convince Khrushchev that conciliation did not mean humiliation. 'If Khrushchev wants to rub my nose in the dirt ... its all over.' But how to convince Khrushchev short of a showdown? 'That son of a bitch won't pay attention to words,' the President said bitterly on another occasion. 'He has to see you move.'[38]

The test came not at Checkpoint Charlie, one of the very rare direct confrontations of the Cold War between Soviet and American ground forces, but the year later during the Cuban missile crisis. If the origins of this crisis are a case study in miscalculation, the record of its conduct is on the whole more encouraging. Kennedy had clearly learned from the Berlin crisis. He soon showed that he had become a much more decisive President, able, as Anne Tusa puts it, 'to act spontaneously without first demanding lengthy re-examinations of every aspect, capable of seeing his problems in full colour rather than black and white simplicities, with the courage to face the worst and the finesse to achieve the best'.[39] Toughness was matched by a willingness to go to great lengths to avoid unnecessary provocation. Kennedy regarded Khrushchev as an intelligent and rational man who given time, would alter his position, and was determined to spare him the alternatives of 'holocaust or surrender', which Kennedy himself had feared over Berlin.[40] Khrushchev in turn tempered bluster designed to try and extract concessions from the Americans in exchange for withdrawing the missiles, with military caution. Soviet strategic nuclear forces do appear to have been placed on heightened alert. Work continued round the clock on the missile sites still under construction in Cuba. But there was no attempt to challenge American naval superiority by running the blockade, or to pressurise the US elsewhere in the world. Indeed Khrushchev tersely rejected a proposal to exert counterpressures on Berlin.[41]

But if a testimony to the managability of nuclear crisis, Cuba is also the classic case study in nuclear risk. Cuba *could* have gone wrong. Tension was very high, particularly on 26 and 27 October when the Cubans became convinced that an American attack was imminent. Both sides could have miscalculated. Each remained uncertain of the other's intentions. Signals and messages were often ambiguous or misunderstood when received.[42] Stress, lack of sleep, and indeed shock and anger, all posed dangers. Looking back Kennedy confessed that had it been necessary to act in the first two days, 'I don't think we would have chosen as prudently as we finally did.' Similarly it took Khrushchev several days to come to terms with the gravity of the situation and recognise that if he did not remove the missiles, then the Americans undoubtedly would.[43]

Equally if not more disturbing, both men had less control over their respective military machines than they realised. When a U2 reconnaissance plane inadvertently strayed over Soviet airspace, precisely the sort of incident Kennedy wished to avoid, the President ruefully remarked that there was always some son of a bitch 'who doesn't get the word'.[44] In the wake of the downing of the American U2 over Cuba on 27 October, Robert Kennedy warned the Soviet Ambassador of strong pressure on the president to respond with fire. 'If we start to fire in response – a chain reaction will quickly start that will be very hard to stop.'[45] Not all the potentially dangerous incidents were known to Excomm. Scott Sagan who has sifted through the evidence now available, reports 'numerous instances of safety violations, unanticipated operational problems, bizarre and dangerous interaction, and unordered risk-taking by senior and junior commanders'.[46] And for all their caution, the Americans may have been overconfident about their ability to control and coordinate the alerting and deployment of forces. One member of Excomm notes that 'at no time did any consideration of nuclear alerts affect us in *any* way. That just wasn't part of our sense of danger.' Key officials in Washington simply did not realise how bureaucratic rigidity, insubordination and human error could undermine their strategy.[47]

Detente may have diminished the worst of these dangers; it did not banish them. Already during the first week of the 1973 Yom Kippur War, Kissinger warned that 'the Middle East may become ... what the Balkans were in Europe in 1914, that is to say, an area where local rivalries ... have their own momentum that will draw in the great nuclear powers into a confrontation'.[48] And that is precisely what threatened to happen at the end of the war when, following a major breach in the cease-fire agreement which Kissinger had negotiated in Moscow, the Soviet Union made its 'threat' of intervention. It was a brief but instructive incident, characterised by a classic combination of misunderstanding and miscalculations. Kissinger and Gromyko had failed to make proper provision for the supervision and enforcement of the cease-fire; neither had accurate information of the military situation on the ground. Kissinger failed to impress sufficiently on the Israelis the importance of observing the agreement. When Israeli forces seemed on the point of encircling the Egyptian Third Army, the Russians believing that the Americans had been acting in bad faith made their threat. The Americans in turn then overreacted.[49]

Victor Israelyan has provided a first-hand account of the Politburo meeting of 25 October.

Using strong language and characterizing Nixon's decision as irresponsible, everybody at the meeting expressed indignation at the news that the Americans were preparing their troops for military action. Some saw no reason for such an action and were plainly taken by surprise. Others saw it in orthodox Marxist–Leninist terms as part of the class struggle in the international arena. Some wondered, 'The Americans say we threaten them, but how did they get that into their heads?' And several believed that the Soviet Union's decisive role in maintaining peace and strengthening international security was making the American imperialists furious.

Very few indeed guessed that the pretext for Washington's decision was Brezhnev's latest message to Nixon. 'What has this to do with the letter I sent to Nixon?', asked Brezhnev, who believed the emphasis in the letter was on joint Soviet–American action in accordance with the understanding reached during Kissinger's visit to Moscow.[50]

The Russians had reason to be baffled. The American decision had been taken hastily, and under the influence of Watergate as well as of strategic concerns. Little attention had been paid to its details, the risks it entailed, or likely consequences. According to Richard Lebow and Janice Stein, American decision-makers did not understand the technical and operational requirements of the alert. Although the immediate crisis quickly blew over – the Soviet Union abstained from any reaction, the Soviet and American navies in the Mediterranean continued operating in dangerously close proximity, targetting one another at point blank range.[51]

1973 was the last of the major Cold War crises. But there was an incident ten years later which offers a disconcerting illustration of the possible dynamics of inadvertent nuclear war. Unlike other crises, it was not occasioned by any form of nuclear diplomacy. Its origins lay in the tense atmosphere of the early 1980s when unguarded American rhetoric was increasingly matched by Soviet paranoia. Unlike his predecessors, Yuri Andropov did not simply regard the US as a real military threat, but appears actually to have feared the possibility of an American surprise attack. What particularly worried the Soviet leadership was the combination of American bellicosity and the old bugbear of simple human miscalculation. 'Reagan is unpredictable', Dobrynin quotes Andropov as saying. 'You should expect anything from him.'[52] It was against this background that Soviet intelligence, which had been ordered to increase vigilance for signs of anything untoward, misinterpreted a 1983 routine NATO exercise, 'Able Archer' aimed at simulating a crisis leading to a nuclear conflict, as a possible indicator of an actual attack. It was, or so at least a statement issued by the Soviet Defence Minister, Marshal Ustinov, claimed, becoming increasingly difficult to distinguish exercises from 'the real deployment of armed forces for aggression'.[53] Thanks to good intelligence, NATO was advised of Soviet suspicions, and was able to change aspects of the exercise.

The 'Able Archer' incident provided an uncomfortable reminder that the nuclear learning process was not self-perpetuating; it could stagnate or indeed go into reverse. As at the time of the Cuban missile crisis, the two sides had again lost touch with one another's concerns. Reagan, by his own subsequent admission, had immense difficulty in realising that the Soviet Union genuinely feared the US. In the climate of anger and self-righteousness which prevailed in the early 1980s, Washington had given little serious attention to the way in which its policy might be perceived in Moscow.[54] This was unfortunate because political leaderships appear to have been at best partially aware of the growing military risks which acute crisis might entail. The Cuban missile crisis had already indicated the problem of what might be called 'concealed risk', previously unrecognised dangers resulting from force deployments, command structures or technical malfunctions which might tip crisis into catastrophe. But Cuba had taken place at a time when arsenals were still relatively small, and warning and intelligence systems relatively rudimentary. This situation changed radically over the following two decades, as the superpowers came to rely on a rapid reaction 'launch on warning' posture, with launch authority, certainly in the United States, delegated to military commanders. This placed a dangerously heavy dependence on early warning systems of 'incomprehensible complexity' but dubious reliability.[55] Not only did the sheer mass of information from intelligence and warning systems threaten to overwhelm political authorities and their staff in crisis, but the close integration of warning systems with nuclear forces meant that the effect of even small perturbations would be amplified around the whole of the nuclear system.[56] Under the wrong circumstances preplanning might precipitate war.

It did not of course happen. Whatever the excesses of the Cold War, judged by the standards of Hitler, and indeed Japan, these were unfanatical adversaries. Believing that history was on its side, the Soviet Union could afford to wait. In his Long Telegram of February 1946 written well before nuclear matters began to dominate considerations of East–West relations, George Kennan noted that:

> Soviet power, unlike that of Hitlerite Germany, is neither schematic nor adventuristic. It does not work by fixed plans. It does not take unnecessary risks. Impervious to logic or reason, and it is highly

sensitive to logic or force. For this reason it can easily withdraw – and usually does – when strong resistance is encountered at any point ... If situations are properly handled there need be no prestige-engaging showdowns.[57]

Memories of the Great Patriotic War and fears of a Third World War reinforced this caution. 'You must understand,' Khrushchev's son told a conference held many years later to discuss the Cuban missile crisis, 'that Khrushchev could not conceive of starting another war, because as he understood it, this would be the end of humanity.'[58]

The result was that crises which in an earlier era might have led to war, were resolved or set aside. 'Prestige-engaging showdowns' were generally eschewed. Both sides showed a striking tolerance for the awkward, artificial and unstable arrangements epitomised by Berlin.[59] They also demonstrated a creative ingenuity in getting round dangerous situations, by such devices as quarantine, blockade and airlift. And where situations did become dangerously tense, more extreme options, although usually put forward, were usually also rejected.

That said, however, the 'long peace' was also a great and irresponsible gamble. *Pace* Khrushchev's rash boast at Vienna, the superpowers made mistakes. Although the superpowers did more than pay lip service to their 'fiduciary' nuclear responsibilities, outside of crises this was rarely their overriding preoccupation. Political leaderships took military risks which they did not fully understand, and did not want to understand. They entered into commitments and adventures without taking sufficient account of the possible dangers and showed themselves overly willing to rely on rules and conventions which provided no more than safety nets. At no point did either side develop sufficient understanding or feel for the other's thinking and motivation. Rather as one academic-practitioner puts it, they behaved

> like two heavily armed blind men feeling their way around a room, each believing himself in mortal peril from the other whom he assumes to have perfect vision. Each side should know that frequently uncertainty, compromise, and incoherence are the essence of policy-making. Yet each side tends to ascribe to the other a consistency, foresight, and coherence that its own experience belies.[60]

Clearly things could have been managed better. But it must also be said that it would not have been easy. Nuclear weapons were an unsolicited legacy of the Second World War. Since they could neither be disinvented, shared, or kept to minimal levels, risk-taking was seen as the lesser of two evils. The Soviet Union could only have eschewed risk at the price of either resigning itself to the acceptance of the international *status quo*, or of depending entirely on diplomacy and the economic and political success of Communism, plus a certain amount of subversion, to bring about change. The United States had fewer options. If it had walked away from nuclear danger, or given the impression of a willingness to appease, it would have placed itself in much greater immediate political peril than it did by standing up against Soviet bluff. In both public and private Kennedy, Eisenhower and Dulles all underscored the point that the side which tried to run away from, or was scared to go to the brink, was lost.[61] It might of course have sought a *modus vivendi* with its rival on unfavourable terms, but saw no reason to do so.

This latter point is worth pausing over, because it underscores the fact that while the superpowers themselves believed that they had no other choice, the notion that this was an imposed gamble is subject to qualification. It was at least in part a matter of political choice. Stalin was offered the prospect of political cooperation with the West in the aftermath of the Second World War, just as he was offered a deal for international control of nuclear weapons. While it is fair to say that acceptance of either deal would have been out of character, the fact remains that the alternatives were there. Once the pattern of superpower rivalry had been established, it was sustained by the belief that while the dangers were real, they were not intolerable. There was after all a widely-held belief that nuclear weapons prevented a repetition of war on a world scale. Whether this was primarily a matter of conviction or of wishful thinking is unclear. It made the acceptance of residual nuclear risk much easier, and is certainly what people wanted to believe. In measure it was probably also true. In the final analysis the superpowers were both victims and accomplices. They were victims of a system which they had helped make, which was neither immediately fatal nor entirely safe. They may not have been very comfortable with the result, but they could at least live with it. Without the collapse of Soviet power, it would have survived longer, although sooner probably than later it would have required substantial modification. A balance of terror is not something which is indefinitely sustainable.

During the Cold War, as for much of the twentieth century, the Powers were operating dangerously near to the margins of manageability. The problem was not complexity *per se*, but the failure to adapt quickly enough to complexity. That failure was at one level 'managerial' – the failure of the German government to develop a decision-making machinery appropriate to the pursuit of *Weltpolitik* under twentieth-century conditions; the failure indeed of generals prior to 1918 to learn how to fight a modern war. The underlying problem however was political. There certainly were times when they had no other choice – one of the worst mistakes of the whole period occurred because first the supporters of the League of Nations and then the appeasers were determined to pretend that they did. But there was also a deep-seated reluctance to accept the need to temper ambitions to military reality. An immense amount flowed from the failure to recognise that power politics had become a dangerous anachronism even before the beginning of the twentieth century. It took two world wars to bring about the change, not just in the culture of international relations, but in national purpose, which provided the only possible guarantee that the nightmare of Zola's driverless train would not materialise. A further forty years of Cold War were to elapse before the Soviet Union was willing to follow suit. Whether accommodatory politics can provide a permanent solution to the problem of power is the question to which we must now turn.

10 A Conditional Achievement

Power politics distorted the history of the twentieth century. It need not and should not have a similarly destructive impact on the twenty-first century. With the defeat of the German and Soviet hegemonial challenges, the only remaining superpower is, paradoxically, the one most hostile to the idea of power politics. Since the beginning of the Cold War, the United States has lost something of its innocence and reforming zeal. It is, in economic and military terms immensely powerful, and is not above throwing its weight around. American political and cultural dominance are inevitably resented and the absence of any kind of counterweight creates unease. This worries the Russians and the Chinese, it worries America's allies; it also worries some Americans.[1] But the problems the US poses for international order centre much more around its latent instincts towards isolationism than any excess of activism, let alone hegemonial ambition.

Though few seem willing to recognise the fact America's end of century preeminence represents a victory of accommodatory over power politics. All the Great Powers active on the eve of the First World War, with the possible exception of Russia, have come to view power politics as a crude anachronism, dysfunctional and disreputable as well as suicidally dangerous. They have come to accept that the pursuit of national interests must be subject to international rules, and that might is decidedly not right. The question now is whether the accommodatory politics of the West can be extended to the states which emerged from the collapse of the old European, Soviet and colonial empires. How long will power politics survive in more than residual form? The answers to these questions provide important clues to the political shape of the twenty-first century.

The long-term trends, certainly as seen from the old cockpit of power politics in Western Europe, point in the right direction. Having failed disastrously to abandon power politics during the earlier phases of the Industrial Revolution, the region has become a model of how an accommodatory future can be made to work. The contrast between the Europe of the first and last decades of the century is striking. The hunger for power which characterised the pre-1914 years, and resurfaced in Fascist form twenty years later, has gone. Wilhemine Germany was a totally different place from the chastened, self-absorbed country which is only now reluctantly assuming duties in international peacekeeping operations. Germany is a leading member of a group of pacifically-inclined states for whom the ideas, values and language of pre-1914 are alien and foreign. The old atavisms of hypernationalism and bellicism, the crude form of Social Darwinism which represented international economic and political relations as a zero-sum game in which only the fittest survived, belong to another, dead world. No respectable politician or academic would today claim that war represents 'motion and life, whereas a too prolonged peace heralds in stagnation, decay and death'.[2] 'The past', in L. P. Hartley's famous phrase, 'is a foreign country: they do things differently there.'[3]

But not entirely differently. The past, as the war in Yugoslavia demonstrated, is too recent, and too incompletely exorcised to be written off as finished business. At the conclusion of Camus' wartime novel, *La Peste*, the narrator, Dr Rieux, listens with unease to crowds cheering the end of the outbreak of plague in the city:

> He knew what those jubilant crowds did not know but could have learned from books: that the plague bacillus never dies or disappears for good; that it can lie dormant for years and years in furniture and linen chests; that it bides its time in bedrooms, cellars, trunks, and bookshelves; and that perhaps the day would come when, for the bane and enlightening of men, it roused up its rats again and sent them forth to die in a happy city.[4]

While such dangers are recognised in the Post-Cold War world, there is no consensus as to how seriously they should be taken. The immediate evidence is ambiguous, providing ammunition for both optimists and pessimists in what has in fact been a surprisingly short-lived debate. On the one hand are those who believe in a long-term secular retreat from doomsday, and see the accommodatory experiment of the post 1945 world as the blue-print for the future; on the other the Cassandras who warn that the decline of power politics represents no more than a benign interlude, rather than a vital stage in a long-term shift from a Hobbesian to a more Lockean world.[5] The Realist argument that without fundamental change in the anarchical structure of the international system, power politics will sooner or later make a comeback, is echoed by Chancellor Kohl's warnings that without further integration, Europe may return to the old balance of power system, and possibly even war. To some this may appear to be a peculiarly German view, one overly burdened by memories of the past. Germany is certainly the only European country where a politician branded as being 'against Europe' is thought 'in favour of the nation state, therefore in favour of nationalism, therefore in favour of competetion between states and therefore in favour of war'.[6] But there are also other straws in the wind. The sudden worsening of trade disputes between Japan and the United States in the early 1990s briefly brought old dislikes and tensions back to the surface. Books appeared with titles such as *A Japan that Can Say No* and *The Coming War With Japan.*[7] In 1996 the United States sent aircraft carriers to warn China off any attempt to use force against Taiwan. While there certainly have been substantial reductions in defence spending since 1989, there has been no headlong rush to disarmament. Mid decade defence budgets for all NATO countries amounted to nearly $473 billon.[8] There has been no disposition to abandon military alliances or other insurance policies. Instead of fading away, NATO is being expanded.

If some of this seems irrational, the stubborn survival of 'old thinking' into a new age, the decline of power politics is far too recent, and too incomplete, to be taken for granted. It would be both imprudent and unrealistic to assume that Russia will automatically become a responsible and predictable member of international society. Although the country has changed, it has not yet succeeded in entrenching a stable and democratic system. *Pace* Gorbachev's good intentions, Russia has yet to decide what role it should play in Europe and the world. Much of the younger generation wants Russia to evolve as a 'normal' country in which they can get on with their lives and make money, without bothering about anybody else. Others including many of those in power, mourn the demise of Great Power status and have made no attempt to rid themselves of their traditional zero-sum view of the world in which some countries become strong only by making others weak.[9] If Vladmir Zhironowsky, with his redemptive nationalism and tendency to hysterical outbursts about nuclear weapons, has faded from prominence, the conditions which encourage people to vote for such a figure are, and are likely to remain, a very real problem. It would also be unwise to discount the possibility of Germany and Japan becoming more heavily armed and politically assertive, if only because there was an element of overreaction in the scale of their postwar abnegation, which sooner or later may need to be corrected. As the memories of the Second World War fade, something of the moral inhibitions which propelled the mid-century rejection of power politics, may yet weaken.

The more fundamental reason for concern, which is closer to the position of the Realists than to the historically-conditioned fears of Kohl, Mitterrand or Thatcher, lies in the *conditional* nature of the accommodatory achievement. This was premised on the old liberal belief that affluent neighbours are the best neighbours. The malign effects of anarchy were finally overcome through the establishment of a prosperous community of democratic states capable of satisfying social needs and national interests without the use of force. The consequent transformation in the culture of the international relations of a small but crucial group of states is, in other words, a reflection of the much more favourable conditions under which politics can now be conducted, rather than of any more fundamental change in human nature. Highly developed democracies have much greater opportunities and incentives to behave well than they had during the first half of the century, when nationalisms were still new and raw, and the process of modernisation was less advanced. If these opportunities continue, and become more widely available, the prospects are good. If they do not, then power politics will linger on, threatening to stage a dangerous come-back.

An immense amount therefore hangs on the continued cohesion of the the groups of accommodatory communities which emerged since the Second World War, and their ability to perpetuate the conditions for their survival. As things stand in the second half of the the 1990s, the prospects are reasonably encouraging. The glass is half full rather than half empty. What is striking about German unification is less the residual fears and doubts harboured across Europe, but the relative ease with which the process was nevertheless managed. This was testimony not simply to US diplomacy but to the roots which the institutions of the accommodatory order, most notably the European Community, have taken. While Japan is less firmly anchored into the Western system, the levels of interdependence which have grown up over a forty year period, have created a strong sense that like it or otherwise, there is no alternative to long-term cooperation and accommodation. The two countries had become so politically and economically intertwined that a rupture, in the words of one commentator 'would be so disastrous as to be virtually unthinkable'.[10]

That said, the end of the Cold War does make the the pursuit of accommodatory politics more difficult. A community of democratic states in which electoral considerations are pressing and strong government uncertain, has inherent weaknesses which only become obvious when the common military threat is removed. Once domestic priorities come to the fore, horizons begin to narrow and it is easy for old obligations and commitments to be kept in less good repair. This new self-centredness seemed in the early and mid 1990s to be matched by a temptation to see a new and potentially dangerous freedom of national manoeuvre. The disarray over Yugoslavia contributed to what at one point began to look like a return to the balance of power politics not seen since the first half of the century. 'Everywhere,' one observer noted in 1994, 'politicians are talking about reasserting national interests.' The message was uncomfortably clear – the complex postwar Western arrangements of accommodation and coopera-tion could yet unravel.[11]

It was not an immediate threat. Much of what took place in the immediate Post-Cold War years could be dismissed as shadow-boxing, a diplomatic charade in which the players nostalgically recreated an old game which had long lost its underlying military sting. It was nevertheless potentially dan-gerous because of the strains it imposed on both the Atlantic alliance and the European Union. The latter's importance had been increased by the very events which were turning some members back to bad ways. The new polit-ics of national manoeuvre threatened to reopen the old fault lines which had never completely closed up during the Cold War. Germany's partners could not have it both ways. They could not at once want the European Germany which Kohl sought to promote, and behave in a way which would ultimately lead a united Germany to doubt its partners. Under these circumstances the old spectre of Rapallo and the Molotov–Ribbentrop Pact would be revived, with Russia again being seen as a vital element in the European balance of power. European unification would then seem to have been a retrogressive rather than a progressive development.

The end of the Cold War also highlighted a second set of potential prob-lems. How do accommodatory communities adjust to major changes in the relative strength between members, and the shifts in confidence and assertiveness which may go with this? The hierarchy of inequality based on the outcome of the Second World War could not provide an indefinite basis for relations between Western countries. The enhanced power of a united Germany is proving relatively easy to manage because it worries the Germans as much as their partners. The enhanced power of Western Europe and Japan *vis-à-vis* the United States is potentially more trouble-some. Japan has so far shown remarkably little sign of rebelling against the overdependence which has marked its relationship with the the US. The pacifism imposed after the defeat 1945 has been translated into a deep-rooted passivism.[12] The United States on the other hand responded badly to suggestions that its economic power might be slipping against it in favour of its Pacific ally. The people of a strong nation, particularly when they have an uneasy sense of decline, do not like to seem losers. No matter that the US remained an immensely wealthy country with a GNP significantly larger than that of Japan. The trends in the early and mid 1990s seemed to be against her; economic primacy suddenly mattered in a way it had not done in a more self-confident era. 'In real politics', as Ronald Steel noted in 1995, 'unlike the world of abstractions where economic theorists live – it is relative gains that count. The key issue politically is not how much the total pie grows when world trade expands, but whose share is getting bigger. The American share is not growing; that of its economic rivals [i.e. Cold War allies] is.'[13]

A key source of accommodatory strength when things are going well, economics become a source of weakness and contention once the going begins to get rougher. The immediate problem in this particular case was exacerbated by a combination of very different economic priorities, cultural dissimilarity and latent racial tensions going back well before the Second World War, which common strategic interests had previously helped to overlay. But the broader lesson, that shared democratic values are no guarantee against serious economic friction, is of much wider applicability. Once populist politicians convince electorates that job losses are the result of 'unfair' competition on the part of allies or partners, or that protectionism provides an easy solution to highly intractable domestic problems of competitiveness, intolerance and xenophobia can still very quickly come back to the surface. The underlying habits of respect and cooperation, the instinct to look for common solutions to common problems on which accommodatory politics are premised, are consequently impaired.

This need not mean breakdown – existing arrangements are probably capable of absorbing a good deal of recurrent tension and friction. But any significant deterioration in relations would make it more difficult to deal with what must be the most serious long-term threat to the accommodatory order, a major international economic or financial crisis.[14] Here we enter on uncharted territory. Institutions such as GATT (General Agreement on Tariffs and Trade), and now the World Trade Organisation, the International Monetary Fund (IMF) and indeed the European Union all evolved during a period of economic boom. While they have coped with stagnation, recession and exchange rate instability, they have never been faced with an economic crisis on the scale of the 1930s. The potential for panic within a worldwide system in which the flow of information has become instantaneous, is considerable. The capacity of existing institutions to prevent or contain a breakdown of such a highly integrated economic and financial system, much of which is not under the full control of national or international authorities, is almost bound to be severely tested at some point. It could be seriously impaired if the world's leading economic power found itself increasingly at odds with its main partners. And it would dwindle to the point of non-existence if geoeconomics, 'the pursuit of adverserial gains by commercial means' ever became a reality, or if free trade gives way to establishment of a series of three rival trading blocs in the form of North American, Asia and Europe.[15]

A major international crisis precipitating a return to the reactionary power politics last seen in the 1930s, is a nightmare scenario because it suggests the kind of circumstances in which nuclear weapons might provide not a safety net, as they did for much of the Cold War, but a trigger. The superpowers had taken risks; they had less control over events and arsenals than they cared to believe. But they were constrained by a healthy fear and respect for what even the most 'limited' nuclear exchange would mean. The strength of this elemental instinct for survival should not be underestimated. A leader who showed signs of extreme nuclear irrationality, might well precipitate a coup. The charge of adventurism over the Cuban missile crisis contributed to Khrushchev's eventual removal two years later. More speedy action by the military or other elements within a government cannot however be taken for granted. On the contrary, the kind of leadership which evolved out of a climate of anger and immoderation brought about by widescale financial loss and economic hardship, would be much more inclined to take risks than any of its predecessors, more difficult to deter, and perhaps most alarming of all, much more capable of effective intimidation.

These however are worst possible case scenarios. While the possibility of regression or even disintegration cannot and should not be excluded – there are real problems here which have yet to be adequately addressed, the balance of probability currently favours the survival and development of the accommodatory order. How far and fast it will extend to 'new' states, which gained *de facto* or *de jure* independence since the Second World War, is much less certain. The question is important because the break-up of empires has opened up a whole new arena for power politics at the very time when it is in decline at the core of the system. While the accommodatory order accounts for the large part of the world's GNP, it accounts for a much smaller part of its population, as indeed of UN membership. Over the mid to long term the situation is likely to change quite dramatically. As Max Singer reminds us, prior to 1900 it was impossible for any country to

> provide most of its citizens with a high school education and with conditions good enough so that they were able to live to see their grandchildren ... Today about one-fourth of the world's people live in wealthy countries. And the wealth is spreading so fast that by the end of the next century more than three-quarters of the world's people are likely to be living in wealthy countries.[16]

The outlook over the short to medium term is less certain. So far the only post-colonial area to which wealth has already spread is East Asia, where it has immediately fed through into increased defence expenditure. Observers are divided. 'Back to the future' realists believe that Asia could easily destabilise with classical balance of power politics dominating its international relations. Others like the Singaporean Kishore Mahbubani, insist that the region would not be so stupid as to turn away from the domestic challenges and opportunities which affluence provide, to engage in military rivalries, thereby snatching 'failure once more from the jaws of victory'.[17]

The case for the accommodatory rationalism rests in the first place on the restraints and disciplines which access to a highly interdependent economic and financial system imposes. States tempted to deviate from the accommodatory norms, must reckon with the fact that assertive or internationally unsocial behaviour may carry a high price in terms of access to international capital, investment, and respectability. This matters in a world in which domestic power is increasingly bound up with the ability to deliver material wellbeing. Governments which come to power through the ballot box must take account of the concerns of a growing middle class whose primary interest is in making money and ensuring a better and freer future for themselves and their children. But even non-democratic governments depend for their legitimacy on their ability to generate economic growth and jobs. All live in a system in which colonies have gone, and in which 'rich country' no longer automatically implies 'strong army' as it did in the days of the rise of Imperial Japan. Effective world power, or so William Pfaff optimistically claims, is now becoming 'economic and cultural. It lies in the success and good order or a nation. The nation that can successfully combine economic success and prosperity with social justice will exercise the greatest long-term influence.'[18]

But if affluence is a necessary precondition of accommodatory politics, it is not of itself a reliable, let alone a sufficient one. Economic sanctions for 'bad' international behaviour are not imposed automatically – and the larger the potential market, the more reluctant the trading nations of the accommodatory world are to take action. China enjoys a particularly wide latitude of dubious action. More generally the success of the Western European experiment after the Second World War indicates just how demanding the conditions for accommodatory politics in fact are. These were not just wealthy, but also democratic countries, interacting in a war-averse, stable enviornment devoid of territorial or other disputes. With the exception of North America, such conditions do not exist in any other part of the world. No other group of countries has gone so far in exorcising history and settling disputes and rivalries. No other group has established such sophisticated accommodatory institutions, combining both elements of supranationality and unprecedentedly high levels of intergovernmental cooperation. Perhaps most important, no other group has had the same chance to put the problems of early modernisation, when instability and overconfidence translated economic growth into expansionist foreign policies, behind them. Modernisation, where indeed it has taken place, is a very recent phenomenon; the economic take-off in East Asia only dates back to the 1980s.

It is still therefore much too early to discount the risk of a reaction to the pressures which rapid social and cultural change exert on what are often very traditional societies, or indeed to economic setback. China's economic modernisation is proving a hugely destabilising phenomenon. It is resulting in large-scale migration of workers, huge income gaps in a country which once prided itself on equality, and much corruption. Millions are entering the workforce without medical care or safety nets. More than 130 million peasants alone, a figure more than half the population of the United States, have been jobless since the decollectivisation of agriculture. Official Chinese projections for the year 2000 suggest that around one in fifty of the population will be unemployed. All this is taking place at a time when an ageing leadership is becoming increasingly unsure about its hold on power.[19] The most obvious beneficiary of resentment in India against economic liberalisation and the opening to Western cultural influences which go with it, is the only political party which overtly supports possession of nuclear weapons, the right-wing nationalist Bharatiya Janata Party (BJP). 'Nuclear weapons', the BJP claims,' will give us prestige, power, standing. An Indian will talk straight and walk straight when we have the bomb.'[20]

Even if the extremes of aggressive hypernationalism of the kind seen in Europe at the beginning of the twentieth century do not materialise, the hard fact is that the trappings if not necessarily the actual substance of power politics exert a strong emotional pull, which the accommodatory alternative does not. There are at this stage no obvious models to follow. The EU is too complex and sophisticated. The 'civilian' status of Germany and Japan is too obviously a function of American protection and defeat. Neither country projects itself as an international model. Arms by contrast still serve a number of obviously useful purposes. They are an easily acquired symbol of modernity and sources of prestige. No child brought up in New Delhi, writes Ranabir Samaddar, can forget the spectacle of the great military parades there. 'More than military pride, it was a mass spectacle, thousands of men, women and children, many from villages outside, witnessing the parade, it was a celebration of power. It was not a circus for bread, it was more – pride, wonder, involvement.'[21]

Arms also continue to serve other traditional purposes. In what are still predominantly conventional military environments, they remain instruments of coercion and influence, as well of course, as Paul Kennedy reminds us, vital requisites of security. 'Like the large powers in the developed world – or, for that matter, traditional Great Powers over centuries – China and India today seek to enhance their prosperity within the economic order *and* to defend their interests in an anarchic international system. Whether one regards their pursuit of greater military security as anachronistic or realistic, the consequence is that neither Beijing nor New Delhi feels able to concentrate all national energies on becoming rich.'[22] On a whole number of counts therefore power is still very much the first temptation.

Emerging Powers at the end of the twentieth and the beginning of the twenty-first century therefore are pulled in two directions – by the atavistic appeal of the armed past, and the more immediate but by no means irresistible future of 'success and good order'. Nowhere is the balance more uncertainly poised than China; nowhere is the outcome more important. China's neighbours are uneasy that the country may wish to resume its old imperial status. The memory of being treated as vassal states is still alive. A menacing China would spur the East Asian arms race and shift Japan into a more overtly military stance. Longer term China is the one country with the potential to contend with the United States for international leadership. The direction it takes, the way it defines its greatness will, in President Clinton words, 'help to decide whether the next century is one of conflict or cooperation'.[23]

History, ideology and ambition all currently dispose China in the direction of power rather than accommodatory politics. Economic take-off and the opening towards the larger world economy which this has entailed, have still to make inroads into old fears and ideas. China has good reason to mistrust the larger world. It has within the last forty years been threatened by both superpowers, and although its relations with Russia have improved, those with the United States are, and are likely to remain uneasy. The Chinese have also yet to accept the legitimacy of the existing international order. Its officials remain highly suspicious of interdependence. While they want membership of international institutions such as the World Trade Organisation, they want it on their own terms, and they want to play by their own rules. They are reluctant to join multilateral security arrangements, and have proved difficult, though not impossible negotiating partners on major international arms control accords.[24]

Growing nationalism in the face of social tensions and waning ideological legitimacy suggest that these attitudes are unlikely to ease much in the immediate future. But while China could still turn out to be the last major practitioner of power politics, it is not at this stage a major military power,[25] and will have to weigh the economic opportunity costs much more carefully than Imperial Germany, the Soviet Union or Imperial Japan needed to do, should it wish to become one. This is no guarantee of political rationality. It may not prevent the use of strong-arm tactics over access to raw materials in areas such as the Spratly Islands to which China lays claim, let alone over the highly emotive issue of Taiwan. But the internationalism which long-term wealth and stability require, goes hand in hand with access to the *fora* which would bring the country to the centre of the world stage. China has the potential to make its voice heard in international affairs much more easily and much more cheaply than previous would-be hegemonial challengers could. Assuming political and social stability can be achieved, over the longer term the accommodatory option may yet prevail.

While wealth and affluence do not make automatically or immediately for accommodatory politics, the link between scarcity and power politics is all too clear. Many of the states which gained their independence after the Second World War and the Cold War, remain poor, insecure and weak. They exist within a Hobbesian environment in which power is still highly functional. Old enmities, territorial disputes, population pressures and economic shortages all militate strongly in favour of the traditional association of might and right.[26] The economic advantages of physically controlling water supplies, oil wells or other sources of raw materials which have long declined in the case of members of the accommodatory order, remain. Iraq's invasion of Kuwait in 1990 is the most obvious case in point. Where, as will often happen, governments are weak and conflicts intractable, coercive politics will continue to be the norm.

This may not at first sight appear too disturbing a prospect in a world in which minor conflicts no longer reverberate across the globe as they did during the Cold War. But that does not mean that they can be safely ignored. Standing idly by while people in 'small countries far away' kill each other, is neither a wise nor in the long run an acceptable option. The argument is in part a moral one. Members of the accommodatory order have a responsibility to expand their system. 'Decent people', as the former British Foreign Secretary, Douglas Hurd argues, should have a 'sound instinct' to 'make some contribution to working for a more decent world'.[27] Power politics, as such people have every reason to know, is a nasty and brutish anachronism which is not in accordance with their principles or values. If they believe that the abuse of human rights and the persecution of minorities are wrong and should be actively discouraged, it is only consistent to approach the continued practice of power politics in a similarly censorious fashion. Both involve not just a breach of law, but a denial of the concepts of international responsibility and civilised behaviour, which are at the core of any contemporary notion of political order to which Western countries subscribe.

Fortunately the moral argument is buttressed by self-interest. If international order is not a seamless web, disorder is contagious in complex and often intangible ways. The problems of Africa cannot be 'ringfenced'. As its economy declines, 'so immigration to southern Europe rises, Moslem extremism intensifies and drug-trafficking increases. Disease, whether Aids or the discovery of bubonic plague in Zaire, will pose a serious health problem; environmental erosion or neglect will lead to the destruction of valuable flora and fauna'.[28] The ease with which ideas and precedents leap over borders, means that democracies, in Brian Beedham's phrase, 'have a keen interest in not letting the world become a place in which they would find it hard to live'.[29] They have an interest in not showing the kind of indifference towards violence and suffering in other parts of the world which breeds domestic cynicism within their own populations, and subverts the culture of accommodation.[30]

All of this is in addition to the more overt strategic concerns relating to the need to uphold the still very fragile norms of international order initially laid down in the Covenant of the League of Nations, into an era in which the proliferation of weapons of mass destruction is still very much of a live issue. The most tangible and pressing reason for concern over the survival of a stubborn core of power politics in what is sometimes described, somewhat misleadingly, as the 'periphery' of the system, lies in the unprecedented ability of medium Powers to destabilise and cause damage. The phenomenon of the 'rogue' state that refuses to live by international rules is fortunately rare. Few leaderships are as ruthless as that of Saddam Hussein. Most Third World states have a relatively limited revisionist agenda. Nevertheless the proliferation of weapons of mass destruction, which is by no means confined to this small but prominent grouping, has come to pose an increased threat. 'The most likely initiators of nuclear threats or the use of nuclear weapons,' notes Robert O'Neill,

> will not be large, well-staffed and well-advised governments who understand and worry deeply about the losses entailed in a nuclear conflict; rather, they will be desperate, hate-driven, small-to-medium sized powers, or subnational groups, who see resort to nuclear force as their only option to break an international system which disfavours them, or

to take revenge on a more powerful force which is subverting their power bases.[31]

Accommodatory states on this reading face both direct and indirect threats. Not only may they themselves be targetted, but their ability to intervene outside their own system, as the American-led coalition did in suport of Kuwait, could be undermined. And they would suffer potentially very serious consequences in the event of a breach of the nuclear taboo, wherever it occurred. In addition to environmental and and financial dangers – even the most limited nuclear exchange would be likely to destabilise world markets – military services would be demoralised and democracy undermined. As unprepared governments fumbled for a response, so demagogues might rush forward convincingly promising protection. Fred Iklé may overstate the case when he argues that were the era of nuclear nonuse to end violently, 'many countries might freely choose dictatorships to survive.'[32] But the prospect cannot be dismissed.

How long and dangerous the coexistence between power and accommodatory politics proves, depends very much on how much the members of the accommodatory order choose to do about it. They have, for the first time, both the means and the opportunity to extend their value system beyond the original Western base established in the late 1940s and early 1950s. No other group of states has the political clout to ensure action, or to turn the much-used concept of 'the international community' into something more than a figure of polite international speech. As a former UN Secretary General, acutely conscious of the limitations of his own power put it, 'The Security Council is Great Britain, is France is United States is Russia. They are the international community. They have decided, they have accepted, they have sent the troops, they are their own troops. The UN depends on the will of the major countries.'[33]

It depends too on their unrivalled set of resources, skills and experience. These range from logistic and technical support for peacekeeping operations to models of regional economic integration or confidence-building regimes which are there for other countries to adapt of develop. Some accommodatory organisations are open to wider membership. NATO and the European Union, are already in the process of expanding to take in new members from Eastern Europe. These are slow and difficult processes, both because they involve costs for the existing accommodatory community and because, in the case of NATO, it begs more than it solves the question of how to handle a Russia which is at once too large and insufficiently stable to be integrated into a European system. But the potential prize of the boldest geopolitical projects of a generation is considerable. On the most optimistic reading, it would mean the completion of the European order originally established by the Marshall Plan, extending the zone of stability and civilised conduct which until now has run from the Atlantic to Elbe, as far as the Urals.[34]

Outside Europe the emphasis is on dealing with the most obviously dangerous manifestations of power politics such as nuclear proliferation and a final settlement of the Arab–Israeli dispute, as well as on extending the underlying conditions of democracy and prosperity, on which accommodatory politics depends. The World Trade Organisation, which has considerably greater powers than its predecessor, is a notable case in point. Expanded membership offers a means not just of promoting free trade but encouraging the kind of domestic economic policies conducive to cooperative and internationally-minded foreign policies.[35]

While this may sound a comprehensive agenda, it is a far cry from the clarion calls for a new world order heard during the two world wars, and again, very briefly from President Bush in 1990. This is partly a reflection of the extent to which the problem of power politics is being subsumed into the wider process of creating a more benign international order which applies similar liberal, non-warrior norms to politics at the domestic and international level. Partly too it is a matter of lessons having been learned – the unrealism of the grand Wilsonian and Rooseveltian designs, the success of the 'indirect approach' pioneered by Bretton Woods, Monnet and the Marshall planners. But it is also a reflection of a mood of incremental, and somewhat weary pragmatism which characterised the immediate Post-Cold War years, as the leading members of the accommodatory order hastened to attend to economic affairs. There was no stomach for grand designs, least of all ones which would be expensive.

This may not be a permanent state of affairs. The patterns set in the immediate Post-Cold War years are still fluid, and are likely to take some time to set. Accommodatory politics may yet enter into a more dynamic and purposeful phase. For the time being, however, our outlook is conditioned by the oddly mixed legacy from the Cold War. While the Western victory was a victory of accommodatory over power politics, providing substantial opportunities for the further expansion of the former at the expense of the latter, the elimination of power politics was never a main political aim of this conflict. Had nuclear controversy taken hold before the 1980s, things might perhaps have been different. As it was the early impact of this weapon was certainly, by Nils Bohr's standards, strikingly unradical, seeming to dull rather than to excite a sense of real danger. For most of the time the hope that deterrence worked, overwhelmed the fear that it might not. The old game could continue with new rules. With the

Cold War over, the immediate instinct is to forget more than to re-evaluate. Superpower arsenals are in the – gradual – process of significant reduction; there is no obvious great threat on the international horizon. All this may be unfortunate, but it is hardly surprising. On the contrary, it is a variation on a classic theme. While power politics makes its presence unmistakeably felt, its absence or recession, like that of any threat, is too easily taken for granted. A great deal has happened since Tirpitz's naval challenge, to move power politics from centre to side stage, but much more will have to be done before it moves permanently into the wings. This is good news, but it is not good enough.

References

1 A Deadly Anachronism

1. Gerhard Weinberg, *A World At Arms – A Global History of World War II* (Cambridge University Press, Cambridge, 1994) p. 894; Alan Bullock, *Hitler and Stalin – Parallel Lives* (Harper Collins, London, 1991) pp. 1086–7.
2. Zbigniew Brzezinski, *Out of Control – Global Turmoil on the Eve of the Twenty-First Century* (Scribners, New York, 1993) p. 10.
3. Eric Hobsbawm, *Age of Extremes – the Short Twentieth Century 1914–1991* (Michael Joseph, London, 1994) p. 1.
4. Martin Wight, *Power Politics* (edited Hedley Bull and Carsten Holbraad) (Penguin Books, Harmondsworth, 1979) p. 29. See also George Schwarzenberger, *Power Politics – A Study of World Society* (Stevens & Sons, London, third edn 1964) p. 14.
5. Henry Kissinger, *Diplomacy* (Simon & Schuster, London, 1995 pb edn) p. 58; Edward Crankshaw, *Bismarck* (Macmillan, London, 1982, pb edn) p. 181; Otto Pflanze, 'Bismarck's *Realpolitik*' in James Sheehan (ed.), *Imperial Germany* (New Viewpoints, New York and London, 1976) p. 176.
6. Quoted in Albert Sorel, *Europe and the French Revolution – The Political Traditions of the Old Regime* (translated and edited Alfred Cobban and J. W. Hunt) (Collins, London, 1969) p. 45.
7. Ernst Haas, 'The Balance of Power: Prescription, Concept or Propaganda?', *World Politics*, July 1953, p. 470.
8. Sorel, op. cit., p. 60.
9. William Fox, *The Super-Powers – The United States, Britain and the Soviet Union – their Responsibilies for Peace* (Harcourt Brace & Co, New York, 1944) p. 5.
10. Ivan Bloch, *Is War Now Impossible?* (Translated W. T. Stead, Grant Richards, London, 1899) p. xxxi.
11. Carsten Holbraad, *The Concert of Europe – A Study in German and British International Theory, 1815–1914* (Longman, London, 1976) p. 166.
12. Nicholas Stargardt, *The German Idea of Militarism – Radical and Socialist Critics 1866–1914* (Cambridge University Press, Cambridge, 1994, pb edn) p. 152.
13. F. H. Hinsley, *Power and the Pursuit of Peace – Theory and Practice in the Relations between States* (Cambridge University Press, Cambridge, 1963) p. 197.
14. Crankshaw, op. cit., p. 352.
15. Richard Elrob, 'The Concert of Europe – A Fresh Look at an International System', *World Politics*, January 1976, p. 170.
16. Ian Clark, *The Hierarchy of States – Reform and Resistance in the International Order* (Cambridge University Press, Cambridge, 1989) p. 125.
17. Hinsley, op. cit., p. 251. See also Paul Schroeder, 'The Nineteenth Century International System', *World Politics*, October 1986, p. 7.

18. Crankshaw, op. cit., p. 246.
19. Cited in Michael Stuermer, *Die Grenzen der Macht – Begegnung der Deutschen mit der Geschichte* (Siedler Verlag, Berlin, 1992) p. 98.
20. 'Anthem for Doomed Youth', *The Poems of Wilfred Owen* (ed. Edmund Blunden), (Chatto & Windus, London, 1964) p. 80.
21. Francois Duchene, *Jean Monnet – the First Statesman of Interdependence* (W. W. Norton, New York, 1994) p. 257.
22. I. F. Clarke, *Voices Prophesying War 1763–1984* (Panther, London, 1970 pb edn), p. 76.
23. David Holloway, *Stalin and the Bomb – The Soviet Union and Atomic Energy, 1939–1946* (Yale University Press, New Haven and London, 1994) p. 307.
24. Dean Rusk, *As I Saw It – A Secretary of State's Memoirs* (I. B. Tauris, London, 1991) p. 217.
25. Hedley Bull and Adam Watson (eds), *The Expansion of International Society* (Oxford University Press, Oxford, 1984) p. 1.
26. Lawrence Freedman, 'The Gulf War and the New World Order', *Survival*, May/June 1991, pp. 195–6.
27. See Chapter 10, note 5.

2 'Militarism Run Stark Mad'

1. Modris Eksteins, *Rites of Spring – The Great War and the Birth of the Modern Age* (Black Swan, London, 1990) p. 92.
2. Robert Asprey, *The German High Command at War – Hindenburg, Ludendorff and the First World War* (Warner, London, 1994 edn) p. 75;
3. James Joll, *The Origins of the First World War* (Longman, Harlow, 1984) p. 182.
4. Joll, op. cit., p. 183–4. See also A. D. Harvey, *Collision of Empires – Britain in Three World Wars 1793–1945* (Phoenix, London, 1992) pp. 208–9.
5. C. Seymour (ed.), *The Intimate Papers of Colonel House – Vol 1* (Ernest Benn, London, 1926) p. 268. See also Eksteins, op. cit., pp. 91–2; Vladimir Dedijer, *The Road to Sarajevo* (Simon & Schuster, New York, 1966) pp. 450–1; John Keiger, *France and the Origins of the First World War* (Macmillan, London, 1983) p. 145.
6. Janet Adam Smith, *John Buchan – a Biography* (Oxford University Press, Oxford, 1985 pb edn) p. 193.
7. Winston Churchill, *The World Crisis 1911–1918* (Four Square, London, 1960) pp. 19, 110–11. See also L. L. Farrar, *Arrogance and Anxiety – The Ambivalence of German Power 1848–1914* (University of Iowa Press, 1981) p. 149; Robert Wohl, *The Generation of 1914* (Harvard University Press, Cambridge, MA, 1979) pp. 211–12; Cf Eric Hobsbawm, *The Age of Empire* (Cardinal, London, 1989 edn) p. 304.
8. Samuel Hynes, *A War Imagined – The First World War and English Culture* (Pimlico, London, 1992 edn) p. 3. See also Barbara Tuchman, *The Proud Tower – A Portrait of the World Before the War 1890–1914* (Macmillan, London, 1966) p. 234.
9. A. J. P. Taylor, *The Struggle for the Mastery of Europe* (Oxford University Press, Oxford, 1954) p. 256.

10. Grey of Fallodon, *Twenty Five Years 1892–1916 – Vol. 2* (Hodder & Stoughton, London, 1928) p. 144. See also Churchill, op. cit., p. 117.
11. David Stevenson, *Armaments and the Coming of War – Europe 1904–1914* (Oxford University Press, Oxford, 1996) pp. 279, 415–16.
12. Ibid., p. 125.
13. Ibid., p. 278.
14. Richard Langhorne, *The Collapse of the Concert of Europe – International Politics 1890–1914* (Macmillan, London, 1981) pp. 105–7; Paul Kennedy, *The Rise of Anglo-German Antagonism 1860–1914* (George Allen & Unwin, London, 1980) p. 456.
15. Richard Cork, *A Bitter Truth – Avant-Garde Art and the Great War* (Yale University Press, New Haven and London, 1994) pp. 13–35.
16. Stefan Zweig, *The World of Yesterday – An Autobiography* (Cassell, London, 1987) p. 164.
17. Seymour, op. cit., p. 255.
18. Joll, op. cit., p. 187.
19. Daniel Pick, *War Machine – The Rationalisation of Slaughter in the Modern Age* (Yale University Press, New Haven and London, 1993) p. 112.
20. Kennedy, op. cit., p. 256.
21. L. L. Farrar, op. cit.
22. David Landes, *The Unbound Prometheus – Technological Change and Industrial Development in Western Europe from 1750 to the Present* (Cambridge University Press, Cambridge, 1969) p. 241.
23. Kennedy, op. cit., pp. 257–8. See also Tuchman, op. cit., p. 312.
24. H. G. Wells, *The War in the Air* (Penguin Books, Harmondsworth, 1979) p. 71.
25. Zweig, op. cit., pp. 154–5.
26. Landes, op. cit., p. 241.
27. Zara Steiner, *Britain and the Origins of the First World War* (Macmillan, London, 1977) p. 164.
28. William Langer, *The Diplomacy of Imperialism Vol. 1* (Alfred A. Knopf, New York, 1935) p. 79.
29. Alfred Kelly, *The Descent of Darwin – The Popularization of Darwinism in Germany, 1860–1914* (The University of North Carolina Press, Chapel Hill, 1981) p. 100. See also H. W. Koch, 'Social Darwinism as a Factor in the "New Imperialism"' in Koch (ed.), *The Origins of the First World War – Great Power Rivalry and German War Aims* (Macmillan, London, 1984).
30. Kennedy, *The Rise of Anglo-German Antagonism*, p. 309.
31. Norman Angell, *The Great Illusion* (Heinemann, London, 1933 edn) p. 107.
32. V. R. Berghahn, *Germany and the Approach of War in 1914* (Macmillan, London, 1983) p. 35.
33. 'Maud' cited in Olive Anderson, *A Liberal State at War – English Politics and Economics during the Crimean War* (Macmillan, London, 1967) p. 20. See also Roland Stromberg, *Redemption by War – The Intellectuals and 1914* (The Regents Press of Kansas, Lawrence, 1982).
34. Geoffrey Best, *Humanity in Warfare – The Modern History of the International Law of Armed Conflicts* (Weidenfeld & Nicolson, London, 1980) p. 145. See also Steiner, op. cit., p. 155. John Mueller, *Retreat from Doomsday – The Obsolesence of Major War* (Basic Books, 1989) pp. 42–3.

35. Howard Weinroth, 'Norman Angell and the Great Illusion – An Episode in pre-1914 Pacifism', *The Historical Journal*, September 1974, p. 551.

36. Nicholas Stargadt, *The German Idea of Militarism – Radical and Socialist Critics 1866–1914* (Cambridge University Press, Cambridge, 1994) pp. 132–4.

37. Michael Howard, *Weapons and Peace* (The David Davies Memorial Institute for International Studies, London, 1983) p. 6–7.

38. I. F. Clarke, *Voices Prophesying War – 1763–1984* (Panther, London, 1970) pp. 120, 122, 127; Robert Wohl, *Aviation and the Western Imagination 1908–1918* (Yale University Press, New Haven and London, 1994) pp. 89–90.

39. Michael Howard, *War in European Society* (Oxford University Press, Oxford, 1976) pp. 110–11.

40. Steiner, op. cit., pp. 155–63.

41. John Gooch, *Studies in British Defence Policy* (Frank Cass, London, 1981) p. 45.

42. Adolf Hitler, *Mein Kampf* (Radius Books, London, 1972) pp. 150–1.

43. Gordon Craig, *Germany 1866–1945* (Oxford University Press, Oxford, 1981) p. 339, 770.

44. Brian Gardener (ed.), *Up the Line to Death – The War Poets 1914–18* (Methuen, London, 1964) pp. 10–11.

45. Robert Wohl, op. cit., p. 216–17; Roland Stromberg, op. cit., p. 83.

46. Churchill, op. cit., p. 111. See also Steiner, op. cit., p. 257.

47. Henry Kissinger, *Diplomacy* (Simon & Schuster, London, 1995) p. 169.

48. Kennedy, op. cit., p. 311.

49. Konrad Jarausch, *The Enigmatic Chancellor – Bethmann Hollweg and the Hubris of Imperial Germany* (Yale University Press, New Haven and London, 1971) p. 143.

50. Michael Howard, *War in Modern History*, p. 124; Jonathan Steinberg, *Yesterday's Deterrent – Tirpitz and the Birth of the German Battlefleet* (Macdonald, London, 1965) pp. 26–7.

51. Joll, op. cit., p. 116.

52. Langer, op. cit., vol. 1, pp. 79–80; vol. 2, p. 416.

53. Steinberg, op. cit., pp. 20–21.

54. Michael Howard, *The Lessons of History* (Oxford University Press, Oxford 1991), p. 68; Kennedy, op. cit., pp. 308–9.

55. 'Memorandum on the present state of British relations with France and Germany', 1 January 1907, FO 371/257, in G. P. Gooch and Harold Temperley (eds) *British Documents on the Origins of the War 1898–1914*, vol. 3 (His Majesty's Stationery Office, London, 1928) p. 416.

56. Stevenson, op. cit., pp. 105–111.

57. Tuchman, op. cit., p. 258.

58. Michael Gordon, 'Domestic Conflict and the Origins of the First World War – the British and German Cases' in Robert Matthews, Arthur Rubinoff and Janice Gross Stein (eds), *International Conflict and Conflict Management – Readings in World Politics* (Prentice Hall, Scarborough, Ontario, 1984) p. 161; See also Wolfgang Mommsen, 'Domestic Factors in German Foreign Policy before 1914' in James Sheehan (ed.), *Imperial Germany* (New Viewpoints, New York and London, 1976) p. 257.

59. Berghahn, op. cit., pp. 212–13.
60. J. C. G. Roehl, *From Bismarck to Hitler – The Problem of Continuity in German History* (Longman, London, 1970) p. 30.
61. Berghahn, op. cit., p. 186; William Wohlforth, 'The Perception of Power – Russia in the Pre-1914 Balance', *World Politics*, April 1987, p. 302.
62. Seymour, op. cit., p. 268. See also Berghahn, op. cit., p. 172.
63. Berghahn, op. cit., p. 186.
64. Robert Massie, *Dreadnought – Britain, Germany and the Coming of the Great War* (Jonathan Cape, London 1992) pp. 856–7.
65. Samuel Williamson Jr., *Austria–Hungary and the Origins of the First World War* (Macmillan London, 1991) pp. 195–7.
66. Kissinger, op. cit., p. 215.
67. Keith Robbins, *Sir Edward Grey* (Cassell, London, 1971) p. 192.
68. Stevenson, op. cit., pp. 372–5; Arden Bucholz, *Moltke, Schlieffen and Prussian War Planning* (Berg, New York and Oxford, 1991) pp. 309–10; Immanuel Geiss (ed.), *July 1914 – The Outbreak of the First World War – Selected Documents* (W. W. Norton and Co., New York, 1974) pp. 62–3; Jarausch, op. cit., pp. 157–9.
69. Geiss, op. cit., pp. 76–7.
70. Ibid., pp. 71–2.
71. Jarausch, op. cit., p. 159; Karl Dietrich Erdmann (ed.), *Kurt Riezler – Tagebuchen, Aufsaetze, Diskurse* (Vaudenhoek und Ruprecht, Goettingen, 1972) p. 183; L. C. F. Turner, *Origins of the First World War* (Edward Arnold, London, 1970) p. 86; Geiss, op. cit., p. 71.
72. D. W. Spring, 'Russia and the Coming of War' in R. J. W. Evans and Helmut Pogge von Strandmann (eds), *The Coming of the First World War* (Oxford University Press, Oxford, 1988) p. 67.
73. D. C. B. Lieven, *Russia and the Origins of the First World War* (Macmillan, London, 1983) p. 65.
74. Geiss, op. cit., p. 154.
75. Spring, op. cit., p. 72.
76. Ibid., p. 65.
77. Jehuda Wallach, *The Dogma of the Battle of Annihilation – The Theories of Clausewitz and Schlieffen and their Impact on the German Conduct of the Two World Wars* (Greenwood Press, Westport, Conn., 1986) p. 98.
78. Stevenson, op. cit., p. 373. See also Wallach, op. cit., pp. 136–8, 146–7; Bucholz, op. cit., p. 176–7; Azar Gat, *The Development of Military Thought: The Nineteenth Century* (Oxford University Press, Oxford, 1992) p. 98; Craig, op. cit., p. 317.
79. Gooch and Temperley, op. cit., vol 11, *The Outbreak of War*, pp. 24–5.
80. Steiner, op. cit., p. 226.
81. Churchill, op. cit., p. 119.
82. Grey, op. cit., p. 217; Geiss, op. cit., pp. 198–9.
83. Marc Trachtenberg, 'The Meaning of Mobilisation in 1914', *International Security*, Winter 1990/91, p. 133.
84. Correlli Barnett, *The Swordbearers – Studies in Supreme Command in the First World War* (Penguin Books, Harmondsworth, 1966) p. 23.
85. Maurice Pearton, *The Knowledgeable State – Diplomacy, War and Technology since 1830* (Burnett Books, London, 1982) pp. 128–9.

3   'This isn't War'

1. Marc Trachtenberg, 'The Meaning of Mobilisation in 1914', *International Security*, Winter 1990–91.

2. Brian Bond, *War and Society in Europe, 1870–1914* (Fontana, London, 1984) p. 47. John Gooch, *The Prospect of War – Studies in British Defence Policy 1847–1942* (Frank Cass, London, 1981) p. 38; Azar Gat, *The Development of Military Thought in the Nineteenth Century* (Oxford University Press, Oxford, 1992) p. 79; James Joll, *The Origins of the First World War* (Longman, Harlow, 1984) p. 178.

3. L. C. F. Turner, 'The Significance of the Schlieffen Plan' in Paul Kennedy (ed.), *The War Plans of the Great Powers 1880–1914* (Allen & Unwin, Boston, 1985) p. 200.

4. Jack Snyder, *The Ideology of the Offensive – Military Decision-Making and the Disaster of 1914* (Cornell University Press, Ithaca and London, 1984) p. 154.

5. Tim Travers, 'Technology, Tactics and Morale: Jean de Bloch, the Boer War and British Military Thought, 1900–1914', *Journal of Modern History*, June 1979, p. 268: Michael Howard, 'Men Against Fire: the Doctrine of the Offensive in 1914', in *The Lessons of History* (Oxford University Press, Oxford 1991) p. 101.

6. Ivan Bloch, *Is War Now Impossible?*, trans W. T. Stead, (Grant Richards, London, 1899) p. xii.

7. Ibid., p. xxxii.

8. Barbara Tuchman, *The Proud Tower* (Macmillan, London, 1966) pp. 235–6.

9. Bloch, op. cit., p. xxvii.

10. Roger Chickering, *Imperial Germany and a World Without War – The Peace Movement and German Society 1892–1914* (Princeton University Press, Princeton, New Jersey, 1975) pp. 389–90. See also Maurice Pearton, *The Knowledgeable State* (Burnett Books, London, 1982) p. 139.

11. Gordon Craig, *War, Politics and Diplomacy* (Weidenfeld & Nicolson, London, 1966) p. 121.

12. Dennis Showalter, 'Total War for Limited Objectives: an Interpretation of German Grand Strategy' in Paul Kennedy (ed.), *Grand Strategies in War and Peace* (Yale University Press, New Haven, 1991) p. 114.

13. Arden Bucholz, *Moltke, Schlieffen and Prussian War Planning* (Berg, New York and Oxford, 1991) p. 178.

14. Samuel Williamson Jr, *The Politics of Grand Strategy – Britain and France Prepare for War 1904–1914* (Harvard University Press, Cambridge, MA, 1969) pp. 187–93, 369.

15. John Terraine, *White Heat – the New Warfare, 1914–1918* (Sidgwick and Jackson, London, 1982) p. 82. See also Michael Howard cited in Stephen von Evera, 'The Cult of the Offensive and the Origins of the First World War', *International Security*, Summer 1984, p. 102

16. Zara Steiner, *Britain and the Origins of the First World War* (Macmillan, London, 1977) pp. 184, 209, 229.

17. George Kennan, *The Fateful Alliance – France, Russia and the Coming of the First World War* (Pantheon Books, New York, 1984) p. 264.

18. Gerhard Feldman, *Army, Industry and Labour in Germany* (Princeton University Press, Princeton, 1966) p. 6.
19. Holger Herwig, 'The Dynamics of Necessity – German Military Policy during the First World War' in Allan R. Millett and Williamson Murray, *Military Effectiveness Vol 1: The First World War* (Unwin, Hyman, Boston, 1988) p. 87.
20. Ibid., pp. 89–90.
21. Jack Snyder, op. cit., p. 112.
22. Martin van Creveld, *Supplying War – Logistics from Wallenstein to Patton* (Cambridge University Press, Cambridge, 1977) pp. 128–34; Herwig, op. cit., p. 85; Jehuda Wallach, *The Dogma of the Battle of Annihilation* (Greenwood Press, Westport, Conn., 1986) p. 110.
23. van Creveld, op. cit., p. 138; Avner Offer, *The First World War – An Agrarian Interpretation* (Oxford University Press, Oxford, 1991) p. 350.
24. Bucholz, op. cit., p. 211.
25. Howard, *The Lessons of History*, p. 99.
26. Bond, op. cit., p. 46.
27. Paul Kennedy, *Diplomacy and Strategy – 1870–1945* (Fontana, London, 1984) pp. 45–6.
28. Barbara Tuchman, *The Guns of August* (Macmillan, New York, 1962) p. 22.
29. Tim Travers, 'Technology, Tactics and Morale', p. 271.
30. Sir Basil Liddell-Hart, 'French Military Ideas Before the First World War' in Martin Gilbert (ed.), *A Century of Conflict 1850–1950 – Essays for A. J. P. Taylor* (Hamish Hamilton, London, 1966) p. 140.
31. Snyder, op. cit., p. 16; Douglas Porch, 'The French Army in the First World War' in Millett and Williamson, op. cit., p. 203.
32. Bond, op. cit., p. 93.
33. Tim Travers, 'The Offensive and the Problem of Innovation in British Military Thought – 1870–1915', *Journal of Contemporary History*, July 1978, p. 539
34. John Ellis, *The Social History of the Machine Gun* (Pimlico, London, 1993) p. 16.
35. Tim Travers, *The Killing Ground – The British Army, the Western Front and the Emergence of Modern Warfare 1900–1918* (Routledge, London, 1990) 63–8.
36. Ellis, op. cit., pp. 17, 50, 56, 60, 69.
37. I. F. Clarke, op. cit., p. 69.
38. Grey of Fallodlon, *Twenty-Five Years*, Vol. 2 (Hodder & Stoughton, London, 1928) p. 145.
39. Immanuel Geiss (ed.), *July 1914* (W. W. Norton and Co, New York, 1974) p. 184; Konrad Jarausch, *The Enigmatic Chancellor* (Yale University Press, New Haven and London, 1971) pp. 151–2, 158.
40. Alistair Horne, *The Price of Glory – Verdun 1916* (Penguin Books Harmondsworth, 1964) pp. 238–9.
41. Michael Howard, *War in European History* (Oxford University Press, Oxford, 1976) pp. 112–13; L. L. Farrar Jr, *The Short War Illusion – German Policy, Strategy and Domestic Affairs, August – December 1914* (ABC-Clio, Santa Barbara, 1973) p. 110.
42. Kennan, op. cit., pp. 256–7.

43. David Stevenson, *The First World War and International Politics* (Oxford University Press, Oxford, 1988) p. 138; Correlli Barnett, *The Swordbearers Studies in Supreme Command in the First World War* (Penguin Books Harmondsworth, 1966) pp. 234–7, 367.

44. Showater, op. cit., pp. 113–14; David Calleo, *The German Problem Reconsidered – Germany and the World Order, 1870 to the Present* (Cambridge University Press, Cambridge, 1980) pp. 44–6.

45. Geiss, op. cit., p. 367.

46. Fritz Fischer, *Germany's Aims in the First World War* (Chatto & Windus, London, 1967) pp. 103–4.

47. Ibid., pp. 607–8; Calleo, op. cit., p. 51.

48. Trevor Wilson, *The Myriad Faces of War – Britain and the Great War, 1914–18* (Polity Press, Cambridge, 1986) p. 99.

49. Kennedy, 'Britain in the First World War' in Millett and Williamson, op. cit., p. 63.

50. Ibid., p. 50.

51. Michael Howard, 'Men Against Fire' in Peter Paret (ed.), *Masters of Modern Strategy* (Oxford University Press, Oxford, 1986), pp. 522–5; Barnet, op. cit., p. 232; Hubert Johnson, *Breakthrough! – Tactics, Technology and the Search for Victory on the Western Front in World War One* (Presidio, Novato, 1994), p. 107

52. Ellis, op. cit., pp. 129–30.

53. Michael Geyer, 'German Strategy in the Age of Machine Warfare', Paret op. cit., p. 536.

54. 'We were all amateurs' quoted from Denis Winter's *Haig's Command: A Reassessment* (Penguin Books, Harmondsworth, 1992) p. 136. See also Wilson, op. cit., p. 318.

55. Travers, op. cit., pp. 85–97.

56. C. S. Forester, *The General* (Penguin Books, Harmondsworth, 1956) p. 173.

57. Paul Kennedy, 'Military Effectiveness in the First World War' in Millett and Williamson, op. cit., pp. 332–3, 345.

58. Johnson, op. cit., p. 184; Porch, 'The French Army in the First World War' in Millet and Williamson, op. cit., p. 216.

59. Herwig, 'The Dynamics of Necessity' in ibid., p. 101.

60. Martin Samuels, *Doctrine and Dogma – German and British Infantry Tactics in the First World War* (Greenwood Press, New York, 1992) pp. 49–50, 88–89. 97.

61. Martin Middlebrook, *The Kaiser's Battle – 21 March 1918; the First Day of the German Spring Offensive* (Penguin Books, Harmondsworth, 1983) pp. 51–5; Barnett, op. cit., p. 321; Robert Asprey, *The German High Command at War* (Warner Books, London, 1994) p. 368.

62. Winters, op. cit., p. 193.

63. Horne, op. cit., pp. 327–8.

64. Porch, 'The French Army in the First World War', Millett and Williamson op. cit., p. 223; Kennedy, 'Britain in the First World War' in ibid., p. 67; Kennedy, 'Military Effectiveness in the First World War' in ibid., p. 333; Howard, 'Men Against Fire' in Paret, op. cit., p. 522.

65. Eugen Weber, *The Hollow Years – France in the 1930s* (Sinclair Stevenson, London, 1995) pp. 11, 16–18.

66. John Terraine, *The Smoke and the Fire – Myth and Anti-Myth of War 1861–1945* (Leo Cooper, London, 1992) p. 109.
67. Arthur Marwick, *British Society and the First World War* (Penguin Books, Harmondsworth, 1967) p. 221.
68. Winters, op. cit., p. 109.
69. Edmund Blunden (ed.), *The Poems of Wilfred Owen* (Chatto & Windus, London, 1946) p. 66.
70. Fred Northedge cited in Kennedy, *The Rise and Fall of the Great Powers*, pp. 346–7; Terraine, *The Smoke and the Fire*, p. 105.
71. Kennedy, op. cit., pp. 353–4.
72. Gordon Craig, *Germany 1866–1945* (Oxford University Press, Oxford, 1981) p. 381. See also Offer, op. cit., pp. 358–61.
73. Terraine, *White Heat*, p. 245.
74. Martin Gilbert, *The Roots of Appeasement* (Weidenfeld & Nicolson, London, 1966) pp. 38–9.
75. Brian Bond, *The Pursuit of Victory – From Napoleon to Saddam Hussein* (Oxford University Press, Oxford, 1996) p. 117.
76. Anthony Adamthwaite, *Grandeur and Misery – France's Bid for Power in Europe, 1914–46* (Edward Arnold, London, 1995) pp. 42–3; David French, *The Strategy of the Lloyd George Coalition 1916–1918* (Oxford University Press, Oxford, 1995) pp. 268–77.

4   A Flawed Experiment

1. Arthur Marwick, *The Deluge* (Penguin Books, Harmondsworth, 1967) p. 261; E.H. Carr, *The Twenty Years Crisis 1919–1939* (Macmillan, London, paperback edn, 1981) pp. 1–2; Philip Windsor, 'The Evolution of the Concept of Security in International Relations' in Michael Clarke (ed.), *New Perspectives on Security* (Brassey's, London and New York, 1993) pp. 62–3.
2. Robert Ferrell, *Peace in Their Time – the Origins of the Kellogg–Briand Pact* (Yale University Press, New Haven, 1952) pp. 13–14.
3. D. C. Watt, *How War Came – The Immediate Origins of the Second World War 1938–1939* (Pantheon Books, New York, 1989 pb edn) pp. 601–2.
4. Harold Nicolson, *Peacemaking 1919* (Methuen, London, 1943) p. 188.
5. John Maynard Keynes, *The Economic Consequences of the Peace* (Harcourt, Brace and Howe, New York, 1920) p. 34.
6. Kalevi Holsti, *Peace and War: Armed Conflicts and International Order 1648–1989* (Cambridge University Press, Cambridge, 1991, pb edn) p. 191.
7. David Watson, *Georges Clemenceau – A Political Biography* (Eyre Methuen, London, 1974) p. 361.
8. Keynes, op. cit., p. 36.
9. Joachim Fest, *Hitler* (Weidenfeld & Nicolson, London, 1987 pb edn), p. 82.
10. Henry Kissinger, *Diplomacy* (Simon & Schuster, London, 1995 pb edn), p. 245.
11. Robert Cecil, *A Great Experiment – An Autobiography* (Cape, London, 1941) pp. 58–9.
12. Nicolson, op. cit., pp. 31–2.

13. Paul Kennedy, *The Rise and Decline of the Great Powers* (Fontana Press, London, 1989 pb edn) p. 259.

14. Barbara Tuchman, *The Proud Tower* (Macmillan, London, pb. edn, 1966) p. 146.

15. Robert Osgood, *Ideals and Self-Interest in America's Foreign Policy – The Great Transformation of the Twentieth Century* (University of Chicago Press, Chicago, 1974 edn) p. 112.

16. Lloyd Ambrosius, *Woodrow Wilson and the American Diplomatic Tradition – The Treaty Fight in Perspective* (Cambridge University Press, Cambridge, 1987) pp. 172, 222, 250.

17. Thomas Knock, *To End All Wars – Woodrow Wilson and the Quest for a New World Order* (Oxford University Press, New York and Oxford, 1992) pp. 9, 19.

18. Ibid., pp. 37–8.

19. Fred Northedge, *The League of Nations – Its Life and Times 1920–1946* (Leicester University Press, Leicester, 1986) pp. 27–8.

20. Nicolson, op. cit., p. 86.

21. Carr, op. cit., p. 28.

22. A. Lentin, *Guilt at Versailles – Lloyd George and the Pre-History of Appeasement* (Methuen, London, 1985 pb edn) p. 6.

23. N. Gordon Levin Jr, *Woodrow Wilson and World Politics – America's Response to War and Revolution* (Oxford University Press, Oxford, 1968) p. 180; Z. A. B. Zeman, *A Diplomatic History of the First World War* (Weidenfeld & Nicolson, London, 1971) pp. 192–3.

24. See Gregor Dallas, *At the Heart of a Tiger – Clemenceau and His World 1841–1929* (Macmillan, London, 1993) p. 565; this quoted in Arno J. Mayer, *Politics and Diplomacy of Peacekeeping – Containment and Counterrevolution at Versailles 1918–1919* (Weidenfeld & Nicolson, London, 1968) p. 193.

25. Michael Howard, *War and the Liberal Conscience* (Temple Smith, London, 1978) p. 31; Lawrence Martin, *Peace Without Victory – Woodrow Wilson and the British Liberals* (Yale University Press, 1958) pp. 2, 13.

26. Robert Skidelsky, *John Maynard Keynes – Hopes Betrayed 1883–1920* (Macmillan, London, pb edn 1992) pp. 368–9, 387, 399.

27. T. S. Eliot, 'Burnt Norton', *Four Quartets* (Faber & Faber, London, 1944) p. 7.

28. Knock, op. cit., pp. 207, 225.

29. Cecil, op. cit., p. 98.

30. Holsti, op. cit., p. 202.

31. Cecil, op. cit., p. 77.

32. Seymour, *The Intimate Papers of Colonel House – Vol IV, The Ending of the War June 1918 - November 1919* (Ernest Benn, London, 1928) p. 22.

33. Dallas, op. cit., p. 565.

34. Holsti, op. cit., p. 210; Sally Marks, *The Illusion of Peace – International Relations in Europe 1918–1933* (Macmillan, London 1976) p. 31.

35. Jean Monnet, *Memoirs* (Collins, London, 1978) p. 96.

36. Howard, op. cit., p. 65; Cecil, op. cit., pp. 237–8.

37. Salvador de Madariaga, *Morning without Noon – Memoirs* (Saxon House, Farnborough, 1974) p. 48.

38. Marks, op. cit., p. 100.

39. Terrance Lewis, *A Climate for Appeasement* (Peter Lange, New York, 1991) p. 170.
40. Monnet, op. cit., p. 85.
41. Stephen Roskill, 'Lord Hankey – The Creation of the Machinery of Government' in *Journal of the Royal United Services Institute*, September 1975, p. 13.
42. Alan Bullock, *Hitler and Stalin: Parallel Lives* (Harper Collins, London, 1991) p. 369. Emphasis in the original.
43. Marks, op. cit., p. 137.
44. Bullock, op. cit., p. 588.
45. N. H. Gibbs, *Grand Strategy Vol 1, Rearmament Policy* (Her Majesty's Stationery Office, London, 1976) p. 98.

5 The Remastery of Power

1. Alan Bullock, *Hitler and Stalin* (Harper Collins, London 1991) pp. 1086–7.
2. Paul Kennedy, 'Appeasement in British Foreign Policy, 1865–1939' in *Strategy and Diplomacy* (Fontana, London, pb edn 1984) pp. 15–16.
3. R. A. C. Parker, *Chamberlain and Appeasement – British Policy and the Coming of the Second World War* (Macmillan, London, 1993) p. 201.
4. Martin Gilbert, *The Roots of Appeasement* (Weidenfeld & Nicolson, London, 1966) p. 9.
5. Ibid., p. 152.
6. Sally Marks, *The Illusion of Peace* (Macmillan, London, 1976) pp. 104–5, 106–7; Cornelia Navari, 'The Origins of the Briand Plan', *Diplomacy and Statecraft*, March 1992, p. 100.
7. Keith Feiling, *The Life of Neville Chamberlain* (Macmillan, London, 1947) p. 321.
8. Keith Middlemass, *Diplomacy of Illusion – The British Government and Germany, 1937–39* (Weidenfeld & Nicolson, London, 1972) p. 47. See also Andrew Roberts, *The Holy Fox – A Life of Lord Halifax* (Papermac, London 1992) p. 63.
9. Middlemass, op. cit., p. 376.
10. Uri Bialer, *The Shadow of the Bomber – The Fear of Air Attack and British Politics 1932–1939* (Royal Historical Society, London, 1980) p. 133.
11. Winifred Holtby, *South Riding* (Fontana, London, 1954 pb edn) p. 89.
12. Anthony Adamthwaite, *France and the Coming of the Second World War 1936–39* (Frank Cass, London, 1977) p. 88.
13. Parker, op. cit., pp. 216, 94; Feiling, op. cit., 365.
14. Roberts, op. cit., pp. 114–20; Gitta Sereny, *Albert Speer – His Battle with Truth* (Picador, London, 1996) p. 208.
15. Parker, op. cit., p. 182, Feiling, op. cit., p. 379.
16. Quoted in Peter Hennesy, *Never Again – Britain 1945–51* (Vintage, London, 1993) p. 5.
17. Feiling, op. cit., p. 358.
18. Bullock, op. cit., p. 802.
19. Wolfram Wette, 'Ideology, Propaganda and Internal Politics as Preconditions of the War Policy of the Third Reich' in Wilhelm Deist, Manfred Messerschmidt, Hans-Erich Volkmann, Wolfram Wette, *Germany and the*

Second World War: Vol 1 – The Build up of German Aggression (Oxford University Press, Oxford, 1990) p. 11. See also Bullock, op. cit., p. 650.

20. Henry Kissinger, *Diplomacy* (Simon & Schuster, London, 1995) pp. 283–4.
21. Alistair Horne, *To Lose a Battle – France 1940* (Penguin Books Harmondsworth, 1979) pp. 645, 649; see also Gerhard Weinberg, *Germany, Hitler and the Second World War* (Cambridge University Press, Cambridge, 1995) p. 130.
22. Bullock, op. cit., p. 798.
23. Joachim Fest, *Hitler* (Weidenfeld & Nicolson, London, 1987 pb edn) pp. 367–8; A. C. Grayling, 'Tales of Resistance to Nazism', *Financial Times*, 6/7 August 1994.
24. Fest, op. cit., pp. 53–6.
25. Fest, op. cit., p. 617.
26. Kalevi J. Holsti, *Peace and War: Armed Conflicts and International Order 1648–1989* (Cambridge University Press, Cambridge, 1991) p. 224. See also David Calleo, *The German Problem Reconsidered* (Cambridge University Press, Cambridge, 1978) p. 104.
27. Weinberg, op. cit., p. 36. See also J. Noakes and G. Pridham (eds), *Nazism 1919–45 – Vol. 3 Foreign Policy, War and Racial Extermination* (University of Exeter, Exeter, 1988) pp. 611–14; Woodruff Smith, *The Ideological Origins of Nazi Imperialism* (Oxford University Press, New York and Oxford, pb edn, 1989) p. 242; Fest, op. cit., p. 214.
28. Ibid., pp. 607, 608.
29. Adolf Hitler, *Mein Kampf* (Radius Books, London, 1972 edn) p. 150; Jeffrey Herf, *Reactionary Modernism – Technology, Culture and Politics in Weimar and the Third Reich* (Cambridge University Press, Cambridge, 1984) pp. 15, 72.
30. Johan Roehl, *From Bismarck to Hitler – the Problem of Continuity in German History* (Longman, London, 1970) p. 153.
31. William McNeill, *The Pursuit of Power* (Basil Blackwell, Oxford, pb edn, 1983) p. 334; James Corum, *The Roots of Blitzkrieg* (University Press of Kansas, Kansas, 1992) pp. 122–4, 167, 191; Michael Howard, *War in Modern History* (Oxford University Press, Oxford, 1976) pp. 131–2.
32. Horne, op. cit., pp. 81–2, 177.
33. Bullock, op. cit., p. 743.
34. Noakes and Pridham, op. cit., p. 778.
35. Bullock, op. cit., pp. 766–7.
36. Ibid., p. 802; R. A. C. Parker, *Struggle for Survival: The History of the Second World War* (Oxford University Press, Oxford, 1989) p. 65.
37. Bullock, op. cit., p. 846, See also Noakes and Pridham, op. cit., p. 831, Weinberg, op. cit., p. 50.
38. Paul Kennedy, *The Rise and Fall of the Great Powers* (Fontana, London, 1989 edn) pp. 457–8.
39. Roberts, op. cit., p. 179.
40. Anthony Read and David Fisher, *The Fall of Berlin* (Pimlico, London, 1993) p. 67.
41. Eric Larrabee, *Commander-in-Chief – Franklin Delano Roosevelt, his Lieutenants and their War* (Andre Deutsch, London, 1987) p. 10.
42. Remi Nadeau, *Stalin, Churchill and Roosevelt Divide Europe* (Praeger, New York, 1990) pp. 62, 76.

43. Ibid., p. 155.
44. Ibid., p. 63.
45. Reed and Fisher, op. cit., pp. 270–1.
46. John Lamberton Harper, *America's Vision of Europe – Franklin D. Roosevelt George F. Kennan, Dean G. Acheson* (Cambridge University Press, Cambridge, 1994) p. 79.
47. Kissinger, op. cit., pp. 400–1, 395.
48. Lloyd Gardner, *Spheres of Influence – The Partition of Europe From Munich to Yalta* (John Murray, London, 1993) pp. 149, 152.
49. Willard Rauge, *Franklin D. Roosevelt's World Order* (University of Georgia Press, Athens, 1959) pp. 108.
50. Robert Nisbet, *Roosevelt and Stalin – The Failed Courtship* (Simon & Schuster, London, 1989) p. 73.
51. Rauge, op. cit., pp. 181–2.
52. Abba Eban, *The New Diplomacy – International Affairs in the Modern Age* (Weidenfield & Nicolson, London, 1983) p. 6. See also Warren Kimball, *The Juggler – Franklin Roosevelt as Wartime Statesman* (Princeton University Press, Princeton, 1991) p. 100.
53. Kissinger, op. cit., pp. 405–9, 419.
54. Gardner, op. cit., p. 202.
55. Paul-Henri Spaak, *The Continuing Battle* (Weidenfeld & Nicolson, London, 1971) p. 141.
56. Bullock, op. cit., pp. 972–3.
57. Albert Speer, *Inside the Third Reich* (Macmillan, New York, 1970) pp. 227–9; Mark Walker, *German National Socialism and the Quest for Nuclear Power 1939–1949* (Cambridge University Press, Cambridge, 1989) pp. 173–4; McGeorge Bundy, *Danger and Survival* (Random House, New York, 1988) pp. 14–23.
58. Richard Rhodes, *The Making of the Atomic Bomb* (Simon & Schuster, New York, 1986) p. 642. Emphasis in the original.

6 A Nuclear Education

1. John Lewis Gaddis, *The Long Peace – Inquiries into the History of the Cold War* (Oxford University Press, New York and Oxford, 1987) p. 20.
2. Thomas Wilson, *The Great Weapons Heresy* (Houghton Mifflin, Boston, 1970) p. 50.
3. William Fox, *The Super-Powers* (Harcourt, Brace & Co, New York, 1944) p. 21.
4. Richard Overy, *Why the Allies Won* (Jonathan Cape, London, 1995) p. 321; R. A. C. Parker, *Struggle for Survival – The History of the Second World War* (Oxford University Press, Oxford, 1989) p. 65.
5. William Curtis Wohlforth, *The Elusive Balance – Power and Perception during the Cold War* (Cornell University Press, Itahaca and London, 1993 pb edn) pp. 131, 103. See also Vladislav Zukov and Constantine Pleshakov, *Inside the Kremlin's Cold War – From Stalin to Khrushchev* (Harvard University Press, Cambridge, MA, 1996) pp. 2–3.
6. Alan Bullock, *Ernest Bevin, Foreign Secretary 1945–1951* (Oxford University Press, Oxford, 1985, pb edn), pp. 129–30, 210; Vladislav Zubok

and Constantine Pleshakov 'The Soviet Union' in David Reynolds (ed.), *The Origins of the Cold War in Europe: International Perspectives* (Yale University Press, New Haven and London 1994) p. 63; Zubok and Pleshakov, *Inside the Kremlin's Cold War,* p. 17.

7. Robin Edmonds, *The Big Three – Churchill, Roosevelt and Stalin in Peace and World War* (W. W. Norton, New York, 1991) pp. 445–6. See also Melvyn Leffler, *A Preponderance of Power – National Security, The Truman Administration and the Cold War* (Stanford University Press, Stanford, California, 1992) pp. 69, 102.

8. Dmitri Volkogonov, *Stalin – Triumph and Tragedy* (Weidenfeld, London, 1991) p. 504.

9. Zubok and Pleshakov, *Inside the Kremlin's Cold War*, pp. 18, 43–5.

10. David Holloway, *Stalin and the Bomb* (Yale University Press, New Haven and London, 1994) p. 167.

11. Kenneth Jensen (ed.), *Origins of the Cold War – the Novikov, Kennan, and Roberts 'Long Telegrams' of 1946* (United States Institute of Peace, Washington, 1991) pp. 3, 6–7; Wohlforth, op. cit., p. 66.

12. Anne Deighton, *The Impossible Peace – Britain, the Division of Germany and the Origins of the Cold War* (Clarendon Paperbacks, Oxford, 1993) p. 81. See also Arthur Schlesinger, 'Origins of the Cold War', *Foreign Affairs*, October 1967, p. 46.

13. Henry Kissinger, *The White House Years* (Weidenfeld & Nicolson and Michael Joseph, London, 1979), p. 114.

14. Leffler, op. cit., pp. 21, 24.

15. Ibid., p. 13.

16. See Chapter 1, note 10.

17. Richard Betts, *Nuclear Blackmail and Nuclear Balance* (Brookings, Washington, D. C., 1987) p. 53.

18. Mary Kaldor, *The Baroque Arsenal* (Abacus Books, London, 1982) p. 48.

19. Gaddis, op. cit., p. 57.

20. John Spanier, *American Foreign Policy since World War II* (Praeger, New York, 1960) p. 32.

21. George Kennan, *Memoirs – 1925–50* (Hutchinson, London, 1968) p. 558.

22. Leffler, op. cit., p. 60.

23. William Manchester, *The Caged Lion – Winston Spencer Churchill 1932–1940* (Cardinal, London, 1988) p. 593.

24. *Khrushchev Remembers* (Sphere Books, London, 1971) pp. 356–7.

25. Anatoly Dobrynin, *In Confidence – Moscow's Ambassador to America's Six Cold War Presidents (1962–1986)* (Times Books, New York, 1995) p. 525.

26. Michael Herman, *Intelligence Power in Peace and War* (Royal Institute of International Affairs/Cambridge University Press, Cambridge, 1996) pp. 241–6.

27. Anne Tusa, *The Last Division – Berlin and the Wall* (Hodder & Stoughton, London, 1996) pp. 83–4.

28. Dean Rusk, *As I Saw It* (I. B. Tauris, London, 1991) p. 209; Betts, op. cit., pp. 4–5.

29. Betts, op. cit., p. 40; Gaddis, op. cit., pp. 115–40.

30. Betts, op. cit., p. 79.

31. Gaddis, pp. 108–9; Holloway, op. cit., pp. 132, 154–6.

32. Holloway, op. cit., pp. 155–6.
33. Gaddis, op. cit., p. 109.
34. Leffler, op. cit., pp. 326–8.
35. Sir Frank Roberts, 'Stalin, Khrushchev and the Berlin Crisis', *International Affairs* (Moscow) November 1991, p. 124.
36. Holloway, op. cit., p. 247.
37. Rusk, op. cit., p. 219.
38. Holloway, op. cit., p. 339.
39. Tusa, op. cit., p. 83; Richard Lebow and Janice Stein, *We All Lost the Cold War* (Princeton University Press, Princeton, New Jersey, 1994) p. 90.
40. James Blight and David Welch, *On the Brink – Americans and Soviets Reexamine the Cuba Missile Crisis* (Hill & Wang, New York, 1989) p. 235; Arnold Horelick and Myron Rush, *Strategic Power and Soviet Foreign Policy* (University of Chicago, Chicago, 1966) p. 81.
41. Lebow and Stein, op. cit., p. 67.
42. Wohlforth, op. cit., pp. 146–7.
43. Zubok and Pleshakov, op. cit., p. 190; Fedor Burlatsky, *Khrushchev and the First Russian Spring* (Weidenfeld & Nicolson, London, 1991) p. 49.
44. Alexei Vasiliev, *Russian Policy in the Middle East – From Messianism to Pragmatism* (Ithaca Press, Reading, 1993) pp. 40–1; See also Betts, op. cit., pp. 65–6.
45. Norman Naimark cited in Melvyn Leffler, 'Inside Enemy Archives – The Cold War Reopened', *Foreign Affairs*, July/August 1996, p. 123.
46. *Khrushchev Remembers*, pp. 415–18; Zubok and Pleshakov, op. cit., pp. 194–8; Dobrynin, op. cit., p. 113.
47. Marc Trachtenberg, *History and Strategy* (Princeton University Press, Princeton, 1991) p. 208.
48. McGeorge Bundy, *Danger and Survival* (Random House, New York, 1988), p. 374.
49. Michael Beschloss, *Kennedy v Khrushchev – The Crisis Years 1960–63* (Faber & Faber, London, 1991) pp. 256–7.
50. Ibid., p. 265.
51. Tusa, op. cit., p. 337. See also Raymond Garthoff, 'Berlin 1961: The Record Corrected', *Foreign Policy*, Fall 1991.
52. Trachtenberg, op. cit., p. 219.
53. Sir Frank Roberts, *Dealing with Dictators – The Destruction and Revival of Europe 1930–70* (Weidenfeld & Nicolson, London 1991) p. 216; Zubok and Pleshakov, op. cit., p. 236.
54. The best study of Khrushchev's nuclear threats remains Horelick and Rush, op. cit.
55. Rusk, op. cit., pp. 199–200.
56. Tusa, op. cit., p. 307.
57. Henry Kissinger, *Diplomacy* (Simon & Schuster, London, 1995 pb edn), pp. 579–80, 587, 590–1; See also Trachtenberg, op. cit., p. 208; Tusa, op. cit., pp. 173–4.
58. Oleg Grinevsky, 'Golden Rules of Diplomacy', *International Affairs* (Moscow) no. 8 1995; Dobrynin, op. cit. pp. 46, 64. Trachtenberg op. cit., p. 193; Wohlforth, op. cit., p. 175.
59. Beschloss, op. cit., pp. 195–212. See also Zubok and Pleshakov, op. cit., p. 184.

60. Rusk, op. cit., p. 217.
61. *Khrushchev Remembers*, p. 454. See also John Gaddis, *'We Now Know'* – *Rethinking Cold War History* (Oxford University Press, New York, 1997) p. 263.
62. Lebow and Stein, op. cit., p. 41.
63. Beschloss, op. cit., p. 329–31.
64. James Blight, Bruce Allyn, David Welch, *Cuba on the Brink* – *Castro, the Missile Crisis and the Soviet Collapse* (Pantheon Books, New York, 1993), pp. 348–9.
65. Raymond Garthoff, *Reflections on the Cuban Missile Crisis* (Brookings, Washington DC, 1989) pp. 138–46; Bundy, op. cit., pp. 417, 420; Dobrynin, op. cit., p. 52.
66. Dobrynin, op. cit., p. 52.
67. Lebow and Stein, op. cit., pp. 76–7.
68. Trachtenberg, op. cit., p. 203. See also *Back to the Brink* pp. 19, 20, 39.
69. Thomas Schwartz, 'The Berlin Crisis and the Cold War', *Diplomatic History*, Winter 1997, pp. 143–4; Mark White, *The Cuban Missile Crisis* (Macmillan, London, 1996) pp. 78–82.
70. Aleksandr Fursenko and Timothy Naftali, *'One Hell of a Gamble'* – *Khrushchev, Castro, Kennedy and the Cuban Missile Crisis* (John Murray, London, 1997) pp. 160–5, 183.
71. Lebow and Stein, op. cit., pp. 89, 92–3.
72. Fursenko and Naftali, op. cit., pp. 190–2.
73. Ibid., pp. 196, 197.
74. Beschloss, op. cit., pp. 382–5.
75. Lebow and Stein, op. cit., p. 92.
76. Fursenko and Naftali, op. cit., pp. 211–13.
77. Lebow and Stein, op. cit., p. 104.
78. Fursenko and Naftali, op. cit., pp. 216–40.
79. Dobrynin, op. cit., p. 79.
80. Beschloss, op. cit., p. 536. Emphasis added.
81. Fursenko and Naftali, op. cit., p. 260.
82. Ibid., pp. 277–8; Beschloss, op. cit., p. 532; *Cuba on the Brink*, pp. 116, 119–21.
83. Gabriel Partos, *The World that Came in from the Cold* – *Perspectives from East and West on the Cold War* (Royal Institute of International Affairs/BBC World Service, London, 1993) pp. 71–2. See also *Cuba on the Brink*, p. 74.
84. Beschloss, op. cit., p. 545.

7 'Great in What?'

1. D. R. Thorpe, *Alec Douglas-Home* (Sinclair Stevenson, London, 1996), p. 246.
2. Mark Kramer, 'The "Lessons" of the Cuban Missile Crisis for Warsaw Pact Nuclear Operations', *Cold War International History Project*, Spring 1995; Raymond Garthoff, *Reflections on the Cuban Missile Crisis* (Brookings, Washington DC, 1989), pp. 154–92.

3. Background interviews for BBC World Service series, *The World that Came in From the Cold*; Seweryn Bialer, *The Soviet Paradox – External Expansion, Internal Decline* (I. B. Tauris, London, 1986) p. 41.

4. Cyrus Vance, *Hard Choices – Critical Years in American Foreign Policy* (Simon & Schuster, New York, 1983) p. 26; William Hyland, *Mortal Rivals – Superpower Relations from Nixon to Reagan* (Random House, New York, 1987) pp. 36–7; David Holloway, *Stalin and the Bomb* (Yale University Press, New Haven and London) p. 155.

5. Richard Nixon, *The Memoirs of Richard Nixon* (Sidgwick & Jackson, London, 1978) p. 577.

6. Henry Kissinger, *Diplomacy* (Simon & Schuster, London, 1995 pb edn) pp. 722–4.

7. Ibid., p. 730; Henry Kissinger, *The White House Years* (Weidenfeld & Nicolson/Henry Joseph, London, 1979) pp. 524, 763–5.

8. Vance, op. cit., p. 26.

9. Kissinger, *The White House Years*, pp. 1244–5; Raymond Garthoff, *Detente and Cooperation – American–Soviet Relations from Nixon to Reagan* (Brookings, Washington DC, 1985) p. 300.

10. Hyland, op. cit., p. 193.

11. Garthoff, op. cit., p. 1069; Richard Lebow and Janice Stein, *We All Lost the Cold War* (Princeton University Press, Princeton, New Jersey, 1994) p. 222.

12. Anatoly Dobrynin, *In Confidence* (Time Books, New York, 1995) p. 276.

13. Nixon, op. cit., p. 373.

14. Timothy Garton Ash, *In Europe's Name – Germany and the Divided Continent* (Vintage, London, 1994) p. 57.

15. Helmut Schmidt, *Men and Powers – A Political Retrospective* (Cape, London, 1990) p. 4; Ash, op. cit., p. 298.

16. Willy Brandt, *My Life in Politics* (Hamish Hamilton, London, 1992) pp. 359–60.

17. Ash, op. cit., pp. 77, 223.

18. Hyland, op. cit., pp. 127–8; Dobrynin, op. cit., p. 347.

19. Texts in *Keesing's Contemporary Archives*, 17–24 June 1972, pp. 25313–14.

20. Ibid.

21. Garthoff, op. cit., pp. 338, 349.

22. Ibid., p. 61.

23. Kissinger, *Diplomacy*, p. 736.

24. Peter Mangold, 'The Soviet Record in the Middle East', in Gregory Treverton (ed.), *Crisis Management and the Super-Powers in the Middle East* (Gower, Westmead, 1981) p. 91.

25. Mohamed Heikal, *Sphinx and Commissar – The Rise and Fall of Soviet Influence in the Middle East* (Collins, London, 1978) pp. 241–2.

26. Peter Mangold, *Superpower Intervention in the Middle East* (Croom Helm, London, 1977) p. 118; Lyndon Baines Johnson, *The Vantage Point – Perspectives of the Presidency, 1963–1969* (Holt, Rinehart and Winston, New York, 1971) pp. 300–3.

27. Victor Israelyan, *Inside the Kremlin During the Yom Kippur War* (Pennsylvania State Press, Pennslyvania, 1995) p. 168.

28. William Quandt, *Decade of Decisions – American Policy towards the Arab–Israeli Conflictl, 1967–1976* (University of California Press, Berkeley and Los Angeles, 1977) p. 205.
29. Vance, op. cit., p. 23.
30. Israelyan, op. cit., p. 37; Dobrynin, op. cit., pp. 329, 362, 371–2, 405, 475–6.
31. Quoted in Willaim Wohlforth, *The Elusive Balance* (Cornell University Press, Ithaca and London, 1993) p. 207.
32. Gabriel Partos, *The World that Came in from the Cold* (Royal Institute of International Affairs/BBC, London, 1993) pp. 217–18.
33. Raymond Garthoff, *The Great Transition-American–Soviet Relations and the End of the Cold War* (Brookings, Washington, 1994) p. 31.
34. Peter Mangold, *National Security and International Relations* (Routledge, London, 1990) pp. 48–9.
35. *Observer*, 8 September 1985.
36. Garthoff, op. cit., p. 33.
37. Ronald Reagan, *An American Life* (Hutchinson, London, 1990) p. 547.
38. George Schultz, *Turmoil and Triumph – My Years as Secretary of State* (Charles Scribner & Sons, New York, 1993) p. 262.
39. Philip Zelikow and Condezza Rice, *Germany Unified and Europe Transformed – A Study in Statecraft* (Harvard University Press, Cambridge, MA., 1995) p. 10
40. Schultz, op. cit., pp. 263, 264, 704–5.
41. Lou Cannon, *President Reagan – The Role of a Lifetime* (Simon & Schuster, New York, 1991) p. 290.
42. See Neil Malcom, 'De-Stalinization and Soviet Foreign Policy: the Roots of the "New Thinking", in Tsuyoshi Hasegawa and Alex Pravda (eds), *Perestroika: Soviet Domestic and Foreign Policies* (Royal Institute of International Affairs/Sage, London, 1990) pp. 189, 190.
43. Jack Matlock, *Autopsy on an Empire – an American Ambassador's Account of the Collapse of the Soviet Union* (Random House, New York, 1995) p. 137.
44. Quoted in Archie Brown, *The Gorbachev Factor* (Oxford University Press, Oxford, 1996) p. 231.
45. Ibid., pp. 134–5.
46. Eduard Shevardnadze, 'Perestroika: Reflections From Atop the Powder Keg', *International Herald Tribune*, 14 May 1990. Emphasis added. See also Shevardnadze, *The Future Belongs to Freedom* (Sinclair Stevenson, London, 1991) pp. 54, 125.
47. Mikhail Gorbachev, *Memoirs* (Doubleday, London, 1996) p. 586.
48. Shevardnadze, op. cit., pp. 131–2; Anatoli Chernaiev, 'Gorbachev and the Reunification of Germany: Personal Recollections' in Gabriel Gorodetsky (ed.), *Soviet Foreign Policy, 1917–1991 – A Retrospective* (Frank Cass, London, 1994) pp. 158–64; Vyacheslav Dashichev, 'On the Road to German Reunification – The View from Moscow', ibid., pp. 170–5.
49. Zelikow and Rice, op. cit., p. 179.
50. Ibid., p. 123, James Baker, *The Politics of Diplomacy – Revolution, War and Peace, 1989–1992* (G. P. Putnam, New York, 1995) p. 241.
51. Gorbachev, op. cit., p. 533.
52. Zelikow and Rice, op. cit., p. 178.

53. Ibid., p. 197.
54. Baker, op. cit., p. 257.
55. Zelikow and Rice, op. cit., pp. 182.
56. Ibid, p. 164.
57. Michael Beschloss and Strobe Talbott, *At the Highest Levels* (Little, Brown, Boston, pb edn, 1994) p. 198. See also Zelikow and Rice, op. cit., p. 266.
58. Zelikow and Rice, op. cit., p. 332.
59. Baker, op. cit., pp. 237–8.
60. Ibid., pp. 253–4; Chenaiev, op. cit., p. 167.
61. Thorpe, op. cit., p. 335. See also Marc Trachtenberg, *History and Statecraft* (Princeton University Press, Princeton, 1991) p. 213.
62. *Soviet News*, 14 December 1988, pp. 459–63.
63. Ibid.

8 Peace in Their Time

1. Quoted in Brian Urquart, '1986 Alastair Buchan Memorial Lecture', *Survival*, September/October 1986, p. 388.
2. Robert Ellwood, *Rebuilding Europe – Western Europe, America and Postwar Reconstruction* (Longman, London, 1992) p. 172; Robert Marjolin, *Architect of European Unity, Memoirs 1911–1986* (Weidenfeld & Nicolson, London, 1989) p. 234.
3. Richard Mayne, *Postwar – The Dawn of Today's Europe* (Thames & Hudson, London, 1983) p. 12.
4. Peter Henessy, *Never Again – Britain 1945–1951* (Vintage, London, 1993 edn) p. 2.
5. Ellwood, op. cit., p. 2.
6. Quoted in Michael Howard, *War and the Liberal Conscience* (Temple Smith, London, 1978) pp. 37, 43–4.
7. Harlen Notter, *Postwar Foreign Policy Preparation, 1939–1945* (Greenwood Press, Westport, Conn., 1975) pp. 23–4.
8. Henry Morgenthau Jr, 'Bretton Woods and International Cooperation', *Foreign Affairs*, January 1945, p. 184.
9. Armand Van Dormael, *Bretton Woods – Birth of a Monetary System* (Macmillan, London, 1978) pp. 2–3; Richard Gardener, 'The Political Setting' in Keith Acheson, John Chant, Martin Prachowny (eds), *Bretton Woods Revisited* (Macmillan, London, 1972) pp. 32–3.
10. Dean Acheson, *Present at the Creation – My Years in the State Department* (Hamish Hamilton, London, 1969) p. 229.
11. Peter Duignan and L. H. Gann, *The United States and the New Europe 1945–93* (Blackwell, Oxford, 1994) pp. 38–9.
12. Acheson, op. cit., p. 727.
13. Henry Kissinger, *Diplomacy* (Simon & Schuster, London, 1995 pb edn) p. 396.
14. Brian Attwood, 'Goals to Make the Common World More Livable', *International Herald Tribune*, 21 May 1996.
15. Don Cook, *Forging the Alliance NATO, 1945–50* (Secker & Warburg, London, 1989) p. 82.

16. Walter Isaacson and Evan Thomas, *The Wise Men – Six Friends and the World They Made* (Faber & Faber, London, 1986) pp. 406–8.

17. Alan Milward, *The Reconstruction of Western Europe 1945–51* (Methuen, London, 1984) pp. 7–19; Melvyn Leffler, *A Preponderance of Power* (Stanford University Press, Stanford, California, 1992) pp. 162–3.

18. George Kennan, *Memoirs 1925–50* (Hutchinson, London, 1968) p. 336.

19. Charles Maier, 'The Two Postwar Eras and the Conditions for Stability in Twentieth Century Western Europe', *American Historical Review*, April 1981, p. 342.

20. Michael Hogan, *The Marshall Plan – America, Britain and the Reconstruction of Western Europe, 1947–52*, (Cambridge University Press, Cambridge, 1989 pb edn) p. 432.

21. Kennan, op. cit., p. 337. See also *Foreign Relations of the United States, 1947, Vol. 3, The British Commonwealth and Europe* (USGPO, Washington, 1970) p. 227.

22. Paul-Henri Spaak, *The Continuing Battle* (Weidenfeld & Nicolson, London, 1971) p. 192; Marjolin, op. cit., p. 220; Peter Duignan and L. H. Gann, *The Rebirth of the West – the Americanization of the Democratic World, 1945–58* (Blackwell, Oxford, 1992) p. 344.

23. Milovan Djilas, *Conversations with Stalin* (Penguin Books, Harmondsworth, 1963) p. 90.

24. Frank Ninkovich, *Germany and the United States – the Transformation of the German Question since 1945* (Twayne, New York, 1995 edn) p. 58; Robert Pollard, *Economic Security and the Origins of the Cold War, 1945–50* (Columbia University Press, New York, 1985) p. 82.

25. Jean Monnet, *Memoirs* (Collins, London, 1978) p. 305.

26. George Ball, *The Past has Another Pattern – Memoirs* (W. W. Norton, New York, 1982) p. 83; Monnet, op. cit., p. 292.

27. Francois Duchene, *Jean Monnet* (W. W. Norton, New York, 1994) pp. 197–8.

28. John Gillingham, *Coal, Steel and the Rebirth of Europe, 1945–1955 – The Germans and France from Ruhr Conflict to Economic Community* (Cambridge University Press, Cambridge, 1991) p. 2.

29. Ibid., p. 18.

30. Duchene, op. cit., pp. 202–4.

31. Monnet, op. cit., p. 290.

32. Duchene, p. 363 Monnet, op. cit., p. 323.

33. Ibid., p. 293.

34. Konrad Adenauer, *Memoirs – 1945–53* (Weidenfeld & Nicolson, London, 1966) p. 257.

35. Michael Charlton, *The Price of Victory* (BBC, London, 1983) p. 105.

36. Adenauer, op. cit., pp. 36–7, 78–9, 419, 427; Marion Doenhoff, *Foe into Friend* (Weidenfeld & Nicolson, London, 1982).

37. Monnet, op. cit., p. 310.

38. Duchene, op. cit., pp. 399–400; Gillingham, op. cit., pp. 231–2.

39. *Treaty Establishing the European Economic Community* (Her Majesty's Stationery Office, London, 1973) p. 30.

40. Josef Joffe, 'With its Western Alliance at Stake, Germany becomes Responsible', *International Herald Tribune*, 22 December 1994; Roy

Jenkins, *A Life at the Centre* (Pan Books, London, 1992) p. 451; Franz-Josef Meiers, 'Germany: The Reluctant Power', *Survival*, Autumn 1995, pp. 83, 84; Hanns Maull, 'Germany and Japan; the New Civilian Powers', *Foreign Affairs*, Winter 1990/1, pp. 91–106.

41. Cited in Josef Janning, 'A German Europe – a European Germany? On the Debate over Germany's Foreign Policy', *International Affairs*, January 1996, p. 35.

42. Ian Buruma, *Wages of Guilt – Memories of War in Germany and Japan* (Cape, London, 1994) p. 33.

43. Gerhard Weinberg, *Germany, Hitler and World War II* (Cambridge University Press, Cambridge, 1995) p. 320.

44. Alan Milward, *The European Rescue of the Nation State* (Routledge, London, 1992) p. 330.

45. Duchene, op. cit., pp. 405–6.

46. Alastair Buchan, 'Technology and World Politics' in Brian Porter (ed.), *International Politics 1914–1969* (Oxford University Press, Oxford, 1972) p. 177; Klaus Knorr, *On the Uses of Military Power in the Nuclear Age* (Princeton University Press, Princeton, 1966) pp. 22–7.

47. Paul Kennedy, *Preparing for the Twenty-First Century* (Random House, New York, 1993) p. 48; Angus Maddison, 'Economic Performance and Policy in Europe' in Carlo Cipallo (ed.), *The Fontana Economic History of Europe – The Twentieth Century, Part 2* (Fontana Books, London, 1976) pp. 476–7; Moses Abramowitz, *Thinking about Economic Growth* (Cambridge University Press, Cambridge, 1989), pp. 199–201; A. G. Kenwood and A. L. Lougheed, *The Growth of the International Economy 1870–1980* (Unwin Hyman, London, 1983) p. 275.

48. Martin Gilbert, *The Roots of Appeasement* (Weidenfeld & Nicolson, London 1966) p. 214.

49. Joseph Schumpeter, *Imperialism and Social Classes* (Basil Blackwell, Oxford, 1951) p. 90.

50. Mary Fulbrook, *Germany 1918–90 – The Divided Nation* (Fontana, London, pb edn, 1991) p. 183; William Patterson and Gordon Smith (eds), *The West German Model – Perspectives on a Stable State* (Frank Cass, London, 1981) pp. 19–20.

51. John Ikenberry, 'The Myth of Post-Cold War Chaos', *Foreign Affairs*, May/June 1996, p. 87.

52. Kennan, op. cit., p. 325; Isaacson and Thomas, op. cit., pp. 413–14.

53. Spaak, op. cit., p. 141; Lloyd Gardner, *Spheres of Influence* (John Murray, London, 1993) p. 263.

54. *The Military Balance 1988–89* (International Institute for Strategic Studies, London, 1988) p. 67.

55. Ninkovich, op. cit., pp. 79–80.

56. Edward Fursdon, *The European Defence Community* (Macmillan, London, 1980) p. 3.

57. Josef Joffe, 'Europe's American Pacifier', *Foreign Policy*, Spring 1984, pp. 75, 81; Ikenberry, op. cit., p. 89.

58. Gillingham, op. cit., p. 297.

59. Philip Zelikow and Condezza Rice, *Germany Unified and Europe Transformed* (Harvard University Press, Cambridge, MA 1995) pp. 206–7.

See also 'How Thatcher Used Tea and Tanks to Outgun Kohl', *The Times*, 3 October, 1996.
60. James Baker, *The Politics of Diplomacy* (Putnam, New York, 1995) p. 234.
61. Zelikow and Rice, op. cit., p. 207.
62. Duchene, op. cit., p. 363.

9 No Other Choice?

1. Karl Jarausch, *The Enigmatic Chancellor* (Yale University Press, New York and London, 1973) p. 165.
2. Albert Hirshmann, *The Passions and the Interests – Political Arguments for Capitalism before its Triumph* (Princeton University Press, Princeton, 1977) p. 34.
3. Correlli Barnett, *The Swordbearers* (Penguin Books, Harmondsworth, 1966) p. 299.
4. Barbara Tuchman, *The Proud Tower* (Macmillan, London, 1966 pb edn) p. 312; David Calleo, *The German Problem Reconsidered* (Cambridge University Press, Cambridge, 1980) pp. 48–9.
5. Arden Bucholz, *Moltke, Schlieffen and Prussian War Planning* (Berg, New York and Oxford, 1991) pp. 309–10.
6. Geoffrey Barraclough, *From Agadir to Armageddon – Anatomy of a Crisis* (Weidenfeld & Nicolson, London, 1982), p. 42. See also Barnett, op. cit., pp. 28–9.
7. James Joll, *The Origins of the First World War* (Longman, London, 1984) p. 21.
8. Marc Trachtenberg, 'The Meaning of Mobilization in 1914', *International Security*, Winter 1990–1, pp. 120, 148–50; David Stevenson, *Armaments and the Coming of War* (Oxford University Press, Oxford, 1996) pp. 307–8.
9. Daniel Pick, *War Machine* (Yale University Press, New Haven and London, 1993) p. 106.
10. Zara Steiner, *Britain and the Origins of the First World War* (Macmillan, London, 1977) p. 216.
11. 'Secrets of the Caribbean Crisis – N. Khrushchev–J. Kennedy Correspondence October–December 1962' A Joint Publication of the US State Department and the Ministry of Foreign Affairs of Russia, *International Affairs (Moscow)*, 1992.
12. Alistair Horne, *Harold Macmillan* (Macmillan, London, 1989) p. 325.
13. Jimmy Carter, *Keeping Faith* (Bantam Books, Toronto and New York, 1982) p. 214.
14. Keith Robbins, *Sir Edward Grey* (Cassell, London, 1971) p. 175.
15. McGeorge Bundy, *Danger and Survival* (Random House, New York, 1988) p. 213.
16. Henry Kissinger, *Diplomacy* (Simon & Schuster, London, 1995) p. 749.
17. Daniel Ford, *The Button – The Nuclear Trigger – Does it Work?* (George Allen & Unwin, London, 1985) pp. 180–1.
18. McGeorge Bundy, 'To Cap the Volcano', *Foreign Affairs*, October 1969, pp. 9–10.

19. David Rosenberg, 'The Origins of Overkill', *International Security*, Spring 1983, pp. 7–8; Carter, op. cit., p. 241; Robert McNamara, *Blundering into Disaster* (Bloomsbury, London, 1987) p. 63.

20. Mikhail Gorbachev, *Memoirs* (Doubleday, New York, 1996) p. 444.

21. Stevenson, op. cit., pp. 366, 421.

22. Avner Offer, *The First World War* (Oxford University Press, Oxford 1991 pb edn) pp. 283–4. See also I. F. Clarke, *Voices Prophesying War* (Panther Books, London, 1970) pp. 104–5.

23. Richard Overy, *Why the Allies Won* (Jonathan Cape, London, 1995) p. 296.

24. Barton Bernstein, 'The Atomic Bombings Reconsidered', *Foreign Affairs*, January 1995, p. 146; Charles Krautenhammer, 'A Moral Difference between Atom Bombs and Firebombing?', *International Herald Tribune*, 24 July 1995.

25. David Rosenberg, '"A Smoking, Radiating Ruin at the End of Two Hours" – Documents on American Plans for Nuclear War with the Soviet Union', *International Security*, Winter 1981/2, pp. 3–38.

26. James Blight, Bruce Allwyn and David Welch, *Cuba on the Brink – Castro, the Missile Crisis and the Soviet Collapse* (Pantheon Books, New York, 1993) p. 183.

27. Robert Jay Lifton and Eric Markusen, *The Genocidal Mentality – Nazi Holocaust and Nuclear Threat* (Macmillan, London, 1990) p. 181.

28. Richard Rhodes, *The Making of the Atomic Bomb* (Simon & Schuster, London, 1986) pp. 526–7.

29. Ibid., p. 645.

30. Ibid., p. 534.

31. McGeorge Bundy, *Danger and Survival*, pp. 167, 182; David Holloway, *Stalin and the Bomb* (Yale University Press, New Haven and London, 1994) pp. 162–3.

32. Bundy, *Danger and Survival*, p. 153.

33. Henry Kissinger, *The White House Years* (Weidenfeld & Nicolson and Michael Joseph, London, 1979) p. 764.

34. Townsend Hoopes, *The Devil and John Foster Dulles* (Little, Brown & Co, Boston and Toronto, 1973) p. 310.

35. Michael Beschloss, *Kennedy v Khrushchev* (Faber & Faber, London, 1991) pp. 196, 320–1.

36. Harold Macmillan, *Pointing the Way, 1959–61* (Macmillan, London, 1972) p. 393;

37. Beschloss, op. cit., p. 255.

38. Arthur Schlesinger, *A Thousand Days – John F. Kennedy in the White House* (Houghton Mifflin, Boston, 1965) p. 391. See also Richard Lebow and Janice Stein, *We All Lost the Cold War* (Princeton University Press, Princeton, New Jersey, 1994) p. 23.

39. Anne Tusa, *The Last Division* (Hodder & Stoughton, London, 1996) p. 349.

40. Robert Kennedy, *Thirteen Days – The Cuban Missile Crisis* (Pan Books, London, 1969) p. 124.

41. Bruce Blair, *The Logic of Accidental Nuclear War* (The Brookings Institution, Washington DC, 1993) pp. 23–4; Lebow and Stein, op. cit., pp. 113, 116–17.

42. Paul Bracken, *The Command and Control of Nuclear Forces* (Yale University Press, New York and London, 1983) p. 211.

43. Lebow and Stein, op. cit., p. 113.

44. Lebow and Stein, op. cit., pp. 331–8. See also Mark White, *The Cuban Missile Crisis* (Macmillan, London, 1996) pp. 118–24; Jerold Post, 'The Impact of Crisis-Induced Stress on Policy-Makers' in Alexander George (ed.), *Avoiding War – Problems of Crisis Management* (Westview Press, Boulder, 1991) pp. 488–9.
45. Aleksander Fursenko and Timothy Naftali, *One Hell of a Gamble* (John Murray, London, 1997) p. 282.
46. Scott Sagan, *The Limits of Safety – Organisations, Accidents and Nuclear Weapons* (Princeton University Press, Princeton, New Jersey, 1993), pp. 115,112.
47. Lebow and Stein, op. cit., p. 344.
48. Ibid., pp. 183, 198.
49. Ibid., pp. 213, 216–219.
50. Victor Israelyan, *Inside the Kremlin During the Yom Kippur War* (Pennsylvania State University Press, Pennsylvania, 1995) pp. 179–80.
51. Lebow and Stein, op. cit., pp. 264–5.
52. Anatoly Dobrynin, *In Confidence* (Times Books, New York 1995), pp. 522–3.
53. Raymond Garthoff, *The Great Transition* (Brookings, Washington DC, 1994) pp. 138–40. See also Don Oberdorfer, *The Turn – How the Cold War Came to an End* (Cape, London, 1992) pp. 66–8; Gordon Brook-Shepherd, *The Storm Birds – Soviet PostWar Defectors* (Weidenfeld & Nicolson, London, 1988) pp. 267–71.
54. Sir Geoffrey Howe, *Conflict of Loyalty* (Macmillan, London, 1994) p. 350; Archie Brown, *The Gorbachev Factor* (Oxford University Press, Oxford, 1996), pp. 227–8.
55. Bracken, op. cit., p. 48; Blair, op. cit., pp. 8–9.
56. Bracken, op. cit., p. 59.
57. George Kennan, *Memoirs, 1925–1950* (Hutchinson, London, 1968) pp. 557–8.
58. Blight, Allwyn and Welch, op. cit., pp. 115–16.
59. John Gaddis, *The Long Peace* (Oxford University Press, New York, 1987) p. 230.
60. Kissinger, *The White House Years*, p. 522.
61. Hoopes, op. cit., p. 310; Stephen Ambrose, *Eisenhower – Vol. 2. The President* (George Allen & Unwin, London, 1984) p. 521.

10   A Conditional Achievement

1. William Pfaff, 'Sole Superpower Status Goes to America's Head', *International Herald Tribune*, 18–19 January 1997.
2. Zara Steiner, *Britain and the Origins of the First World War* (Macmillan, London, 1977) p. 155.
3. L. P. Hartley, *The Go-Between* (Penguin Books, Harmondsworth, 1958) p. 7.
4. Albert Camus, *The Plague* (Penguin Books, Harmondsworth, 1960 edn) p. 252.
5. Charles Kegley and Geogory Raymond, *A Multipolar Peace? – Great Power Politics in the Twenty-First Century* (St Martins Press, New York, 1994),

pp. 7–8; John Mearscheimer, 'Back to the Future – Instability in Europe after the Cold War' in Sean Lynn-Jones, *The Cold War and After – Prospects for Peace* (MIT Press, Cambridge, MA, 1991); Kenneth Waltz, 'The Emerging Structure of International Politics', *International Security*, Fall 1993. Stephen van Evera, 'Primed for Peace – Europe after the Cold War' in Lynn-Jones, *The Cold War and After*; John Mueller, *Retreat from Doomsday* (Basic Books, New York, 1989).

6. 'Fragility of France Heightens Kohl Angst about War', *Times*, 8 December 1995; George Brock, 'Germans Grumble at Euro but no Popular Revolt will Save Mark', *Times*, 24 February 1997.

7. George Friedman and Meredith LeBard, *The Coming War with Japan* (St Martin's Press, New York, 1990); Shintharo Ishihara, *The Japan that Can Say No* (Simon & Schuster, London, 1991).

8. *The Military Balance – 1996/7* (International Institute for Strategic Studies, London, 1996) p. 306.

9. Fred Hiatt, 'Russia Should Quit Carping and Focus on Its Future Role', *International Herald Tribune*, 25 February 1997.

10. Don Oberdorfer, 'US–Japanese Ties: A Deepening Anger', *International Herald Tribune*, 2 March 1992; Stephen Rosenfeld, 'The World Needs US–Japanese Teamwork', ibid., 30 April 1990; T. R. Reid, 'For America and Japan the Pacific is Shrinking', ibid., 18 June 1991.

11. Flora Lewis, 'Next Should Come Europe's 21st Century, Not the 19th', *International Herald Tribune*, 30 December 1994; Brian Beedham, 'Russia Gains, Germany Loses, America Should Stay', ibid., 15 December 1994; Brian Clark, 'Each State for Itself', *Financial Times*, 6 January 1994.

12. Shozo Azuma, 'Tokyo Needs to Take off its Blinders and Join the World', *International Herald Tribune*, 20 December 1996.

13. Ronald Steel, 'Internationalism: the Sensible Ideology for America Today?' and 'Internationalism as a Complement to Nationalism', *International Herald Tribune*, 7 and 8 June 1995; Samuel Huntington, 'Why International Primacy Matters', *International Security*, Spring 1993.

14. Susan Strange, 'The Transformation of the World Economy' in Lidija Babic and Bo Huldt (eds), *Mapping the Unknown – Towards a New World Order* (Hurst & Co, London, 1993) pp. 48–9.

15. Edward Luttwak, 'From Geopolitics to Geo-Economics – Logic of Conflict, Grammar of Commerce', *The National Interest*, Summer 1990, pp. 17–23; Luttwak, 'For America, Again, the World is a New Ball Game', *International Herald Tribune*, 23 September 1991.

16. Max Singer, 'Wealth Without Precedent is Spreading Over All the Earth', *International Herald Tribune*, 2 January 1988. See also Max Singer and Aaron Wildavsky, *The Real World Order: Zones of Peace/Zones of Turmoil* (Chatham, New Jersey, 1993) pp. 44–50.

17. Barry Buzan and Gerald Segal, 'Rethinking East Asian Security', *Survival*, Summer 1994; Kishore Mahbubani, 'The Pacific Way', *Foreign Affairs*, January/February 1995, p. 104.

18. William Pfaff, 'Today's Balance of Power Makes Rivals out of Allies', *International Herald Tribune*, 19 April 1994.

19. William Pfaff, 'In China, the Interregnum Won't Necessarily Be Peaceful', *International Herald Tribune*, 25 February 1995.

20. 'Nuclear South Asia?', *International Herald Tribune*, 1 February 1993; Shekhar Gupta, *India Redefines its Role* (Adelphi Paper 293, International Institute for Strategic Studies, London, 1995) p. 65.

21. Ranabir Samaddar, 'Distant Guns and the Enchanted Mind' in Samaddar (ed.), *Cannons Into Ploughshares – Militarization and the Prospect of Peace in South Asia* (Lancers, New Delhi, 1995) p. 1.

22. Paul Kennedy, *Preparing for the Twenty-First Century* (Random House, New York, 1993) p. 179.

23. 'Clinton – Preparing for Manila Summit', *International Herald Tribune*, 21 November 1996; Paul Dibb, 'Asians are Arming: A Prospect of Trouble Ahead', *International Herald Tribune*, 26 November 1993; Paul Dibb, *Towards a New Balance of Power in Asia* (Adelphi Paper 295, International Institute for Strategic Studies, London, 1995) p. 26.

24. Gerald Segal, 'Get Through and Beyond Chinese Nationalism', *International Herald Tribune*, 14 November 1996; David Shambaugh, 'Growing Strong – Challenge to Asian Security', *Survival*, Summer 1994, pp. 44–5.

25. Patrick Tyler, 'While Quick to Rattle, Chinese Saber is Dull' *International Herald Tribune*, 4 December, 1996.

26. John Ravenhill, 'The New Disorder on the Periphery' in Richard Leaver and James Richardson, *Charting the Post-Cold War Order* (Westview, Boulder, 1993) p. 73.

27. *Hansard*, 23 February 1993, Vol. 219, col. 783.

28. Michael Holman, 'The Sounds of a Continent Cracking', *Financial Times*, 23/24 July 1994.

29. Brian Beedham, 'NATO Troops Could Do the Job if the Politicians So Ordered', *International Herald Tribune*, 15 August 1995.

30. Leslie Gelb, 'Never Again? Beware, Europe, Cynicism is Contagious', *International Herald Tribune*, 14 December 1992.

31. Robert O'Neill, 'Britain and the Future of Nuclear Weapons', *International Affairs*, October 1995, p. 748.

32. Fred Iklé, 'The Second Coming of the Nuclear Age', *Foreign Affairs*, January–February 1996, p. 128.

33. 'UN Chief Backs Use of Force to Ensure Bosnia Peace', *Times*, 3 March 1993.

34. Bruce Clark and Chrystia Freeland, 'A Diplomatic Mountain', *Financial Times*, 22/23 February 1997.

35. David Sanger, 'Phone Pact: the Exporting of US Values', *International Herald Tribune*, 18 February 1997.

Index

ABM (anti-ballistic missile)   106, 145
Abyssinia   63
accommodatory politics   9, 11, 12,
    13, 122, 125, 129, 133, 135, 136,
    137, 138, 139, 140, 142, 158, 159,
    160, 161, 162, 163, 164, 165, 166,
    167, 168, 169, 170, 171, 172
Acheson, Dean   126
Adenauer, Konrad   97, 130, 132,
    134–5
Afghanistan   85, 110, 113, 116, 117
Africa   2, 42, 73, 94, 112, 176
Agadir crises   22, 27, 144
Ahlefeld, Hunold von   21
Aids   170
Alaska   86
Aldershot   47
Ancillon, J.P.F.   2
Andropov, President Yuri   154
Angell, Norman   4; *The Great
    Illusion*   4, 22
Anglo–Egyptian treaty (1936)   110
Anglo–French Staff talks (1906)   27, 38
Anglo–French naval talks   27, 38
Angola   109, 112
Anschluss   73, 77
anti-Semitism   74
appeasement   6, 26, 49, 54, 60, 67,
    68, 71, 88, 114, 142, 158
Arab–Israeli conflict   10, 172
Arab states   110
Arbatov, Georgi   113
arbitration   7, 59, 60, 61
Argentina   64
Arizona   58
arms control   10, 65, 117, 145, 168
arms race   6, 17, 27, 28, 59, 64, 83,
    85, 87, 99, 106, 113, 114, 115,
    116, 120, 145, 147, 148, 150
artillery   46, 56
Asia   87, 91, 94, 105
Asquith, Herbert   20, 38, 53
Assad, President Hafez   110

Atlantic   7, 57, 68, 136, 149, 172
Atlantic alliance   163
Atlantic community   128, 140
Atlantic Monthly   59
atomic bomb   9, 83, 86, 87, 92, 96
attrition   49, 52, 76
Attwood, Brian   127
Auschwitz   134
Austria–Hungary   16, 17, 18, 24, 29,
    30, 31, 32, 40, 45, 98
Axis Powers   67, 78

Baden-Powell, Lt-Col. Robert   22
Bahr, Egon   108
Baker, James   119, 140
balance of power   5, 6, 19, 25, 27, 29,
    33, 53, 59, 79, 80, 81, 88, 92, 105,
    122, 123, 124, 127, 136, 160, 162,
    163, 166
Balkans   17, 18, 30, 82, 126, 153
Ball, George   129
Barraclough, Geoffrey   144
Baruch Plan   150
Basic Principles of Relations
    (US–Soviet)   108, 109
battleship   25–6, 57, 65
Beedham, Brian   170
Belgian neutrality   32, 33
Belgrade   29
bellicism   6, 22, 41, 73, 76, 124, 160
Benelux   132
Beria, Laventry   93
Berlin   15, 18, 22, 28, 29, 33, 51, 62,
    73, 78, 79, 80; American
    ambassador in   16; 1948 crisis
    87, 92; 1958–61 crisis   95–8, 99,
    100, 101, 113, 120; Wall   96, 97,
    107, 118, 146
Beschloss, Michael, 101
Bessmertnykh, Alexander   104
Bethmann Hollweg, Theobold von
    25, 26, 29, 30, 31, 32, 33, 44, 45,
    142, 144

Bevin, Ernest 86
Beyen, Johan 130
Bismarck, Count Otto von 4, 5, 19,
   24, 25, 28, 38, 39, 75, 77
BJP (Bharatiya Janata Party) 167
Black Sea 68
'blank cheque' 16, 30, 32, 50, 51, 98
Bloch, Ivan 3, 36–7, 40, 42, 43, 88;
   The Future of War 3, 36
Blitzkrieg 7, 76, 77
Boer War 19, 41, 43
Bohlen, Charles 80
Bohr, Nils 150, 151, 172
Bolivia 64
Bolshevism 61, 78
bomber 70, 76
'bomber gap' 90
Bosnia crisis (1908) 17
Boulogne 45
Boy Scouts 22
Bradley, General Omar 80
Brandt, Willy 108
Brest-Litovsk (treaty) 45
Bretton, Woods 7, 125, 126, 137, 172
Brezhnev, President Leonid 104,
   107, 108, 112, 117, 154
Brezhnev doctrine 106
Briand, Aristide 69
Briey 45
Brinkmanship 10, 94, 98, 104, 151
Britain 17, 19, 20, 24, 51, 57, 59, 62,
   63, 64, 65, 67, 71, 73, 77, 79, 80,
   85, 87, 88, 89, 96, 97, 110, 113,
   123, 124, 126, 128, 137, 138, 140,
   142, 143, 171; army 41, 42,
   46–7, 62, 76; and origins of First
   World War 15, 26–7, 32–3,
   38–9; reaction against First World
   War 7, 8, 49–50, 53–4, 69, 70
Brooke, Rupert 6, 23; *Peace* 23
Brussels 123
Brzezinski, Zbgniew 1
bubonic plague 170
Bucholz, Arden 38
Budapest 80
Buelow, Prince Bernhard von 25,28
Bull, Hedley 11
Bullock, Alan 74
Bundy, McGeorge 101, 146

Burton, Montague 53
Bush, President George 11, 118, 119,
   172
Bykov, Oleg 113
Byrnes, James 92

Cambridge 59
Camus, Albert 166; *La Peste* 166
Caribbean 102
Carter, President Jimmy 112, 113,
   145
Casablanca 79
Castro, President Fidel 99, 100
Catherine the Great 2
Caucasus 68
cavalry 37, 41–2, 46–7
Cecil, Lord Robert 59
Central Powers 50, 60
Chamberlain, Houston Stewart 75
Chamberlain, Neville 8, 54, 69, 70,
   71, 72, 81
Channel 46
Channel ports 33
Checkpoint Charlie (Berlin) 96
Chernenko, President Konstantin 139
Chernobyl 116
'Chicken' 91
China 13, 68, 88, 89, 105, 143, 159,
   161, 166, 167, 168–9; rivalry with
   Soviet Union 100, 105–6, 111
Churchill, Sir Winston 2, 16, 24, 79,
   80, 82, 82, 84, 90, 148, 149, 150
CIA (Central Intelligence Agency)
   90
Clarke, I.F. 22, 43
Clemenceau, Georges 55, 56, 59, 60,
   61, 63, 65, 66, 69
Clinton, President Bill 168
Cobden, Richard 36
Cold War 6, 10, 11, 12, 17, 65, 85,
   86, 88, 89, 93, 95, 98, 101, 104,
   105, 109, 111, 113, 114, 115, 116,
   117, 120, 121, 123, 139, 142, 145,
   146, 147, 148, 151, 152, 154, 155,
   157, 158, 159, 162, 163, 165, 169,
   172, 173
Colin, Jean 35
collective security 6, 7, 62
Coming War with Japan, The 161

Commitee of Imperial Defence (CID) 38, 39
common security 116
Communism 69, 89, 96, 98, 99, 100, 105, 106, 112, 113, 118, 127, 157
Concert of Europe 4, 5, 28
Congo 98
Congress, US 58, 100, 101
Congress of Vienna 4, 54, 107
Congress system 123
Cook, Don 127
Creveld, Martin van 40
Crimean War 5, 21–2
Crowe, Sir Eyre 27, 31
Cruise missile 114
CSCE (Conference on Security and Cooperation in Europe) 108
Cuba 100, 101, 102
Cuban missile crisis 10, 85, 91, 95, 98–103, 104, 107, 116, 120, 144, 145, 152–3, 154, 155, 156, 165
Czechoslovakia 106

Daladier, Edouard 71
Damascus 111
Danube 86
Darwin, Charles 20, 21; *Origin of Species* 20
Delbruck, Hans 37
democracy 8, 9, 12, 58, 60, 81, 114, 121, 126, 128, 134, 136, 137–8, 149, 161, 162, 164, 166, 170, 171, 172
Depression 61, 63, 67, 73, 74 125, 136
Detente 10, 11, 100, 104, 106, 107, 108, 109, 110, 112, 113, 114, 128, 153
deterrent 43, 113, 114, 139, 149, 172
Deutschmark 124
Dienbienphu, battle of 91
Dilke, Sir Charles 35
disarmament 58, 59, 64, 65, 114, 161
Disraeli, Benjamin 19
Djilas, Milovan 128
Dobrynin, Anatoly 100, 107, 154
Donovan, William 89
Draft Treaty of Mutual Assistance (1923) 62

Dresden 149
Dreyfus affair 139
Dual Alliance 39
Duchene, François 7, 130, 135–6
Dulles, John Foster 91, 94, 151, 157
Dunkirk 45

East Asia 165, 167, 168
East Germany 95, 96, 97, 108, 119
Eastern Europe 18, 80, 81, 90, 96, 107, 108, 117, 118, 120, 139, 171
Eastern Front 35, 48, 108
ECSC (European Coal and Steel Community) 129, 130, 131–3, 139, 140
EDC (European Defence Community) 133, 139–40
EEC (European Economic Community) 123, 128, 133, 135–6, 137, 138, 139, 162
Egypt 110–11, 112, 120, 153
Eisenhower, President Dwight 80, 88, 91, 95, 96, 100, 121, 147, 157
Elbe 88, 91, 172
Eliot, Charles, 57
Eliot, T. S. 61
El Salvador 64
Elser, George 74
Engels, Friedrich 35
Erhard, Ludwig 137
Ethiopia 109, 112
EU (European Union) 12, 118, 140, 163, 164, 167, 171
Eupen-Malmedy 73
Europe 2, 4, 5, 7, 15, 20, 23, 24, 25, 28, 33, 34, 35, 36, 43, 45, 55, 56, 57, 58, 59, 60, 61, 66, 69, 70, 73, 74, 75, 78, 79, 80, 81, 82, 86, 87, 88, 89, 96, 99, 107, 114, 117, 118, 123, 125, 126, 127, 128, 129, 131, 132–3, 134, 135, 138, 145, 151, 159, 160, 161, 164, 167, 170
Excomm 10, 101, 144, 146, 153

Falklands War 15, 137
Far East 20, 26, 63, 68
Farrar, L. L. 20
Farrell, Robert 53
Fascism 7, 69, 159

Fest, Joachim 74
firepower 37, 40, 41, 42, 44
First World War 1, 4, 5, 6, 7, 8, 12,
    21, 26, 35, 39, 44–52, 53, 58, 64,
    66, 68, 70, 72, 73, 76, 77, 82, 124,
    125, 129, 143, 144, 145, 148, 151,
    159
Fisher, Admiral Sir John 148
fission 150
Florida 101
Flottenverein 27
Foch, Marshall Ferdinand 55
Force de Frappe 133
Foreign Office 18, 27, 33, 79, 137
Forester, C. S. 47; *The General* 47
Fourteen Points 58
France 7, 8, 20, 27, 31, 33, 36, 39,
    45, 48, 51, 53, 57, 58, 59, 62, 63,
    65, 67, 71, 73, 85, 88, 97, 110,
    124, 126, 127, 129, 139, 142, 143,
    171; army 28, 41, 47, 48, 49, 50,
    77; Franco–German relations
    17, 69, 129, 130, 131–2, 133; and
    origins of First World War 16,
    17, 18; reaction to First World
    War 49; and Versailles treaty
    55–6, 59–60
Franco–Prussian War 4, 19, 20, 35,
    41, 43, 55
Franz Ferdinand, Archduke 15, 29
Franz Joseph, Emperor 30
Frederick the Great 5
Frederick William IV 2
free trade 36, 61, 124, 125, 136, 141,
    172
French, Field Marshal Sir John 46
French revolution 24
Frontserlebnis 76
Fulbrook, Mary 138
Fursenko, Aleksandr 102

Gardner, Lloyd 87
Garthoff, Raymond 109
Gas 27, 50, 65
Gasperi, Alcide de 130
Gatling, Richard 42
GATT (General Agreement on Tariffs
    and Trade) 23, 137, 164
Gaulle, President Charles de 97, 107

Geneva disarmament conference
    (1932) 65
Geneva peace conference (1973) 111
Geneva Protocol (1925) 64
'geoeconomics' 164
Germany 5, 6, 9, 11, 15, 19, 20, 22,
    37, 38, 39, 40, 52, 54, 55, 56, 60,
    64, 65, 66, 67, 69, 75, 85, 88, 90,
    142, 155, 157, 159, 160, 161, 163,
    167, 169
    German army 7, 48, 49, 51, 56, 78;
        General Staff 7, 34, 39, 50,
        56, 77, 133; navy 1, 25;
        nuclear programme 83, 90;
        and origins of the First World
        War 16, 17, 18, 24–6, 27,
        28–34; and First World War
        45, 50–1; and origins of Second
        World War 71, 73, 143; and
        Second World War 78, 79,
        80; post-1945 86, 87, 95, 97,
        126, 128–9; rearmament 133,
        139–40; unification 108,
        118–20, 135, 140, 162
    German Democratic Republic
        (GDR) 95, 97, 108
Geyer, Michael 47
Gladstone, William 4, 68
Gobineau, Comte Joseph-Arthur de 75
Goltz, Colonel von der 35, 41
Gooch, G. P 23
Gorbachev, President Mikhail 1, 10,
    11, 112, 116, 117, 118, 119, 120,
    121–2, 123, 128, 147, 148, 161;
    Perestroika (book) 116
Grandmaison, Colonel de 41
Grayling, A. C. 74
Great Patriotic War 156; *see also*
    Second World War
Greece 80, 100
Grey, Sir Edward 17, 18, 28, 29, 30,
    32, 38, 43–4, 64
Gromyko, Anatoly 97, 100, 108, 109
Grosse Ostaufmarsch (military plan)
    32
Grossman, Vasilii 105
G7 12
Guerre de Demain, La 22
Gulf War 11, 137

Haig, Field Marshal Douglas 47
Hague disarmament conferences
    (1899, 1907) 27, 28, 37, 64
Halifax, Lord Edward 71
Hamburg 149
Hankey, Maurice 66
Harriman, Averill 96
Hartley, L. P. 166
Harvard 126, 127, 151
Havana 100
Heligoland 26
Henessy, Peter 124
Herald, The 60
Herriot, Edouard 67
'high politics' 123, 135
Hindenburg, Field Marshal Paul von
    46
Hinsley, F. H. 5
Hiroshima 10, 83, 85, 92, 149
Hirsch, Etienne 130
Hitler, Adolf 1, 7, 15, 23, 54, 61, 63,
    65, 67, 68, 69, 70, 71, 72, 73, 74,
    75–6, 77, 78, 79, 81, 82, 83, 86,
    121, 139, 140, 155; *Mein Kampf*
    72, 75, 77
Hobson, J. A. 19; *Psychology of
    Jingoism* 19
Hogan, Michael 127
Hollywood 115
Holocaust 1, 134
Holtby, Winifred 70; *South Riding*
    70
Honecker, Erich 108
Horne, Alistair 44, 48; *The Price of
    Glory* 44
'hotline' 104, 110–11
House, Colonel Edward 18, 29, 59, 62
House of Commons 16, 54
Howard, Michael 22
Hull, Cordell 80, 81, 125, 126
Hurd, Douglas 169
human rights 105, 108, 112, 122,
    169
Hydrogen (H) bomb 9, 92, 145, 147
hypernationalism 19, 44, 160, 167

ICBM (intercontinental ballistic
    missile) 94, 99
Iklé, Fred 171

IMF (International Monetary Fund)
    12, 123, 125, 164
India 33, 87, 167, 168
Indochina 88, 143
Industrial Revolution 3, 4, 5, 20, 25,
    131, 137, 142, 159
Institute of International Law 22
Inter Allied Supply Committee 129
International Atomic Development
    Authority 150
International Relations (academic
    discipline) 53
International Steel Cartel 130
Invasion of 1910, The 22
Iraq 169
IRBM (intermediate range ballistic
    missile) 100
Isaacson, Walter 127
Israel 110, 111, 120, 133
Israelyan, Victor 111, 153
Italy 5, 45, 63, 86, 126, 127, 132

James, Henry 17
Japan 7, 9, 11, 28, 63, 64, 68, 83,
    88, 122, 134, 137, 143, 155, 161,
    163, 166, 167, 168, 169; and
    Second World War 78, 83, 85,
    143, 144
Jenkins, Roy 135
jingoism 19, 53, 57
Joffre, General Joseph 36
Johnson, President Lyndon Baines
    138, 146
Julius Caeser 137
July crisis (1914) 17, 19–34, 35,
    88–9, 98, 144
Junkers 28, 137
Jupiter (missile) 100, 101, 102

Kandinsky, Wassily 18
Kazan 76
Kellogg–Briand Pact 64
Kennan, George 6, 44, 89, 127, 128,
    129, 155
Kennedy, President John F. 96, 121,
    146, 149; and Cuban missile crisis
    98, 101, 102, 103, 104, 120, 145,
    152–3
Kennedy, Paul 168

Kennedy, Robert 102, 153
Keynes, John Maynard 55, 56, 60–1, 62, 69, 125; *Economic Consequences of the Peace* 69
Khan, Genghis 76
Khrushchev, Nikita 90, 93–4, 107, 120, 139, 145, 151, 156, 165; and Berlin crisis 95–8, 152; and Cuban missile crisis 98–103, 104, 152–3; and nuclear weapons 93–4
Khrushchev, Sergei 100
Kiel 21
Kissinger, Henry 2, 24, 56, 80, 87, 105, 107, 109, 112, 114, 146, 151, 153, 154
Kitchener, Field Marshal Lord 36, 46
Kohl, Helmut 118, 134, 140, 160, 161, 163
Korea 20, 86
Korean War 91, 92, 95, 139
Kuwait 169, 171

Laffargue, Captain 48; *The Attack in Trench Warfare* 48
Laos 98
Larabee, Eric 79
Latin America 99
'launch-on-warning' 153
League of Nations 58, 59, 60, 61, 62, 64, 65, 67, 71, 116, 130, 141, 158, 170
Lebensraum 8, 75, 136
Le Bourget (airport) 71
Lebow, Richard 154
Leger, Alexis 71
Lendlease 126
Lenin, Vladimir 4, 57, 59
Leningrad 69
Linchnowsky, Prince 32
Liddel Hart, Basil 60
Lifton, Robert 149
Light Brigade 60
Litvinov, Maxim 87
Lloyd George, David 16, 46, 51, 54, 59, 60
Locarno Pact 63, 67, 69
London 70, 94, 129, 150; German ambassador in 43–4

London Council of Ministers (1945) 92
'Long Peace' 156
'Long Telegram' 155
Loos, battle of 47
Louis XIV 5
Lowes Dickinson, Goldsworthy 59
Ludendorff, General Erich 7, 46, 48, 49, 51

machine gun 32, 42–3, 46, 47
Machtpolitik 1
Macmillan, Harold 72, 97, 145, 151
Madaraga, Salvador de 64
Mafeking 22
Mahan, Admiral Alfred 25, 41, 57
Mahbubani, Kishore 166
Malenkov, Georgii 93
Manchester Guardian 69
Manchuria 63, 68, 81, 86, 143
Manhattan Project 83, 150
Marc, Franz 18; *Apocalyptic Landscape* 18
Marjolin, Robert 123, 138
Markusen, Eric 149
Marne, battle of 40, 46, 48, 49
Marshall Aid 127, 128
Marshall, General George 126, 130, 137, 138
Marshall Plan 12, 61, 125, 126, 128, 137, 172
Martin, Lawrence 60
Marx, Karl 21; *Das Kapital* 21
Marxism–Leninism 99, 112, 154
'massive retaliation' 96
Materialschlacht 78, 120
Matsu 91
Maurice, Colonel 35; *War* 35
McNamara, Robert 147
Mediterranean 26, 33, 154
Mediterranean Fleet 110
Meidner, Ludwig 18
Menshikov, Mikhail 152
Metternich, Prince 107
Mexico 58, 100
Middle Ages 8
Middle East 110, 111, 153
Mikoyan, Sergo 103
Mill, John Stuart 124

miscalculation 142, 151, 152, 153, 154
'missile gap' 90, 146
Mitterrand, President François 161
mobilisation 18, 30, 31, 33, 35, 39
Molotov, Vyacheslav 81, 86, 87, 92, 109
Molotov–Ribbentrop Pack 163
Moltke, Field Marshall von (the Elder) 22, 36, 41
Moltke, Field Marshall von (the Younger) 29, 32, 33, 34, 36, 41, 44
Monnet, Jean 7, 63, 66, 129–33, 134, 136, 137, 139, 172
Monroe Doctrine 58
Montesquieu, Charles de Secondat 2
Montreux Convention 86
Morgenthau, Henry 125, 129
Morocco 17
Moscow 7, 91, 96, 100, 104, 109, 113, 118, 153, 154; British ambassador in 104
Munich crisis 15, 54, 71, 72, 73, 77, 98, 121
Munich *Putsch* 74
Muscovy 46
Mussolini, Benito 63
Mutual Assured Destruction 88, 114

Naftali, Timothy 102
Nagasaki 83, 85, 149
Napoleonic War 85
Nash, Paul 49
nationalism 4, 5, 12, 22, 29, 58, 68, 74, 82, 89, 110, 124, 131, 134, 161, 162, 168
Nationalist China 123
NATO 12, 95, 118, 119, 120, 140, 154, 155, 161, 171
Navy League 22
Nazism 1, 7, 22, 74, 102, 138
Nehru, Jawaharlal 88
Netherlands 143
New Deal 123
New Mexico 58
'new thinking' 3, 10, 11, 117, 121–2, 129
new world order 11, 59, 84, 87, 123, 125, 172

Nicholas II, Tsar 15, 31, 37, 64
Nicolson, Harold 55, 56
Nietzsche, Friedrich 25, 74, 143
Nivelle, General Robert 48
Nixon, President Richard 105, 106, 107, 112, 146, 154
Nobel, Alfred 37
North America 164, 166
Northern Ireland 63
NSC (National Security Council) 91
nuclear alerts 11, 153–4
nuclear diplomacy 10, 91, 93, 94, 95, 101, 109, 110, 154
nuclear parity 101, 112
nuclear proliferation 172
nuclear risk 104, 142, 151–4, 156–7, 165
nuclear taboo 91, 149, 171
nuclear weapons 11, 12, 13, 68, 83–4, 85, 86, 88, 98, 99, 105, 114, 115, 116, 121, 133, 139, 146, 149, 150–1, 156, 157, 161, 165, 167, 170–1
Nuremburg (rallies) 73

Obruchev, General Nikolai 39
Oder–Neisse line 97
OECD 123, 128
OEEC 128
Offer, Avner 40
Ogaden 89
oil 8, 82, 136, 143
O'Neill, Robert 170–1
Operation Barbarossa 77–8
Operation *Sichelschnitt* 77
OSS 89
Ostpolitik 108
Ottoman Empire 82
Oval Office 149
overkill 2, 114, 149
Overy, Richard 149
Owen, Wilfred 6, 50; *Dulce et Dulcorum est* 50
Oxford 72

Paine, Thomas 60; *Rights of Man* 60
Paris 54, 59, 94
Parker, R. A. C. 71

Partial Test Ban Treaty 97, 104
Passchendaele, battle of 49, 144
peace 5, 6, 11, 41, 43, 53, 56, 57, 58,
      61, 62, 63, 65, 81, 85, 107, 123,
      125, 132, 140
'peaceful coexistence' 93
peacekeeping 12, 62, 159, 171
Pearl Harbor 35, 78, 80, 126
Peloponnesian War 85
Pentagon 150
Perestroika 1, 118
Pershing, General John 51
Pershing missile 114
Peter the Great 46
Pfaff, William 166
Philippines 20
Phillimore, Sir Walter 59
Pleven, René 139
Poincaré, President Raymond 55
Poland 36, 45, 67, 71, 73, 76, 96
Politburo 108, 111, 153–4
Portuguese colonies 26
Postsdam 30
power politics 1, 2, 3, 4, 5, 6, 8, 10,
      11, 12, 13, 14, 18, 25, 44, 53, 54,
      55, 56, 57, 58, 59, 63, 66, 67, 68,
      71, 72, 73, 77, 80, 81, 83, 84, 85,
      88, 93, 113, 125, 128, 131, 133,
      134, 137, 138, 142, 159, 162, 164,
      167, 170, 171, 172; decline/
      refutation of 7, 9, 11, 122, 124,
      136, 139, 140, 150, 158, 160, 161,
      165, 169, 173
Prague 80
Prevention of Nuclear War agreement
      (PNW) 108, 109
Princeton 56
protectionism 21, 125, 164
proxies 85, 95, 110, 111, 121
Prussia 19, 40, 46, 132
Punic War 85

Quai d'Orsay 71
Quemoy 91

race 75
RAF 96
railway timetables 35, 144
raison d'état 2, 4, 7, 11

Rapallo treaty 119, 163
Reagan, President Ronald 114–5,
      116, 154, 155
Realism 12, 57, 160, 161, 166
Realpolitik 2, 16, 19, 66, 73, 86, 106,
      142
Red Army 91, 99
Reichstag 1, 26, 38
reparations 56, 61, 87, 126
Reykjavik summit 116
Rhine 23, 39, 130
Rhineland 55, 56, 67, 73, 77
Rhodes, Cecil 20
Riesler, Kurt 25, 51, 142
Riga 48
Ritter, Gerhard 40
Roberts, Sir Frank 96, 107
Rohan, Duke of 143
Rolland, Romain 143
Romania 80
Roosevelt, President Franklin D. 54,
      79, 80–2, 84, 87, 123, 126, 150,
      172
Roosevelt, Theodore 2
Royal Navy 1, 26, 47, 57
Ruhr 69, 129
Rusk, Dean 10, 91, 93, 97, 149
Russell, Bertrand 15
Russia 12, 16, 17, 18, 19, 20, 27, 28,
      29, 32, 36, 45, 68; and origins of
      First World War 31, 33; and
      mobilisation in 1914 30, 31, 32,
      39; post-1991 159, 161, 168,
      171
Russo–Japanese War 42, 43
Rwanda 12

Saar 73, 129
SAC (Strategic Air Command)
      149
Sadat, President Anwar 110, 111
Sagan, Scott 153
SALT (Strategic Arms Limitation
      Treaty) 106–7, 112, 146, 148
Samaddar, Ranabir 167
Sarajevo 15, 30, 151
Sazonov, Sergei 31, 32
Scandinavia 45
Schlesinger, Arthur 152

Schlieffen, Count Alfred von   32,
    39–40, 50; Schlieffen Plan   32,
    39–40, 77
Schmidt, Helmut   108
Schumann, Robert   129, 130, 132,
    139
Schwarz Hans-Peter   134
Scott, CP   69
Scowcroft, General Brent   119
SDI (Strategic Defense Initiative)
    115
seapower   25, 41
Second World War   6, 7, 8, 11, 12,
    66, 68, 74, 79, 83, 89, 90, 95, 98,
    105, 109, 117, 130, 134, 143, 156,
    157, 161, 162, 164, 165, 166, 169
Serbia   15, 29, 30, 31
Shepilov D. T.   94
Shevardnadze, Eduard   117, 119
Shirer, William   73
Shultz, George   115, 116
Singer, Max   163
SIOP (single integrated operations
    plan)   147
Six Day War   110
Skidelsky, Robert   61
smokeless powder   37
Smuts, General Jan   59
Social Darwinism   20–1, 25, 26, 55,
    74, 75, 90, 131, 160
Social Democrats   28
Social Imperialism   5
Somalia   12, 111, 112
Somme, battle of   47, 49, 144
Southey, Robert   9
Soviet Union   1, 8, 10, 11, 35, 82, 88,
    114, 135, 140, 142, 149, 150, 159,
    163, 169; and Cold War   86, 89,
    90, 91, 92, 95, 98, 99, 114, 115,
    120, 121, 129, 139, 145, 146, 147,
    154–5, 158; and *detente*   104–5,
    107, 108, 109, 110, 112–13; and
    end of Cold War   116–20; and
    Middle East   109–11, 153–4; and
    nuclear weapons   9, 10, 11, 91,
    92, 93, 121; and Second World
    War   77–8, 79, 80, 86, 143; and
    Third World   94, 109, 110
Spaak, Paul-Henri   82, 128, 130, 139

Spanish–American war   57
Spanish Civil War   77
Speer, Alert   71, 83
Spencer, Herbert   5
spheres of influence   45, 80, 81, 82,
    87, 98, 109, 123
Spratly islands   169
Sputnik   91, 94, 99
SS 20 missile   114, 147
Staff Collage   42, 47
Stalin, Joseph   10, 54, 78, 81, 82, 94,
    123, 139, 157; and Cold War
    86, 87, 90, 128, 143; and nuclear
    weapons   84, 92–3, 150–1
Stargardt, Nicholas   4
State Department   115, 127
Stead, Wickham   36
Steel, Ronald   163
Stevenson, David   17, 32, 148
Stimpson, Henry   83, 92
Strachey, Lytton   4
Straits   86
strategic bombing   149
Strauss, Richard   143; *Also Sprach
    Zarathustra*   143
Stresemann, Gustav   63, 73, 130
Stuka (aircraff)   77
St Petersburg, French ambassador in
    15
submarine   47, 51, 57, 146, 148
Suez Crisis   94–5, 138
supranationalism   66, 129, 136, 151,
    167
Swanson, Senator   65
Syria   110, 120
Szögyény, Count Ladislaus   30

Taegliche Rundschau   15
Taiwan   91, 161, 169
tank   48, 76, 77
Taylor, A. J. P.   17
Tehran Summit   81
Tennyson, Lord Alfred   22
Texas   58
Thames, 26
Thatcher, Margaret   140, 161
Third World   12, 13, 85, 90–1, 99,
    105, 108–9, 116, 170
Third World War   103, 156

Thomas, Evan 127
Times The 38, 87
Tirpitz,Admiral Alfred von 1, 3, 26, 128, 173
Tokyo 149
Tours 18
Trachtenberg, Marc 35
Treaty of Rome 7, 128, 133
Treaty of Westphalia 54
Treaty of Friendship and Cooperation (Egyptian–Soviet) 110
Treitschke, Heinrich von 19
'Triangular diplomacy' 106
Triple Alliance 17
Triple Entente 17, 27, 32
Tripolitania 86
Truman, President Harry 91, 92, 145
Truman Doctrine 89, 127
Turkey 36, 86, 99, 101, 102
Tusa, Anne 97
Twentieth Party Congress (Soviet) 94
Twenty-Fourth Party Congress (Soviet) 109

U2 (aircraft) 99, 102–3, 153
Ulster 33
unconditional surrender 51, 54, 79, 126
United Nations 12, 66, 121, 123, 125, 171
United States 7, 10, 11, 20, 62, 64, 78, 123, 139, 140, 145, 159, 163, 167, 168, 171; Chiefs of Staff 79, 88; and Cold War 87, 88, 89–90, 92, 93, 97, 99, 104, 113, 114, 115, 121, 152, 155, 157; and Cuban missile crisis 98, 100–2, 152–3; and *detente* 106, 107, 112; and European reconstruction 125–129, 130; 'exceptionalism' 6, 57; and First World War 45, 51, 53, 57–8; and German unification 118–20, 140, 162; isolationism 55, 57–8, 80, 81, 88, 125, 142, 159; and League of Nations 58, 59, 62, 63, 66; and Middle East 109–10, 111, 153–4; and nuclear weapons 9, 91–2, 114, 116, 145, 146–7, 150–1;

and power politics 80–2, 89; and Second World War 79, 86, 143, 144
Upper Volta 91
Urals 172
Uri, Pierre 130
Ustinov, Marshall 155
Usurri river 106

Vance, Cyrus 106
Verdun, battle of 44, 48, 49, 144
Versailles Conference and Treaty 6, 7, 45, 51, 54, 55, 56, 58, 60, 65, 67, 69, 72, 119, 125, 126, 129
Vienna 29, 30, 72, 74, 80; British ambassador in 25; French ambassador in 29
Vienna Summit (1961) 98, 107, 151, 156
Vietminh 88
Vietnam 85, 89, 90, 105, 110, 113, 138
Vladivostok 88
Vosges 45

Wagner, Clauss 21
war 2, 3, 6, 7, 8, 9, 10, 13, 15, 16, 17, 18, 21, 22, 23, 24, 29, 30, 31, 40, 41, 42, 43, 53, 55, 62, 66, 68, 72, 73, 75, 76, 94, 96, 107, 112, 121, 125, 130–1, 132, 133, 137, 142, 143, 144, 145, 148, 149, 150, 151, 157, 160; fear of 49, 64, 70, 71, 113–14
Warsaw Pact 95, 105
Washington, DC 10, 101, 104, 123; British embassy in 89, 121; Soviet ambassador in 87, 100
Washington Naval Treaty (1922) 64
Washington Summit (1973) 107
Washington, President George 57
Watergate 112, 154
Watson, Adam 11
weapons of mass destruction 12, 170
Weber, Eugen 49
Wehrmacht 124
Weimar Republic 138
Weisaecker, President Richard von 108

welfare state   124, 125
Wells, H. G.   20, 70
Weltkrieg, Der   22
Weltpolitik   1, 25, 28, 45, 157
West   8, 12, 85, 87, 93, 94, 95, 96,
  120, 135, 157, 159
West Germany   95, 108, 122, 128–9,
  132, 133–5, 137–8, 139
Western Europe   9, 82, 99, 113, 124,
  127, 132, 135, 139, 140, 159, 166
Western Front   3, 7, 35, 42, 44, 47,
  48, 49, 53, 56, 68, 72, 75, 86, 140,
  144, 149
Western Hemisphere   101
White House   97, 107, 115
Wilhelm II, Kaiser   16, 18, 25, 28, 29,
  30, 31, 32, 33, 36, 40, 98, 143, 144
Wilson, President Woodrow   6, 7, 51,
  54, 55, 56–9, 60, 61, 62, 65–6, 71,
  80, 82, 105, 110, 116, 130, 131,
  135, 141, 172

Wirtschaftswunder   137
wishful thinking   4, 8, 16, 116, 144,
  157
World Bank   12, 123, 125
WTO (World Trade Organisation)
  12, 164, 168, 172

Xinjiang   86

Yalta Conference   81
Yazov, General   116
Yemen   64, 109
Yom Kippur War   111, 153–4
Yugoslavia   12, 140, 162

Zaire   170
Zhirinowsky, Vladimir   161
Zimmermann, Arthur   31, 58
Zola, Emile   145, 158; *La Bête
  Humaine*   145
Zweig, Stefan   18, 20